ID0687458

BRITISH TANKS and FIGHTING VEHICLES
1914 – 1945

BRITISH TANKS
and
FIGHTING VEHICLES
1914 – 1945

B. T. White

LONDON

IAN ALLAN

First published 1970

SBN 7110 0123 5

*Published by Ian Allan Ltd, Shepperton, Surrey and printed
in the United Kingdom by A. Wheaton & Co., Exeter*

Contents

Part 2: Armoured Cars

Part 3: Specialised Armour

Part 4: Self-propelled Guns & Carriers

Jacket pictures: *top left* — Sherman V Adder (page 215)
top right — Beaver–Eel (page 159)
bottom—Covenanter III (page 61)

Introduction

THIS book attempts to cover, for what is believed to be the first time, all British tanks and armoured vehicles, tracked and wheeled, from 1900 until 1945—from the period of their conception, through World War I to the end of World War II.

Also covered are a few special examples of fighting vehicles which are not armoured, and some tracked but unarmoured towing vehicles and amphibians.

All the major types are described in some detail, although for the less important vehicles briefer coverage is given and for some the inevitable restriction on space has allowed only a mention. Some of the AFVs built in British Commonwealth countries are included but, in the main, this is restricted to vehicles used in action outside the country of origin—for this reason, the Canadian Ram tank is included only in its armoured personnel carrier version.

American-built tanks played a very important part in the equipment of British and Commonwealth armies in World War II but in this book only those adapted with British equipment for specialised tasks can be included.

The photographs have been chosen to show typical vehicles as far as possible so that by cross reference some idea can be gained of the appearance of other types not illustrated.

The book, for convenient treatment, has been divided into four sections (the first two of which were first published separately and are now included in expanded and revised form) as follows:

Tanks

Armoured Cars (covering all wheeled armoured vehicles)

Specialised Armour

Self-Propelled Guns and Carriers (including artillery tractors and tracked landing vehicles).

In each section, the treatment is chronological as far as possible, although in some cases it has been found desirable to group together vehicles of a type.

The following conventions have been followed in this book.

Machine gun calibres are: Hotchkiss, Lewis, Maxim or Vickers-Maxim, Bren—0.303in; Vickers—0.303in or 0.5in; Besa—7.92mm or 15mm. The heavy models of the Vickers and the Besa where they occur are specified as such in the text.

Diesel (compression ignition) engines are noted as such; otherwise an engine may be taken in this book to be of the internal combustion (petrol) type. In descriptions of wheeled vehicles the system has been used of indicating the number of wheels, followed by the number driven, e.g. "4 × 2" for a normal four wheeled vehicle with drive to two wheels—normally the rear wheels—only. Twin rear wheels on an axle are counted as singles in this notation. Ranks and titles used are normally those applicable at the period referred to in the text.

The writer wishes to record his grateful thanks to the many people and organisations who have given assistance in connection with this book, including, firstly, his friends Col Robert J. Icks, R. M. Ogorkiewiez, B. H. Vanderveen, D. Nicholas, D. Fletcher and P. Leslie. The Librarian and Photographic Librarian of the Imperial War Museum and the Curator of the RAC Tank Museum have given help from the resources of their collections—which any reader of this book is strongly recommended to visit. The Hillingdon Borough Library has also given great help by obtaining reference material, and the following organisations and individual gentlemen have assisted on particular points:

AC Cars Ltd
AEC Ltd
The Air Ministry
W. G. Allen & Sons (Tipton) Ltd
Earl Annesley
Major G. Atkinson
British Motor Corporation Ltd
F. W. Bromley (of Humber Ltd, who was closely associated with the testing and development of wartime Rootes Group vehicles)
W. E. Bullock
The Canadian Department of National Defence
The late Donald Campbell CBE
G. Clarkson
Concrete Ltd
P. R. Crowe
Major General Sir C. Dunphie
Brigadier A. H. Fernyhough, CBE, MC
F. M. Fish
Fluidrive Engineering Co
L. Gutteridge
Guy Motors Ltd
P. Handel
Harland & Wolff Ltd
Humber Ltd
F. W. Hutton-Stott
The Irish Department of Defence
Leyland Motors Ltd
London Transport Executive
N. C. Macnamara
Ministry of Defence, Army Department
Brigadier R. A. G. Nicholson, CBE, DSO
The Nuffield Organisation (T. J. Clements and D. M. Lowe)
Brigadier J. L. Proudlock, DSO
G. J. Rackham
Ransomes, Sims & Jefferies Ltd (L. J. Orvis)
W. Rigby
Rootes Ltd
The Royal Artillery Institution
The Royal Marines Historian
Self-Changing Gears Ltd
Simms Motor Units Ltd
C. S. R. Stock
Stothert & Pitt Ltd
Sunbeam-Talbot Ltd (E. M. Lea-Major)
The Vulcan Foundry Ltd
Viscount Wimborne
R. J. Wyatt

Abbreviations

AA	Anti-aircraft ("ack-ack")
AC	Autocarrier Ltd
AEC	Associated Equipment Company Limited
AFV	Armoured Fighting Vehicle
amp/hr	amperes per hour
AMRA	Anti-Mine Roller Attachment
ARV	Armoured Recovery Vehicle
atr	anti-tank rifle (Boys 0.55in)
BARV	Beach Armoured Recovery Vehicle
BEF	British Expeditionary Force
bhp	brake horsepower
Bn	Battalion
BSA	Birmingham Small Arms Ltd
CDL	Canal Defence Light
CIRD	Canadian Indestructible Roller Device
cm	centimetre(s)
DD	Duplex Drive (tank floatation equipment)
GOC	General Officer Commanding
GT	Gun Tractor
HP	High Power
hp	horsepower
HQ	Headquarters
IP	Indian Pattern
IWM	Imperial War Museum
lb/sq in	pressure, pounds per square inch
LGOC	London General Omnibus Company Limited
LMSR	London Midland & Scottish Railway
LP	Low Power; Local Pattern
LPTB	London Passenger Transport Board
MCW&F Co	Metropolitan Carriage, Wagon & Finance Company
mg	machine gun
Mk	Mark
MLM	Mobile Land Mine
mm	millimetre(s)
mph	miles per hour
OAC	Obstacle Assault Centre
OP	Observation Post
pr	pounder (preceded by the approximate weight of the shell; designation for many British guns)
PWD	Petroleum Warfare Department
RA	(The) Royal (Regiment of) Artillery
RAC	Royal Armoured Corps
RAF	Royal Air Force

RE	(The Corps of) Royal Engineers
REME	(The Corps of) Royal Electrical and Mechanical Engineers
SBG	Small Box Girder bridge
S-P	Self-propelled (Gun) followed by calibre
s-p	self-propelled
TOG	"The Old Gang"—type of heavy tank (World War II)
UDF	Union Defence Force
USA	United States of America
USSR	Union of Soviet Socialist Republics
v	volt(s)
WD	War Department

Part 1

TANKS

Tank, Mark I (Male) moving up to attack Thiepval, 25th September, 1916

[Imperial War Museum]

Development

THE BRITISH TANKS which went into action for the first time on the Somme on 15th September 1916 were the first practical realisation of the very old military desire for mobile and protected fire power. Some of the elements of the tank can be traced as far back as the Assyrians, but the development of the first practical armoured fighting vehicle with cross-country ability dates from the first time that the need arose when the mechanical means to fulfil it had reached a useful state of progress. The two main mechanical factors were the internal combustion engine, producing a high power-weight ratio, and a form of continuous track suspension to facilitate cross-country movement.

Armoured motor cars had been tested, and in some cases adopted, by the armies of several European countries from about 1902 onwards. Although as early as 1902 an armoured car designed by F. R. Simms was built by Vickers Sons and Maxim, armoured cars were not taken up by the British Army. Not long after the outbreak of War in 1914, however, the Royal Naval Air Service added light armour to armed patrol cars used for the protection of naval aircraft bases in Belgium and Northern France. Later, fully-armoured cars were developed by the RNAS.

After the German advance had been halted towards the end of 1914, a state of deadlock ensued as opposing trench systems, protected by barbed wire and machine guns, were built facing each other in a continuous front stretching from Switzerland to the sea. The lack of cross-country ability and dependence on roads of the RNAS armoured cars led to the formation of a Committee, largely at the instigation of Mr Winston Churchill, then first Lord of the Admiralty, to investigate the possibility of an armoured cross-country "land ship". The Admiralty Landship Committee took as its starting point a specification drawn up by Lt Col E. D. Swinton in October 1914 and submitted, without much effect, to the War Office.

The first major projects of the Landship Committee were a machine utilising two Pedrail tracks and a machine with very large diameter wheels. The latter was abandoned when detailed investigation had shown more clearly the design problems and disadvantages involved. At the same time that design and construction work connected with these main projects was in progress, several other lines of investigation were followed up. One was an armoured tracked machine designed by Lieutenant Macfie, RNAS, and Mr A. C. Nesfield and work was commenced on a prototype built up on the basis of an Alldays 5–ton lorry chassis, although never completed because of disagreement between the two designers. Other experiments were intended to test out features of the designs by Colonel Crompton for articulated landships and to ascertain the potential for landship use of the Bullock Creeping Grip and Killen-Strait tractors and their tracks ordered from the USA. The Killen-Strait tractor gave a spectacular performance at a demonstration on 30th June 1915; following this in July, the RNAS placed an armoured car body on the tractor, thus creating what has been claimed to be the first completed tank. This vehicle appears to have had no direct effect on the later designs which formed the true prototypes of the British tanks which were put into production beyond, no doubt, giving encouragement and incentive to the other landship designers.

The machine designed by Mr William Tritton (following abandonment of the big wheel landships, with which he was at first associated) for the Landship

15

Committee was very promising, although it was unable to meet new requirements for trench crossing laid down by the War Office which, from 29th June 1915, had joined the Landship Committee. This model, Little Willie, was followed by a new type of landship with an entirely different hull shape, the upturned bows of which were said to have been derived from the profile of the lower part of the large diameter wheels of the big wheel landship designs. The new machine—Big Willie, later more widely known as Mother—proved infinitely better than Little Willie in organised trails over various obstacles in which both took part and Mother became the prototype of all the British heavy tanks produced during the First World War.

The first action in which the tanks were used was in a failing offensive: they were in small numbers and the ground was unsuitable and not properly reconnoitred but, nevertheless, the little they achieved brought a demand for production in numbers. Requirement for urgent mass production, except for one period towards the end of 1917, continued throughout the War, permitting improvements to be introduced only gradually. The heavy tanks at the end of the War were very similar in appearance to Mother, but improvements had nevertheless been made in the system of steering, armour protection, ventilation and in many other details.

The first of a series of medium tanks, intended for more mobile roles than the heavy tanks were capable of, was introduced early in 1918. The only light tanks used by the British Army in World War I were a few 6-ton Renault tanks supplied by the French. The plans for 1919 provided for a massive frontal attack on the enemy defences with 3,000 heavy and medium tanks. About 300 new fast tanks were also required to create destruction behind the enemy lines. The War ended before this plan could be put into effect.

RNAS Delaunay-Belleville armoured car body on Killen-Strait tractor chassis

Mark II tank in Arras, 1917   [*Imperial War Museum*

After the Armistice, production of all tanks, except for a few nearly completed Medium Cs, was stopped. The development of the fast tank envisaged in the 1919 plan continued. It was hoped that this tank, Medium D, and lighter vehicles known as the Light Infantry Tank and the Tropical Tank, designed by Lt-Col P. Johnson of the Tank Design Department, would fill the post-war needs of the Army. These designs were rather ahead of their time, and proved unsatisfactory, due mainly to trouble with the wire rope suspension system. A rival design by Vickers in 1921 (known as the Vickers Nos. 1 & 2 tanks) was also not a success, as the transmission system and the speed attained did not come up to expectations. Wartime heavy and medium tanks remained in service for several years after the war, but the new tank which was eventually accepted for the Army was another Vickers design which was known as Tank, Light Mark I (and later as Medium Mark I). This tank featured a rotating turret and an aircooled engine (to avoid difficulties with water supply in some overseas territories) which gave it a reasonably good speed upwards of 15mph. Some Vickers Medium tanks remained in service until after the outbreak of the Second World War.

Financial control on Army expenditure was very rigid in the 1920s, but it was decided to develop a new heavy tank design to be available for production in quantity if the need arose. The outcome of the specification drawn up, A1E1, was usually known as the Independent. It had a 3-pr gun in a central turret and four auxiliary turrets with one machine gun in each: one of these was on an anti-aircraft mounting.

Tracks wore out rapidly on the early tanks. The effort to reduce wear by making the tracks laterally flexible, tested on the Light Infantry Tank by Lt-Col Johnson, was not a success. Between 1926 and 1928 Vickers produced a wheel and track version of the Medium Tank Mark I and a number of other special vehicles capable of running on wheels or tracks. Performance on roads was greatly improved, and track wear was saved, but the device was rather cumbersome and the tank tended to be unstable on its wheels. The development of these wheel-cum-track tanks was not pursued, as improvements in the design of tracks enhanced their lasting qualities.

It was felt by some after the First World War that very small cheap tanks in large numbers to support the infantry would be a better proposition than a lesser number of the relatively costly Medium tanks. To test the practicability of this idea, Lt-Col G. le Q. Martel in 1925 built privately a one-man tank. This used an ordinary motor car engine and had a speed of about 15mph. After it had been demonstrated, a number of similar machines were built by Morris Motors and, later, some prototype one-man and two-man tanks were produced by Messrs. Carden and Loyd. Eight Morris-Martel and eight improved Carden-Loyd machines were ordered and used by the Mechanized Force on manœuvres in 1927 and 1928. These Tankettes, as they were called, were not used for in-fantry support but as reconnaissance vehicles and led to a War Office requirement for a fully armoured light tank with a turret. The Light Tank Mark I, which appeared in 1929, was evolved from the Carden-Loyd tankettes.

The Vickers-Armstrongs concern designed most of the light tanks sub-sequently used by the Army, as well as several experimental designs, including three types of amphibious light tank, and light and medium commercial models. One of the most successful commercial designs was the 6-ton tank which was sold to many foreign countries as far afield as Portugal and Thailand. The first amphibious light tank type was bought by China as well as other countries. There were also private venture designs for light tanks by Alvis-Straussler and Vivian Loyd.

The Vickers firm also built three prototype tanks to the A6 specification between 1928–1929. These were a great improvement in layout over the Medium Marks I-II; weight distribution was much better and they were capable of a speed of 30mph. These vehicles were expensive, however, and a specification, A9, for a lighter and cheaper medium tank was drawn up. The tank which emerged used a commercial AEC engine and weighed 12 tons. The A9 when completed was designated a "cruiser" tank, instead of a Medium, and a similar type, A10, with thicker armour on a 30mm basis, which was completed at about the same time, was intended specifically for the support of infantry. This marked the beginning of the policy which persisted to the end of World War II of having two types of tank: one with heavy armour for infantry support, and the other,

Tank, Medium Mark D   [*RAC Tank Museum*

Light Tank, "Tropical"   [*RAC Tank Museum*

with the stress on mobility at the expense of armour thickness, for a mobile role. The weakness of this policy was that it tended to neglect the most important quality of a tank—its gun.

At the outbreak of war in 1939, the following main types of tank were in use or coming into service: Light Tank Mark VI, Infantry Tanks Marks I and II, Cruiser Tanks Marks I-IV. The best of these were the Infantry Mark II and the Cruisers Marks III-IV. The former had very good armour protection and the cruiser tanks with the Christie suspension were probably some of the fastest tanks in service anywhere at the time. All of these tanks were armed with the same gun, the 2pr armour-piercing weapon, except the Infantry Mark I and the Light Mark VI, which had machine guns only. The Light Tank, which was available in the greatest numbers, was really only a reconnaissance vehicle.

Nearly all the tanks of the British Expeditionary Force were left behind after the evacuation of the British Army from France in 1940. All the tanks in the United Kingdom, including some old machines and others intended for export to some of the Dutch colonies, were pressed into service for Home Defence together with numerous improvised armoured cars. The first Valentine tanks started coming off the production line during the year and development of the Churchill was rushed through: a necessity at the time, but the cause of troubles later.

In the meantime, General Wavell's success in Libya in 1940–1941 was considerably aided by the small number of Matildas in his command. Later defeats in this theatre of war tended to be blamed upon the short-comings of British tanks, both in design and in numbers, although in many cases the lack of success was due to faulty employment of our armour. Supplies of the new British Crusader cruiser tanks were received and were in action in Libya by mid-1941, but it was the American tanks—Lees, Grants, Stuarts—which began to arrive in the Middle East in the middle of 1942 that helped largely to restore the balance. Some Sherman tanks were first received in September 1942 in time to take part in the Alamein battle. The availability of this efficient tank in increasingly large numbers from America tended to make for a lack of urgency in the development of British cruiser tanks. The Sherman was, numerically, the most important tank to be used by the British armies in the Italian and North-West Europe campaigns. American tanks were employed exclusively in the British-Indian tank brigades in the Burma campaign of 1944–1945.

New versions of the Churchill and the Crusader armed with 6pr (57mm) guns appeared on the battle fronts in 1942. In the same year, however, the German Tiger Tank armed with an 88mm gun was first used on the Russian front; it was encountered by the 1st Army in Tunisia in the spring of 1943.

The Normandy campaign opened with the glider-borne arrival of a few Tetrarch tanks of the 6th Airborne Division; this was the first operation of its

Experimental Heavy Tank, A.1 El-Independent   [*War Office*

Medium Tank with wheel-cum-track device, 1926   [*Imperial War Museum*

[*Imperial War Museum*

Tankette, Morris-Martel (one-man type)

[*Imperial War Museum*

Light Tanks used for training in 1940—
Mark VIB (nearest), Mark IIB, two Mark
IVs, a Mark VIB and a Mark IV

[*Imperial War Museum*

Vickers-Armstrongs 6-ton tank, Type B in use for training in 1940

Vickers-Carden-Loyd Light Amphibious Tank (LIE3) (1939)   [*B.T. White*

A Matilda I and two Medium tanks, Mark II**   [*Imperial War Museum*

kind. The principal tanks used by the 21st Army Group in the Normandy battles were Churchill infantry tanks (including some of the later Marks with 6-inch frontal armour) and Cromwell and Sherman cruiser tanks. Nearly all of these types were armed with 6pr or 75mm guns, but there were some Challengers and Shermans armed with 17pr guns. The Comet cruiser tank with a 77mm gun was the only other major type of British tank to join the 21st Army Group before the end of the War.

Field-Marshal Montgomery, the 21st Army Group Commander, in July 1944 suggested abolishing the distinction between infantry and cruiser tanks and, furthermore restricting armoured units to one type of tank only—a medium, which he defined as a Capital Tank. The policy of having two classes of tank lasted through to the end of the war, however. The spectacular progress made by the three British Armoured Divisions equipped with Sherman and Cromwell cruiser tanks in the advance up to Belgium in September 1944 and, on the other hand, the reduction of the heavily defended Channel ports by infantry tanks and specialised armour were operations cited in justification of the infantry and cruiser tank policy. These were operations of rather an exceptional nature, however, and did not materially alter the fact that a tank needed to be a versatile vehicle designed around a powerful all-purpose gun and striking a reasonable compromise between armour protection and mobility. The Centurion tank, a few protoytpes of which were completed in 1945, (and excluded here, as its main development was postwar) had a fair measure of these qualities and, when the ideas advocated by Field-Marshal Montgomery were adopted just after the war, became the first "Capital Tank".

Crusier Mark Is at Tobruk, 1941   [*Imperial War Museum*

[*Imperial War Museum*

Churchill IV (N.A.75) with Sherman gun mounting in Italy, 1944

Cromwell moving up east of Caen, July 1944   [*Imperial War Museum*

Totals of 420 Male and 595 Female Mark IVs were produced, and the type was used in action from June 1917 (at Messines) to the end of the war. Mark IVs took part in the battle of Cambrai in November 1917, the first battle in which tanks were successfully used in large numbers under suitable conditions.

A few Female tanks were fitted with Male (6pr) right sponsons. These tanks were known as "Hermaphrodites" and were produced as the outcome of the first encounter with German tanks in April 1918 when two Female Mark IVs found themselves helpless without heavier armament than machine guns.

Tank, Mark IV (Male) showing unditching beam in use   [*Imperial War Museum*

Tank, **Mark V**

Weight:	29 tons (Male)	Armour:	14mm/6mm
	28 tons (Female)	Armament:	2 × 6pr, 4 Hotchkiss
Length:	26ft 5in		mg (Male)
Width:	13ft 6in (Male)		6 Hotchkiss mg (Female)
	10ft 6in (Female)	Engine:	Ricardo, 150hp
Height:	8ft 8in	Crew:	8
Speed:	4.6mph	Range:	45 miles

The Mark V was the first heavy tank that could be controlled by one man. The four earlier Marks needed four men to drive them: the driver, at the front with the tank commander (who operated the brakes) and two gearsmen, who were also gunners. The latter sat at the rear and operated the secondary gears to each track in response to hand signals from the driver. Demand for rapid production of the earlier models prevented radical changes, but an epicyclic gear system operated by the driver alone was designed by Major W. G. Wilson and incorporated in the Mark V.

A specially designed Ricardo engine of 150hp was used, and proved reliable in service. The radiator was, however, inside the tank and ventilation was less effective than in earlier Marks.

Two hundred Female and two hundred Male Mark Vs were produced in 1918; the first battle in which they took part was at Hamel in July 1918. They were subsequently used in action until the end of the war.

An earlier experimental model, also designated Mark V, was produced in wooden mock-up form by William Foster's in 1916. It was similar in appearance to the Mark IV but had a rear cab and modified machine gun mounts. This design was not accepted.

Experimental versions of Mark V and Mark IV were built with a device called the Tadpole Tail. This extension, added to the rear, increased the trench crossing ability of these tanks to 14 feet. It lacked rigidity, however, and a more conventional method of increasing the length of the tank was adopted in the Marks V* and V**.

Tank, Mark V (Male)   [*Imperial War Museum*

Tank Mark IV with Tadpole Tail   [*Imperial War Museum*

Tank, Mark V* (Female)   [*Imperial War Museum*

Tank, Mark V** (Male)   [*F. Mitchell*

Tanks, **Marks V* and V****

	MARK V*	MARK V**
Weight:	34 tons (Male)	35 tons (Male)
	33 tons (Female)	34 tons (Female)
Length:	32ft 5in	32ft 5in
Width:	13ft 6in (Male)	13ft 6in (Male)
	10ft 6in (Female)	10ft 6in (Female)
Height:	8ft 8½in	9ft 0in
Speed:	4mph	5.2mph
Armour:	14mm/6mm	14mm/6mm
Armament:	2 × 6pr, 5 Hotchkiss mg (Male)	2 × 6pr, 5 Hotchkiss mg (Male)
	7 Hotchkiss mg (Female)	7 Hotchkiss mg (Female)
Engine:	Ricardo, 150hp	Ricardo, 225hp
Crew:	8	8
Range:	40 miles	67 miles

The Mark V* was an adaptation by the Tank Corps Central Workshops in France to increase the trench crossing capacity of the standard Mark V tank. The hull length was increased by three extra panels added near the rear. This allowed a trench about 14 feet wide to be crossed, or about 4 feet more than the Mark V. These tanks were first used in action at the Battle of Amiens in August 1918, where they carried four additional machine gun crews in each tank. These machine gunners were to be carried forward and dismounted during the battle to support the cavalry divisions. This plan was not successful, because the machine gunners were affected by the heat and fumes during their ride in the tanks and in no condition to fight on arrival at their objective.

The Mark V** had the same length and trench crossing ability as the Mark V*, but was built as a new tank. The layout was rearranged and various other improvements were drawn up by the designer of the Mark V, Major W. G. Wilson. A more powerful Ricardo engine of 225hp was used.

Only a small number of Mark V** tanks, Male and Female, were completed, just after the Armistice in 1918, so they were never used in action, but some were adapted for use after the war as experimental "RE tanks" to carry and lay bridges, or operate mine-destroying rollers. Some were also fitted with trench digging devices or cable burying ploughs.

Tank, Mark VI (wooden mock-up)   [*Imperial War Museum*

Tank, **Mark VI**

A wooden mock-up of this design by Major W. G. Wilson was completed by William Foster & Co Ltd in April 1917. One 6pr gun was mounted in the front between the horns and there was a central fighting compartment with four mg mountings as well as two further mg mountings at either side of the hull near the front. The engine (a real one was used in the mock-up) was located at the rear on the right hand side and was a 150hp Ricardo. Compared with the Mark V, ground pressure was lower through the use of wider tracks, and a higher speed was anticipated. The estimated weight was 30 tons, and 14mm was to be the maximum armour fitted.

This design was not accepted because of the urgent need at the time for mass production of existing types, and an American order for 600 was later cancelled in favour of the Mark VIII.

Tank, Mark VII   [*Imperial War Museum*

Tank, **Mark VII**

Weight:	33 tons	Armour:	14mm/6mm
Length:	29ft 11in	Armament:	2 × 6pr, 5 Hotchkiss mg
Width:	13ft 6in	Engine:	Ricardo, 150hp
Height:	8ft 8in	Crew:	8
Speed:	4.5mph	Range:	50 miles

This tank, the prototype of which was completed in November 1918, was externally very similar to the Mark V but three feet longer, so the trench crossing ability was rather better than that of the earlier model.

The main improvement over earlier Marks lay in the adoption of Williams-Janney hydraulic transmission, which had earlier been tested in a Mark IV. The engine was fitted with an electric self-starter, and improved cooling systems were used for the engine and crew compartments.

The production order for Mark VIIs was cancelled after the Armistice.

Tank, Mark VIII

Tank, **Mark VIII**

Weight:	37 tons	Armament:	2 × 6pr, 7 Hotchkiss mg
Length:	34ft 2½in	Engine:	Liberty, 300hp or
Width:	12ft 4in		Ricardo, 300hp
Height:	10ft 3in	Crew:	8
Speed:	5.2mph	Range:	55 miles
Armour:	16mm/6mm		

After the entry of the United States into the war in 1917, the possibility of joint Allied production of tanks was explored. Agreement was reached for co-operation in the production of a tank to be manufactured in a new factory in France; the United Kingdom was to supply the armament and most of the materials for the hull, and the USA to supply the engine, transmission, and other mechanical parts. The production of 1,500 tanks was planned for 1918.

The general specification for this tank was laid down by army representatives at GHQ in France in December 1917, but the design was placed in the hands of a committee under Lt-Col A. G. Stern and Major J. A. Drain (USA) consisting of Sir Eustace d'Eyncourt, Major H. W. Alden (USA) and Captain A. Green (Tank Corps). The detailed drawings were produced by Lieut G. J. Rackham.

The Mark VIII, "Allied" or "Liberty" tank was based on the fruits of British experience, and was similar in layout to the earlier heavy tanks, but the trench crossing capacity was increased to no less than 15 feet. (A Mark VIII*, projected but not built, was designed to cross an 18-foot trench.)

The first Mark VIII to be completed was a hull made in England and shipped in July 1918 to the USA, where the power unit, a "Liberty" aero engine of 300hp, and the transmission were fitted.

After the Armistice the large order for Allied tanks was cancelled, but 100 were completed in America and seven in England. The first British tank had a Rolls-Royce engine, but later this and all the others were fitted with two 6-cylinder 150hp Ricardo engines geared together as one unit.

Tank, Mark IX   [*Imperial War Museum*

Tank, **Mark IX**

Weight:	37 tons	Armour:	10mm
Length:	31ft 10in	Armament:	2 Hotchkiss mg
Width:	8ft 1in	Engine:	Ricardo, 150hp
Height:	8ft 5in	Crew:	4
Speed:	4mph		

For the transport of infantry into battle the Mark V* had been tried—without success, due to poor ventilation—and obsolete Mark I, II, and, later, Mark IV battle tanks as well as Gun Carriers were modified to carry supplies. The Mark IX was the first tank specially designed (by Lieut G. J. Rackham in September 1917) to carry infantry or supplies. The engine was placed well forward, just behind the driver's cab, leaving a long clear compartment with access via two large oval doors on either side. Ten tons of stores or 50 infantrymen could be carried. The mechanical features of the design were based on the Mark V with an extended driving shaft, but the Mark IX, due to its increased weight, was rather more underpowered than the earlier model.

The Mark IX was never used in action, as the first one was not completed until October 1918, and only 35 were built by the end of the war.

An amphibious version was experimented with after the war. This was known as Mark IX Duck, and flotation was achieved by means of long air drums attached to the sides.

Medium Mark A

Tank, Medium, **Mark A**

Weight:	14 tons	Armour:	14mm/5mm
Length:	20ft 0in	Armament:	4 Hotchkiss mg
Width:	8ft 7in	Engine:	2 Tylor, total 90hp
Height:	9ft 0in	Crew:	3
Speed:	8.3mph	Range:	80 miles

The prototype of the Medium A was a tank designed in November 1916 by Sir William Tritton to meet a War Office requirement for a lighter and faster machine more capable of co-operating with the cavalry than were the standard heavy tanks. Tritton's Light Machine, or the "Tritton Chaser", as it was called, was completed at the beginning of February 1917. It used two 45hp Tylor engines side by side, one to drive each track. The driving shafts could be locked together for steering straight ahead, and turning was achieved by controls which opened the throttle of the engine driving one track and closed that of the other. A high degree of driving skill was required, as it was not difficult to stall one or both engines.

The tank, designated Medium Mark A, which went into production, 200 being completed by the end of the War, was similar to the Tritton Chaser except that to simplify manufacture a fixed turret mounting four Hotchkiss machine guns was used instead of the prototype's revolving turret with one Lewis machine gun. The petrol tank was mounted at the front inside an armoured box, instead of at the rear; and the maximum armour protection was increased to 14mm—the same as on the heavy tanks.

In March 1918 the Medium As, or "Whippets" as they were usually known, went into action for the first time at Colincamps, where they routed two German infantry battalions and closed a gap in the front. Eight Whippets supported the Guards' advance between Mons and Maubeuge on 5th November 1918, and this proved to be the last tank action of the war.

The Medium Mark As, like all the British tanks of World War I, had unsprung tracks, but one tank was modified with track rollers on leaf springs by the Tank Corps Central Workshops in France, under Lt-Col P. Johnson. When this same tank was later fitted with a 360hp Rolls-Royce Eagle aero engine in place of the Tylor engines, a speed of 30mph was reached.

Medium Mark B   [*Imperial War Museum*

Tank, Medium, **Mark B**

Weight:	18 tons
Length:	22ft 9½in
Width:	9ft 3in
Height:	8ft 5in
Speed:	6.1mph
Armour:	14mm/6mm
Armament:	4 Hotchkiss mg
Engine:	Ricardo, 100hp
Crew:	4
Range:	65 miles

Forty-five of these tanks were produced by the Metropolitan Carriage, Wagon and Finance Co late in 1918 to the design of Major W. G. Wilson.

A single 100hp Ricardo engine was used, with Wilson epicyclic transmission. A 2pr gun was provided for in the original design, but the only Medium Bs completed were "Female" tanks, armed with four Hotchkiss machine guns with seven alternative mountings. An interesting feature in the design was the provision of a sulphonic acid device over the exhaust pipe to make a smoke screen when required.

Although easy to control, compared with the Medium A, this tank was slow for a medium, with a speed of only 6mph; also the engine was very inaccessible and the crew compartment was cramped.

Medium Mark C

[*F. Mitchell*

Tank, Medium, **Mark C**

Weight:	19.5 tons	Armour:	14mm/6mm
Length:	25ft 10in	Armament:	4 Hotchkiss mg
Width:	8ft 10½in	Engine:	Ricardo, 150hp
Height:	9ft 7½in	Crew:	4
Speed:	7.9mph	Range:	75 miles

The Medium C would have played an important part in the plans for a breakthrough on the German front in 1919. The war ended, however, before the Medium C was ready and only the 36 that were nearly completed at the end of the war were finished after the Armistice. These formed the main post-war equipment of the Tank Corps until 1923.

The Medium C, also known as "Hornet", was designed by Sir William Tritton in December 1917. The track contour was similar to that of the heavy tanks, but the armament was concentrated in a fixed turret raised above the tracks. The Female tanks had 4 Hotchkiss machine guns and the Male version (none of which were completed) one 6pr gun and three Hotchkiss machine guns.

This type was the last of the wartime designed tanks with unsprung tracks, but it nevertheless had several advanced features based on wartime experience in design and operation. These included much better provision for the stowage of spare parts and of crew's requirements, a revolving cupola on the turret for the tank commander, and an anti-aircraft machine gun mounting.

Tanks, Medium, **Marks I-III**

	MEDIUM MARK I	MEDIUM MARK IIA	MEDIUM MARK III
Weight:	11.75 tons	13.45 tons	18.75 tons
Length:	17ft 6in	17ft 6in	21ft 5in
Width:	9ft 1½in	9ft 1½in	9ft 0in
Height:	9ft 3in	9ft 10½in	9ft 9in
Speed:	18mph	18mph	30mph
Armour:	6.5mm	8mm	14mm
Armament:	1 × 3pr, 4 Hotch-kiss mg (turret), 2 Vickers mg (hull	1 × 3pr, 1 Vickers mg (co-axial), 2 Vickers mg (hull)	1 × 3pr, 1 Vickers mg (co-axial), 2 Vickers mg (auxiliary turrets)
Engine:	Armstrong Siddeley, 90hp	Armstrong Siddeley, 90hp	Armstrong Siddeley, 180hp
Crew:	5	5	6
Range:	120 miles	120 miles	100 miles

The backbone of the Royal Tank Corps between the two World Wars was the Vickers Medium Tank. About 160 of these tanks were delivered by Vickers Ltd and the Royal Ordnance Factory between 1923 and 1928, and some were still in service for training purposes as late as 1941. The Medium Mark I was the design chosen to replace the Medium Mark C and various wartime vehicles: it was at first designated Tank, Light Mark I but (together with the Mark II) was reclassified when lighter tanks of less than five tons came along later.

The Vickers Mediums were the first fast tanks to go into service (the top speed was officially about 18mph, although they were capable of nearly 30mph) and were the first British tanks in service with revolving turrets. An air-cooled engine was chosen to avoid the problem of water supply in hot countries.

The Mark II was similar in appearance and layout to the Mark I, but was redesigned to give improved accessibility to the engine, the armour was slightly thicker and the suspension was protected by armoured skirting. During the years that they were in service, many modifications were made to tanks of both Marks, including the fitting of a co-axial Vickers mg with the 3pr in the Mark IA* and the Marks II* and II**. The Mark IIA had various improvements built in during manufacture, including better suspension units, extra turret rollers and differently arranged track return rollers.

The A6 specification was for an improved medium tank of around 16 tons, and three experimental vehicles, A6E1, E2 and E3, were built in 1928/1929. The layout was much more satisfactory than that of the earlier Mediums and the armament—one 3pr gun and five Vickers machine guns—was more powerful than that of the 31-ton Independent heavy tank. Various types of engine and transmission and suspension were tried out. The design was well ahead of its time but was relatively costly, and only three production vehicles followed—designated Tanks, Medium Mark III—built in 1930–1931.

The A6 specification was followed by A7, for which three experimental vehicles were built between 1929 and about 1937. Although not even three production A7s were built for issue to the Army a variety of experimental work on the power unit, transmission and suspension was carried out right up to the outbreak of World War II and much of the result of this work was incorporated in the Matilda infantry tank. Weights and dimensions varied between all three tanks built, but particulars for A7E3 were: weight 18.2 tons; dimensions—22ft 6in long, 8ft 11½in wide, 9ft 1in high; speed 30mph; armour 14mm/6mm; armament 1 × 3pr, 1 Vickers mg (coaxial) and 1 Vickers mg in a hull gimbal mounting; engine two AEC Diesel; crew 5; range 150 miles.

Although none of the Medium tanks described above was used in action in World War II, some were employed for defence or training in England in the early years of the War and some of the Mk IIs in Egypt were finally dug in to form part of the fixed defences around Mersa Matruh in 1940.

[*Imperial War Museum*

Medium Mark IIA used for driver training with armament removed

Medium Mark III   [*Imperial War Museum*

46

Light Mark IIB   [*Imperial War Museum*

Tanks, Light, **Marks I-V**

	LIGHT MKS. IIA AND IIB	LIGHT MK. III	LIGHT MK. IV	LIGHT MK. V
Weight:	4.25 tons	4.5 tons	4.25 tons	4.75 tons
Length:	11ft 9in	12ft 0in	11ft 2in	12ft 10in
Width:	6ft 3½in	6ft 3½in	6ft 8½in	6ft 9in
Height:	6ft 7½in	6ft 11in	6ft 11½in	7ft 3in
Speed:	30mph	30mph	36mph	32.5mph
Armour:	10mm/4mm	12mm	12mm	12mm
Armament:	1 Vickers mg	1 Vickers mg (0.303in or 0.5in)	1 Vickers mg (0.303in or 0.5in)	1 Vickers 0.303in mg 1 Vickers 0.5in mg
Engine:	Rolls-Royce, 66hp	Rolls-Royce, 66hp	Meadows, 88hp	Meadows, 88hp
Crew:	2	2	2	3
Range:	150 miles	150 miles	130 miles	130 miles

The Vickers light tanks were derived from the series of Carden-Loyd one-man tanks, tankettes and carriers produced from 1926 onwards (the Carden-Loyd firm was taken over by Vickers-Armstrongs in 1928).

The first turreted light tank designed by Sir John Carden was known as the Carden-Loyd Mark VII. A development of this, the Mark VIII, was accepted in service in the British Army in 1929 and designated Tank, Light Mark I. This vehicle was a two-man tank, armed with one Vickers 0.303-inch machine gun and the armour maximum was 14mm. The suspension was the Horstmann type with leaf springs and the top road speed was 30mph. Several experimental models of the next type, Mark IA, were built. These had more effectively sloped armour and, on some models, the coil spring Horstmann suspension was introduced. Four tanks of this type were tested in India in 1931, and led to subsequent orders by the Government of India for light tanks similar to those currently in use in the British Army, but with slight modifications for local conditions.

The next mark, Light Mark II, had coil spring suspension and the same hull form as Mark IA but with a larger, rectangular turret and a Rolls-Royce engine instead of the Meadows. The few that were available at first were used mainly as command vehicles. The Marks IIA and IIB that followed were produced in greater numbers. These Marks introduced improvements to the turret and the engine cooling and had rearranged petrol tanks. Tanks supplied to India had commanders' cupolas added.

Tank, Light Mark III was similar in layout to the Marks IIA and IIB. Twin spring suspension units were used and some tanks had a Vickers 0.5-inch machine gun instead of the 0.303-inch previously standard.

The suspension of Mark IV had no separate rear idler wheel and set a pattern followed by the later Marks V-VI. This tank appeared in 1932: there was an Indian pattern with a different turret. A Meadows engine was again used in this and the later Marks of light tank.

The Light Mark V was the first three-man light tank to enter service. Two machine guns—Vickers 0.303 inch and 0.5 inch—were fitted in the turret, which was mounted on a crowded ball-race. Apart from the turret, which had a sloping rear plate and slightly thinner frontal armour, this tank was very similar in appearance and specification to the Mark VI series which followed and was built in far greater numbers.

Light Mark V

About 160 Light Tanks, Marks II-V were built for the Army, apart from those ordered by the Government of India. Production was shared roughly equally between Vickers-Armstrongs and the Royal Ordnance Factory, although the greater part of the design work was undertaken by Vickers.

Most of the types mentioned above were used for training purposes in the early years of World War II, but a small number of Light Tanks Marks IIB and III took part in the opening stages of the Western Desert campaign. A few light tanks of the South African Tank Corps were used in the Abyssinian campaign in 1941: these were also Mark IIBs and IIIs.

As well as the types that were accepted by the British Army, Vickers-Armstrongs produced a number of commercial designs of light tank. Some of these, which were similar in layout to the Mark II-IV light tanks, were sold abroad in many countries. A number intended for the Netherlands East Indies was taken over and used by the British Army after the outbreak of war.

One of the most successful commercial ventures of Vickers-Armstrongs was the Six-ton Tank. This was bought or copied by numerous foreign countries but was not adopted in Britain. The suspension was similar to that of the Infantry Tank Mark I.

Three designs of amphibious light tank by Vickers were tested by the Army but were not accepted into service, although, again, some were purchased by foreign countries, including China.

Tanks, Light, **Marks VI, VIA, VIB and VIC**

Weight:	5.2 tons (Mk VI 4.85 tons)
Length:	12ft 11½in
Width:	6ft 9in
Height:	7ft 3½in (Mk VIC 7ft 0in)
Speed:	35mph
Armour:	14mm/4mm
Armament:	1 Vickers 0.303in mg, 1 Vickers 0.5in mg (Mk VIC—1 7.92 mm Besa mg, 1 15mm Besa mg)
Engine:	Meadows, 88hp
Crew:	3
Range:	130 miles

This type, which first came into service in 1936, was the final development of the series of machine gun-armed light tanks produced by Vickers-Armstrongs for the British Army. The Light Mark VI was a three-man tank generally similar to the Mark V but had a redesigned turret with extra space for the wireless equipment at the rear. The Horstmann suspension with double spring units was the same as that on the Light Mark V.

The Light tank Mark VIA was very similar to the Mark VI but had the track return rollers attached to the hull instead of to the top of the front bogey unit. The next type, the Mark VIB, which was the most widely used British Light Tank in the Second World War, was very similar to the Mark VIA but had a round instead of multi-sided turret cupola and a single armoured louvre over the radiator at the front, instead of two as on the earlier models. About half a dozen tanks of the Mark VIB type were experimentally modified to include rear idler wheels, so that the suspension was similar to that of the earlier Light Tanks

Marks II-III. It was hoped that this would improve the cross-country performance and some were tested in France with the 1st Armoured Division.

The Light tank Mark VIC, the final version, was generally similar to the Mark VIB but was armed with the Besa machine guns (co-axial 15mm and 7.92mm) that were becoming standard on all British built AFVs. The turret differed slightly from that of the Mark VIB and had no cupola.

Successive improvements were made in the Meadows engines fitted in all these light tanks, which were quite handy vehicles although lightly armoured and lacking in cross-country performance. They were used chiefly for reconnaissance.

The Light Mark VIB was used with the BEF in France in 1939–1940, where it formed a high numerical proportion of the total tank strength. Mark VIBs, together with numbers of the earlier Marks of light tank, were also used in the early stages of the campaign in Libya: some continued longer in service fitted out as artillery observation post vehicles.

Before the war the Government of India purchased a number of Light tanks Mark VIB for use by the Indian Army. Some of these tanks, which differed from the British Army ones in not having turret cupolas, were used by the Indian Army when Persia was occupied by British and Russian forces in 1941.

The Light Mark VIC was used in small numbers by the 1st Armoured Division in France in 1940, and, later, a few tanks of this type were with the garrison of Malta.

Light Mark VIA   [Imperial War Museum

Light Mark VIC in Malta camouflage   [*Imperial War Museum*

Tank, Light, **Mark VII Tetrarch**

Weight:	7.5 tons
Length:	13ft 6in
Width:	7ft 7in
Height:	6ft 11½in
Speed	40mph
Armour:	16mm/4mm
Armament:	1 × 2pr, 1 Besa mg (in Tetrarch I CS, a 3in howitzer replaced the 2pr)
Engine:	Meadows, 165hp
Crew:	3
Range:	140 miles

The Light Tank Mark VII was a radical change in design from its predecessor in service. This was the first British light tank mounting a 2pr gun to go into production, and an entirely new system of steering was employed. The four equal sized road wheels (the rear one carrying the driving sprockets) could be turned in a curve, thus warping the tracks so that the vehicle could be driven round the less sharp bends, although skid turning was available for more abrupt corners. Control was normally by steering wheel, but the brake lever, operating on either track, was used for sharp turns.

The prototype Mark VII, which was similar to the later models except that it had a Vickers 40mm gun and Vickers 0.303-inch co-axial machine gun instead of the 2pr and Besa, was completed by Vickers-Armstrongs in December 1937.

The production series was delivered by the Metropolitan-Cammell Carriage and Wagon Co Ltd between 1940 and 1942; an air raid on the factory caused a serious delay in output. A number of Tetrarchs were supplied to the Russians and were in action early in 1942, and a half-squadron of these light tanks also took part in the Madagascar campaign in May 1942, but the remainder of the limited number produced (total 171) was put into reserve for future airborne operations as they were then the only suitable tanks for this purpose. The General Aircraft Hamilcar glider was designed specially to carry the Tetrarch. About half a dozen Tetrarchs in Hamilcar gliders were sent to Normandy with 6th Airborne Division on the eve of D-Day, 1944. One tank plunged through the nose of its glider over the Channel, but those of the remainder that survived the landing gave useful service mainly as dug-in or mobile machine gun posts in support of the parachute troops.

A Tetrarch was experimentally fitted with collapsible canvas floatation screens designed by Nicholas Straussler. This device was first tested in June 1941 and led to the production of Valentine and, later, Sherman DD tanks based on the design.

Tetrarch I CS leaving a Hamilcar glider   [*Imperial War Museum*

Harry Hopkins I   [*War Office*

Tank, Light **Mark VIII, Harry Hopkins**

Weight:	8.5 tons
Length:	14ft 3in
Width:	8ft 10½in
Height:	6ft 11in
Speed:	30mph
Armour:	38mm/6mm
Armament:	1 × 2pr, 1 Besa mg
Engine:	Meadows, 148hp
Crew:	3
Range:	125 miles

This Light Tank was a development of the Tetrarch, to which it was mechanically very similar. The same method of steering by curving the tracks was used, but to reduce the driver's effort the steering controls were hydraulically assisted. The Harry Hopkins had a redesigned hull and turret, and the armour maximum was increased to 38mm. The armament was the same as Tetrarch's and, as with that tank, the 2pr was sometimes fitted with the Littlejohn adaptor with tapered bore, which greatly increased the muzzle velocity.

Vickers-Armstrongs designed the Harry Hopkins, but production totalling 102 vehicles (including prototypes) was undertaken by the Metropolitan-Cammell Carriage and Wagon Co and completed in 1944. The Harry Hopkins was never used in action; it was the final wartime development of the British light tank, although the Alecto SP gun, using the same interesting steering system, was derived from it.

Cruiser Mark I   [*Imperial War Museum*

Tank, **Cruiser**, **Mark I**

Weight:	12 tons
Length:	19ft 3in
Width:	8ft 4in
Height:	8ft 4in
Speed:	25mph
Armour:	14mm/6mm
Armament:	1 × 2pr, 3 Vickers mg (3.7in howitzer instead of 2pr in Cruiser Mk I CS)
Engine:	AEC, 150hp
Crew:	6
Range:	100 miles

A design to replace the old Medium Tanks, Marks I and II, the earliest of which had been delivered in 1923, was sought after in the late 1920s. A very good type, the A6 (usually known as the "Sixteen-tonner") was abandoned, due to its high cost, after a total of six had been built, and so the design of a very much cheaper medium tank, using a modified version of an AEC bus engine, was undertaken by Sir John Carden of Vickers-Armstrongs. The pilot model of the new tank first appeared in April 1936 but proved to be unreliable, often shedding its tracks. After a further period of development the first contract for a limited number of these vehicles was placed in August 1937. Due to a change in the concept of the employment of tanks when the first Service models of this tank appeared, they were designated "cruiser" tanks instead of mediums.

Cruiser Mark Is, or A9s as they were frequently known at the time, were used by the 1st Armoured Division in France in 1940 and also by the 2nd and 7th Armoured Divisions in the Middle East up to about the end of 1941.

54

This was the first type of British tank to have powered traverse for the turret. The main armament was at first the 3pr, as used in the earlier Medium tanks, but later the 2pr was substituted and was used in production machines. The close support models had instead the 3.7in howitzer which fired high explosive or smoke ammunition. The secondary armament consisted of three 0.303in Vickers machine guns, two of which were in cramped auxiliary turrets either side of the driver's position at the front.

Production of the A9 amounted to only 125 tanks, and it was soon succeeded by the very much better A13 cruiser, but the suspension and much of the mechanical design formed the basis of the very successful Valentine.

Cruiser Mark IIA   [*Imperial War Museum*

Tanks, **Cruiser, Marks II and IIA**

Weight:	13.75 tons
Length:	18ft 1in
Width:	8ft 3½in
Height:	8ft 6in
Speed:	16mph
Armour:	30mm
Armament:	1 × 2pr, 1 Vickers mg (Cruiser Mk II); 1 × 2pr, 2 Besa mg (Cruiser Mk IIA); 1 × 3.7in howitzer, 2 Besa mg (Cruiser Mk IIA CS)
Engine:	AEC, 150hp
Crew:	4 (5 in Cruiser Mk IIA)
Range:	100 miles

The A10 was developed as a parallel design to the A9 (Cruiser Mk I), of which it was intended to be an infantry version with thicker armour and, due to increased weight, a lower speed. The design, also by Sir John Carden, was commenced in 1934, shortly after that of the A9. The increased armour thickness was achieved by bolting extra armour plates on the hull, making a maximum thickness of 30mm compared with the 14mm of the A9. By the time the design was ready for production, however (the first contract was placed in July 1938), a much heavier armour thickness was felt necessary for an infantry tank (the Infantry Mk I had 60mm and the Infantry Mk II had 78mm maximum) and the A10 was re-classified as a "heavy cruiser" tank.

The last tanks of the A10 type, which had only a limited production, were completed (by the Metropolitan-Cammell Carriage and Wagon Co) in September 1940. Cruiser Mk IIs were in action in 1940 in France and in the Western Desert up to about the end of 1941.

The turret armament was a 2pr with Vickers co-axial mg, and some models (Cruiser Mk IIa) had also a Besa mg position in the front hull to the right of the driver. The Cruiser Mk IIa in some cases also had a Besa in the turret instead of the Vickers mg. An extra plate was added over the gun mounting in some tanks armed with the 2pr and Vickers mg. As with the Cruiser Mk I, there were close support versions of the A10 armed with the 3.7in howitzer.

Cruiser Experimental, A.14EI

Cruiser, Experimental, A.16EI   [*RAC Tank Museum*

Tanks, **Experimental, Cruiser, A14 and A16**

Orders for prototypes of these two specifications for "heavy cruiser" tanks were placed in 1938, that for the A14 with the London, Midland & Scottish Railway and with Nuffield Mechanisations and Aero Ltd for the A16. Neither type subsequently went into series production but useful experimental work on suspension, transmission and steering systems was carried out on them.

The suspension of the A14 was of the Horstmann type, with grouped small bogey wheels, and the power unit an adapted Thornycroft marine engine of 500hp, with a Wilson 8-speed pneumatically controlled epicyclic gearbox. Weight of this tank was 29.35 tons.

The A16, which weighed 21.75 tons, had Christie type suspension of heavier pattern than that used for the A13 series, a Nuffield Liberty engine of 414hp with a 4-speed transmission: it was later modified to incorporate the Merritt controlled differential steering system and the A16 was the first tank in which this was used. Incidentally, Thomson and Taylor Ltd, the Brooklands firm well known for their racing car work, were called in to deal with a major design fault in this tank which cropped up at one stage and some redesigned components were manufactured and delivered in a very short time.

Both the A14 and the A16 were intended for the same armament (which was never, in fact, fitted) of a 2pr gun and coaxial Besa mg in the main turret, and two small auxiliary turrets with one Besa mg in each.

Cruiser Mark III

Tank, **Cruiser**, **Mark III**

Weight:	14 tons	Armour:	14mm/6mm
Length:	19ft 9in	Armament:	1 × 2pr, 1 Vickers mg
Width:	8ft 4in	Engine:	Nuffield Liberty, 340hp
Height:	8ft 6in	Crew:	4
Speed:	30mph	Range:	90 miles

The Russian manœuvres of 1936 were attended by Lt-Col (later General) G. le Q. Martel, who was very impressed with the BT type tanks which had been developed by the Russians from originals designed by Mr J. Walter Christie, an American engineer. As a result of Col Martel's persuasion, the War Office asked Morris Cars Ltd to purchase one of Christie's tanks from the USA: this was done in November 1936, the tank being shipped as a "tractor", and the turret was sent separately.

The fighting body of the Christie tank was not very advanced in design but the suspension, using large diameter road wheels on swinging arms controlled by coil compression springs, permitted very high speeds (up to 50mph on roads) and also gave a good cross-country performance.

A medium tank, using this Christie type of suspension, was developed by the Morris Commercial Cars company. The engine used was a modification of the American Liberty aero engine, designed in the first World War but the most suitable type available at the time. The first production models of the new tank, A13, now designated a cruiser tank, were delivered by Nuffield Mechanisations and Aero Ltd (a company formed with a nucleus of staff from the Morris firm) at the end of 1938.

A number of these tanks, finally known as Cruiser Mark III, were used with the 1st Armoured Division in France in 1940. The Christie type of suspension was used in all the later British cruiser tanks in World War II.

Cruiser Mark IVA

Tanks, **Cruiser, Marks IV and IVA**

Weight:	14.75 tons	Engine:	Nuffield Liberty, 340hp
Length:	19ft 9in	Crew:	4
Width:	8ft 4in	Range:	90 miles
Height:	8ft 6in		
Speed:	30mph		
Armour:	30mm/6mm		

Armament: 1 × 2pr, 1 Vickers mg (Cruiser Mk IVA had a Besa mg instead of the Vickers)

The Cruiser Mark IV, or A13 Mark II, was very similar to the Cruiser Mark III from which it was developed. The chief differences lay in the turret, which had extra plates and undercut sides, and in the armour maximum which was increased from 14mm to 30mm. The Cruiser Mark IV had the same armament as the Mark III, but in the Mark IVA the co-axial machine gun was changed to a Besa instead of a Vickers. Mechanically, the Mark IVA differed from the earlier models in having a Wilson combined gearchange and steering gearbox. Some Cruiser Mark IIIs were later modified to approximately the same standard as the Mark IV by the addition of extra plates to the turret.

There were several variations in the gun mountings in these tanks: some Mark IVs had an extra plate fitted over the front, and the later Mark IVs and IVAs had axle-shaped mantlets instead of the earlier rectangular type shown above. Production of cruisers Mk III, IV and IVA amounted to 335.

Tanks of this type were used by the 1st Armoured Division in France in 1940 and in the earlier battles in Libya up to about the end of 1941. Although rather lightly armoured and prone to mechanical breakdowns, their speed was an asset in the Desert campaign.

Covenanter I CS   [*Imperial War Museum*

Covenanter III   [*Imperial War Museum*

Tank, **Cruiser, Mark V, Covenanter**

Weight:	18 tons
Length:	19ft 0in
Width:	8ft 7in
Height:	7ft 4in
Speed:	31mph
Armour:	40mm/7mm
Armament:	1 × 2pr, 1 Besa mg (Covenanters I CS, II CS, III CS and IV CS had a 3in howitzer in place of the 2pr)
Engine:	Meadows, 300hp
Crew:	4
Range:	100 miles

It was pre-war Government policy to give small orders for tanks to various concerns engaged in heavy engineering so as to enable them to acquire experience in tank design and production. Accordingly, the London, Midland & Scottish Railway were asked in June 1937 to co-operate in the design of A14, a cruiser tank. A pilot model was built by the LMSR but the type was abandoned in favour of a cheaper and lighter tank. The new design by the LMSR, A13 Mk III, became the Cruiser Mk V, later known as the Covenanter. It was basically a development of the earlier A13 Mk II (Cruiser Mk IV) but with increased armour thickness, a turret with more effective use of angled plates, and a specially designed tank engine.

Unfortunately, the Covenanter had many troubles, chiefly connected with the engine cooling system, and, although it was developed through four Marks in attempts to solve these problems, it was never used in battle. Altogether 1,771 Covenanters were built by firms under the production "parentage" of the LMSR, and these were used for training in the United Kingdom and, in very small numbers, in the Middle East. Some Covenanters were converted for use as bridgelayers and a few of these were used by the Australians.

The main differences between the Marks of Covenanters were as follows:

Covenanter II—modifications in Army workshops to Covenanter Is to improve engine cooling. The front armoured louvres over the radiators were removed in some instances.

Covenanter III—improved cooling system, with vertical louvres at extreme rear of vehicle. Stowage boxes added at either side of front headlamp.

Covenanter IV—engine cooling louvres on rear top plates behind turret. Similar air cooling system to Covenanter II but built as new vehicle and incorporating improvements introduced in Covenanter III.

Tank, **Cruiser, Mark VI, Crusader**

	CRUSADER I	CRUSADER II	CRUSADER III
Weight:	19 tons	19 tons	19.75 tons
Length:	19ft 8in	19ft 8in	19ft 8in
Width:	8ft 8in	8ft 8in	8ft 8in
Height:	7ft 4in	7ft 4in	7ft 4in
Speed:	27mph	27mph	27mph
Armour:	40mm/7mm	49mm/7mm	51mm/7mm
Armament:	1 × 2pr, 2 Besa mg	1 × 2pr, 1 or 2 Besa mg	1 × 6pr, 1 Besa mg
	(Crusader ICS and IICS had a 3in howitzer in place of the 2pr)		
Engine:	Nuffield Liberty, 340hp (Crusader I-III)		
Crew:	5	4–5	3
Range:	100 miles	100 miles	100 miles

The Crusader was designed as a "heavy cruiser", although the main armament—a 2pr gun—was the same as on earlier models. Nuffield Mechanisations and Aero Ltd was the parent company to the group of nine firms responsible for the total of 5,300 Crusaders made. The first tanks were running in July 1939: their design incorporated the results of experience with the A13 cruiser. The same type of Christie suspension (but with an extra pair of road wheels) was used and also the Nuffield-developed Liberty engine.

The first two Marks had a small auxiliary turret at the front with one Besa mg, but this turret was often removed in the field to provide additional stowage space. The Crusader II and III had extra frontal armour, and the latter, of which the first production models came out in May 1942, was fitted with the 6pr gun.

Crusaders were first used in action in the Western Desert near Capuzzo in June 1941; they fought in most of the subsequent engagements in the North African campaign. Excluding later replacements, 105 of the 6pr-armed Crusaders took part in the Alamein battle in 1942; Crusader IIIs were also used by the 1st Army in Tunisia.

Breakdowns under desert conditions were not infrequent at first: the engine fan drive often broke and the air cleaner gave trouble. The Crusader's armour was too thin, but it was nevertheless liked by its crews and admired by the Germans for its excellent turn of speed—officially 27mph, but often bettered.

Crusaders were fitted experimentally with the Meteor engine during its development by Leyland Motors for the Cromwell series of tanks.

Adaptations of the original Crusader took part in the North West Europe campaign as AA tanks and as armoured 17pr gun tractors.

Crusader I   [*Imperial War Museum*

Crusader II CS
[*Imperial War Museum*

Crusader III
[*Imperial War Museum*

Cavalier I

Tank, **Cruiser, Mark VII, Cavalier**

Weight:	26.5 tons	Engine:	Nuffield Liberty, 410hp
Length:	20ft 10in	Crew:	5
Width:	9ft 5½in	Range:	165 miles
Height:	8ft 0in		
Speed:	24mph		
Armour:	76mm/20mm		

Armament: 1 × 6pr, 1 or 2 Besa mg (hull mg position plated over in some tanks)

By the end of 1940 the need was anticipated for a cruiser tank with heavier armour and armament than the Crusader, and a new heavy cruiser tank with an armour basis of 76mm and armed with the 6pr gun was specified. It was hoped to fit this type with a modified version of the Rolls-Royce Merlin aero engine, but as it became apparent that this engine would not be available for some time, and to simplify and speed up production, an interim design, the A24, was brought out. The prototype of this tank, which was completed in January 1942, was made by the Nuffield organisation and used many of the mechanical features of that concern's Crusader, including the Liberty engine, the Mechanisations and Aero gearbox and drive, and side radiators.

This tank was known originally as Cromwell I, but was later renamed Cavalier, Cromwell being kept as the designation of the later Meteor-engined tanks. Only a few hundred Cavaliers were produced, and they were never used in battle as gun-tanks, as the faster and more reliable Cromwells had become available in quantity by 1944, but a version modified as an Observation Post tank was used by some units of the Royal Artillery in North West Europe.

Centaur IV of Royal Marines Armoured Support Group in Normandy, 1944

Tank, **Cruiser, Centaur**

Weight:	27.5 tons
Length:	20ft 10in
Width:	9ft 6in
Height:	8ft 2in
Speed:	27mph
Armour:	76mm/20mm
Armament:	1 × 6pr, 1 or 2 Besa mg (Centaur I)
	1 × 75mm, 1 or 2 Besa mg (Centaur III)
	1 × 95mm, howitzer, 1 or 2 Besa mg (Centaur IV)
Engine:	Nuffield Liberty, 395hp
Crew:	5
Range:	165 miles

The second interim version of the heavy cruiser tank to succeed the Crusader was known at first as Cromwell II but afterwards as Centaur. This tank, which was the same basic hull and turret as the Cavalier, was redesigned by Leyland Motors Ltd with the Merrit-Brown gearbox and modified suspension. The radiator position and layout of the engine compartment were altered to correspond closely to that of the Meteor-engined Cromwell. This simplified the changeover in production from the Centaur to the Cromwell when the Meteor engines later became available in quantity. Eventually, in the middle of 1943, the Leyland Company became design and production "parents" of the Centaur/Cromwell series and responsible for the whole group of manufacturers making these tanks.

65

The first pilot model of the Centaur was completed in June 1942, after delays caused by a temporary decision to revert to the Cavalier design in order to achieve earlier production. Trials revealed the need for more power and greater reliability in the Liberty engine, and Leylands developed a new model which was fitted in later production Centaurs.

The only Centaurs to go into action as gun-tanks were those of the Royal Marines Armoured Support Group. This formation, equipped with eighty Centaurs armed with 95mm howitzers, and twenty Sherman control tanks, was intended to support the D-Day landings with gunfire from its tanks shackled down in landing craft offshore, but in the event the tanks were landed and continued to give fire support several miles inland. Centaurs modified as AA tanks and as bulldozers also took part in the campaign in North West Europe.

Cromwell (with 75mm gun)   [*Imperial War Museum*]

Tank, **Cruiser, Cromwell**

Weight:	27.5 tons (28 tons Cromwell VII-VIII)
Length:	20ft 10in
Width:	9ft 6½in (Cromwell VII-VIII 10ft 0in)
Height:	8ft 2in
Speed:	40mph (32mph Cromwell IV-VIII)
Armour:	76mm/8mm (101/10mm on welded models)
Armament:	1 × 6pr, 2 Besa mg (Cromwell I-III)
	1 × 75mm, 2 Besa mg (Cromwell IV, V, VII)
	1 × 95mm, howitzer, 2 Besa mg (Cromwell VI, VIII)
Engine:	Rolls-Royce Meteor, 600hp
Crew:	5
Range:	165 miles

The design of this heavy cruiser tank was worked out by the Birmingham Railway Carriage and Wagon Co with the co-operation of Rolls-Royce Ltd, whose famous Merlin aero engine had been selected for development as a new tank engine to power it. The first batch of the new engines, de-supercharged and adapted for tank use and renamed Meteor, were made by Rolls-Royce themselves. This was to save time, but arrangements were made for other manufacturers to take over production, leaving Rolls-Royce free to concentrate on aero engines. The Birmingham Railway Carriage and Wagon Co finished the first pilot model of the A27M, Cromwell M or Cromwell III, as it was variously called in its early days, in January 1942. After trials, regular production of the Cromwell began in January 1943. Vauxhall Motors built some prototypes of the Cromwell and they were intended to have been responsible for the whole production of this type. Continuing production of Churchills by Vauxhalls was demanded, however, and eventually, in the middle of 1943, Leyland Motors Ltd undertook the parentage of the group of manufacturers of both the Cromwell and the Centaur.

The Cromwell was one of the fastest tanks of World War II and was capable of a speed of 40mph. This was geared down in later models to a maximum of 32mph to avoid undue wear and tear on the suspension, which was of the Christie type. The Cromwell was also the first British tank with (on some models) all welded construction of the hull.

The Armoured Reconnaissance Regiments of all the British Armoured Divisions in the North West Europe campaign were equipped with the Cromwell: its good speed made it suitable for this type of unit. In the 7th Armoured Division in Normandy, the Cromwell also formed the major part of the tank strength of the Armoured Brigade.

All Marks of the Cromwell were, apart from the armament, almost identical. The Cromwell Vw and VIIw were versions with welded hulls. Various modifications were introduced during production, including a front gunner's side escape hatch, a lower ratio final drive, and a driver's side escape hatch.

Tank, **Cruiser, Challenger**

Weight:	31.5 tons
Length:	26ft 4in
Width:	9ft 6½in
Height:	8ft 9in
Speed:	32mph
Armour	102mm/20mm
Armament:	1 × 17pr, 1 × 0.30in Browning mg
Engine:	Rolls-Royce Meteor, 600hp
Crew:	5
Range:	105 miles

The Challenger was a modification of the Cromwell design with a longer hull and modified suspension, including an extra pair of road wheels. A larger turret, designed and developed by Stothert and Pitt Ltd, was fitted, mounted with the 17pr gun and a co-axial 0.30in Browning machine gun. This type of tank was used in small numbers in the campaign in North West Europe to stiffen up the fire power of regiments equipped with British cruiser tanks.

The initial design of the Challenger was drawn up in 1942 by the Birmingham Railway Carriage and Wagon Company, and a total of 200 tanks was produced under the parentage of this firm.

A Challenger II, with a lower turret, was not produced beyond the prototype.

Challenger I

Tank, **Cruiser, Comet**

Weight:	32.5 tons
Length:	25ft 1½in (21ft 6in excluding gun)
Width:	10ft 0in
Height:	8ft 9½in
Speed:	29mph
Armour:	101mm/14mm
Armament:	1 × 77mm, 2 Besa mg
Engine:	Rolls-Royce Meteor, 600hp
Crew:	5
Range:	123 miles

Battle experience indicated the need for a cruiser tank with a gun heavier than a 75mm, so in July 1943 Leyland Motors Ltd, then responsible for the production of Centaur and Cromwell tanks, began the design of a new "heavy

Comet I   [*War Office*

cruiser" to be armed with a new gun. This weapon, known as the 77mm, was a version of the 17pr with a shorter barrel and a somewhat lower muzzle velocity. The new tank, named Comet, was similar in layout to the Cromwell and had the same Meteor engine. The hull and turret were all welded, however, a method that had been tried out on some marks of the Cromwell, and had thicker armour. The improved suspension system of the Comet included track return rollers (although these were absent on the prototype).

The first prototype was ready for test in February 1944, and after several modifications to the design the production models began to be delivered from September of the same year.

The Comet was not used in action until after the Rhine crossing in early 1945. It was very successful, as it proved to be fast and reliable and the 77mm gun was highly accurate.

Light Anti-Aircraft Tanks

An experimental version of the Light Tank Mark I appeared about 1930 with the turret replaced by an open ring mounting with two 0.5in. Vickers anti-aircraft machine guns. Little further attention was paid to this type of specialised vehicle until Mark VIA and Mark VIB Light Tanks were modified in 1940 to take a special turret equipped with four 7.92 mm Besa machine guns for anti-aircraft use. When available, four of these tanks formed part of the regimental headquarters squadron of British armoured regiments. The first version was known as Tank, Light, AA Mark I; a later model, Tank, Light, AA Mark II, had a modified turret with improved sighting arrangements, and extra stowage on the rear of the hull. An experimental Light AA Tank had four Browning machine guns in a power operated turret and another type had two 15mm Besa machine guns.

Light AA Tanks were on active service during the North African campaign.

Tank, Light A.A. Mark I   [*Imperial War Museum*

Crusader A.A. II   [*Imperial War Museum*

Centaur A.A. II   *[War Office*

Crusader A.A. I   *[Imperial War Museum*

71

Cruiser Anti-Aircraft Tanks

Before the invasion of Normandy in 1944 a new series of AA tanks was developed, using the chassis of obsolescent cruiser tanks. In the Crusader III AA I, the turret was removed and a 40mm Bofors light AA gun mounted in the fighting compartment behind a large four-sided thinly armoured shield which was attached to the gun mounting. Some early models, however, had only the same flat shield as the normal Bofors on the wheeled carriage. A Crusader chassis fitted with a triple 20mm Oerlikon mounting without a shield was also in service.

The Crusader III AA II had a specially designed turret mounting twin 20mm Oerlikon cannon; the Crusader III AA III was similar, but the wireless was transferred to the front compartment next to the driver, leaving more space for the commander/gunner in the rearranged turret.

The Centaur AA I was a similar adaptation to the Crusader AA II, but used the Polsten, a simplified form of the Oerlikon cannon, in a twin mounting; and the Centaur AA II had a modified form of the Crusader AA III turret, also with twin Polsten cannon. The Centaur III or IV chassis, which had the improved Nuffield Liberty Mark V engine, was used for both the AA I and AA II versions of this tank.

All these AA tanks on Crusader or Centaur chassis were employed in the Normandy campaign, but the overwhelming Allied air superiority allowed them few aerial targets, so the AA troops in British armoured regiments were disbanded not long after D-Day.

Infantry Mark I

[*Imperial War Museum*

Tank, Infantry, **Mark I**

Weight:	11 tons
Length:	15ft 11in
Width:	7ft 6in
Height:	6ft 1½in
Speed:	8mph
Armour:	60mm/10mm
Armament:	1 × 0.303in Vickers mg or 1 × 0.5in Vickers mg
Engine:	Ford, 70hp
Crew:	2
Range:	80 miles

The A11 was the first tank designed from the start for infantry support in accordance with the official division of battle tanks into two main types: infantry tanks and cruiser tanks. The designer, Sir John Carden of Vickers, was restricted by cost limitations and the Infantry Mark I adhered closely to essentials. The armour was on a 60mm basis (and proved invulnerable to all German anti-tank guns in 1940); the crew consisted of two men and the armament of one machine gun. The suspension and transmission were similar to that of earlier Vickers-Armstrongs tracked vehicles and the power unit was a Ford V-8 engine geared down to give a speed of only 8mph. This low speed was, however, considered adequate for a tank to support infantry in the assault.

The first production contract for Infantry Mark I tanks was placed in April 1937, so that by 1940 they formed the greater proportion of the equipment of the 1st Army Tank Brigade in France. Within their limits the A11s gave a good account of themselves before being abandoned at the evacuation of the British Expeditionary Force. Only 139 of these tanks were built, as they were soon superseded by the Infantry Mark II, designed to a more generous specification.

Tank, Infantry, **Mark II, Matilda**

Weight:	26.5 tons
Length:	18ft 5in (19ft 9in with auxiliary fuel tank)
Width:	8ft 6in
Height:	8ft 0in
Speed:	15mph
Armour:	78mm/20mm
Armament:	1 × 2pr, 1 Besa mg (Vickers mg on Matilda I)
	1 × 3in howitzer, 1 Besa mg (Matilda III CS and IV CS)
Engine:	2 AEC Diesel, total 174hp (Matilda I-II)
	2 Leyland Diesel, total 190hp (Matilda III-V)
Crew:	4
Range:	70 miles

An infantry tank mounting the 2pr gun and with armour sufficient to withstand projectiles of the same calibre was called for in the A12 specification. The essentials of the design to meet these requirements were worked out at Woolwich Arsenal using the mechanical features and general layout of the experimental A7 Medium tanks of 1929–1937 as a basis. The detail design and eventual production was undertaken by the Vulcan Foundry Ltd. The pilot model (which differed externally from later models in having six mud chutes each side) was ready for trials in April 1938 and production began in the following year. A total of nearly 3,000 Matildas of all Marks was eventually produced by a group of manufacturers under the "parentage" of the Vulcan Foundry.

The name Matilda was originally applied unofficially to the smaller Infantry Mark I tank before becoming eventually the official description of the Infantry Mark II.

The Infantry Tank Mark II was used in small numbers in France, together with larger numbers of the Infantry Mark Is, by the 4th and 7th Battalions, Royal Tank Regiment. Although, with a maximum speed of 15mph, they lacked mobility, their armour was very effective even against field artillery. The Matilda had its greatest impact in the earlier Western Desert battles until mid-1941, when the German 88mm gun was introduced.

Apart from the Western Desert (where the Germans themselves used a number of captured Matildas), the Matilda was used in the Eritrean campaign, in Crete, and in the defence of Malta. Matildas were supplied under Lend-Lease to the USSR and were also used by the Royal Australian Armoured Corps in the Pacific theatre. A few continued in use with some Australian territorial units as a training vehicle as late as 1953.

The Matilda formed the basis of several types of flail tank (some were used in action at Alamein), tank bulldozers, a flamethrower used by the Australians, and as an interesting experimental wireless controlled vehicle.

All Marks of the Matilda, except for the Matilda I which had a Vickers co-axial machine gun, were externally almost identical. The Matilda IV and V were usually fitted with auxiliary fuel tanks at the rear. The Matilda V had an air servo mounted on top of the gearbox to assist gear changing, instead of being incorporated in the control linkage as on the previous model.

Matilda (typical of Marks II-III)   [*Imperial War Musem*

74

Matilda IV CS   [*Imperial War Museum*

Valentine (typical of Marks I, II and IV)   [*Imperial War Museum*

Valentine XI   [*Imperial War Museum*

Tank, Infantry, **Mark III, Valentine**

Weight:	16 tons (17 tons Valentine VIII-XI)
Length:	17ft 9in (19ft 4in Valentine VIII-XI)
Width:	8ft 7½in
Height:	7ft 5½in
Armament:	1 × 2pr, 1 Besa mg (Valentine I-V and
	early models of Valentine VI)
	1 × 2pr, 1 0.30in Browning mg (Valentine VI-VII)
	1 × 6pr (Valentine VIII and IX)
	1 × 6pr, 1 Besa mg (Valentine X)
	1 × 75mm, 1 Besa mg (Valentine XI)
Engine:	AEC 135hp (Valentine I)
	AEC Diesel, 131hp (Valentine II, III and VIII)
	General Motors Diesel, 138hp (Valentine IV and IX)
	General Motors Diesel, 165hp (Valentine X-XI and some IXs)
Crew:	3 (4 in Valentine III and V)
Range:	90 miles
Height:	7ft 5½in
Speed:	15mph
Armour:	65mm/8mm

The Valentine was a Vickers-Armstrongs design using many mechanical components which were similar to those of two earlier Vickers tanks—the Cruiser Tanks Marks I and II. This tank was not the outcome of a War Office specification as was usually the case, and the name Valentine was derived from the fact that the proposal for the type was submitted by Vickers to the War Office two days before St Valentine's Day, 1938. A contract for the first 275 tanks was placed in July 1939. No pilot model was produced because the main features of the mechanical design were well proven and the first production model was ready for trials in May 1940. Manufacture of the Valentine ceased in early 1944, after a grand total of 8,275 of eleven main Marks had been produced. Of this total, 1,420 Valentines were made in Canada and all of these, except the first 30 tanks which were retained for training, were sent to Russia, where, together with some 1,300 UK built Valentines, many were in action shortly after arrival.

The Valentine was designed as an infantry tank, with an armour basis of 65mm, but, owing to the shortage of cruiser tanks in the United Kingdom in 1940–1941, was used to equip the newly raised armoured divisions, although rather slow for this function. It was also delivered to the army tank brigades in its proper role of infantry support. Valentines were first used in action with the 8th Army in the desert in 1941; they took part in many subsequent battles in this theatre of war, including Alamein, until the end of the North African campaign. The 6th Armoured Division of 1st Army in Tunisia was also equipped with some Valentines. Some of the Valentines of 23rd Armoured Brigade, from Alamein onwards, covered over 3,000 miles each on their own tracks. A squadron of Valentine and light tanks took part in a short but fierce action in Madagascar in 1942, and Valentines (some with 2pr guns replaced by 3-inch howitzers) supported the 3rd New Zealand Division in the Pacific campaign. By 1944 the Valentine had been mainly superseded as a gun tank, but a number were used in North West Europe as command vehicles (though retaining their main armament) with self-propelled anti-tank batteries. The Valentine was also employed as the basis of a number of specialised armoured vehicles, including bridgelayers and DD (amphibious) tanks. Some of the latter were used in the Italian campaign.

The Valentine III and V differed from other Marks in having a three-man turret. The Valentine VI and VII were Canadian built, the later tanks having cast nose plates—this innovation being introduced also in the later Marks built in Britain.

Tank, Infantry, **Mark IV, Churchill**

Weight:	38.5 tons (Churchill I-II)
	39 tons (Churchill III-VI)
	40 tons (Churchill VII-VIII)
Length:	24ft 5in
Width	10ft 8in (11ft 4in Churchill VII-VIII)
Height:	8ft 2in (9ft 0in Churchill III-VIII)
Speed:	15.5mph (12.5mph Churchill VIII-VIII)
Armour:	102mm/16mm (152mm/25mm Churchill VII-VIII)
Armament:	1 × 2pr, 1 Besa mg, 1 × 3in Howitzer (in hull) (Churchill I)
	(turret 2pr, replaced by second 3in Howitzer in Churchill I CS)
	1 × 2pr, 2 Besa mg (Churchill II)
	1 × 6pr, 2 Besa mg (Churchill III-IV)
	1 × 75mm, 1 × 0.30in, Browing mg, 1 Besa mg (Churchill IV (NA 75))
	1 × 95mm Howitzer, 2 Besa mg (Churchill V and VIII)
	1 × 75mm, 2 Besa mg (Churchill VI-VII)
Engine:	Bedford, 350hp
Crew:	5
Range:	90 miles

A new specification, A20, was drawn up in September 1939 for an infantry tank to succeed the Matilda, and the first of the 4 prototypes originally ordered was completed by Harland and Wolff Ltd, of Belfast, by the middle of 1940. These tanks were designed, like those of World War I, to have good trench-crossing ability and were originally intended to have 2pr guns in sponsons on either side, although no armament at all was ever fitted. The A20 did not go into production but was used as the starting point for the design of the A22 infantry tank, later known as the Churchill, which was worked out at Vauxhall Motors Ltd by Dr. H. E. Merritt (Director of Tank Design) with Vauxhall engineers. Because of the emergency situation after Dunkirk, production within one year was required, and from the design commenced only in July the first pilot model was running in December 1940; the first fourteen production models were delivered by the end of June 1941. The possibility of faults in design due to such rapid work was anticipated but accepted by the authorities, and various modifications had to be made to the Churchill after it had been issued to the armoured regiments. After the faults had been ironed out, however, the Churchill became a very reliable vehicle.

The only tank gun available in 1940 was the 2pr, and this was used in the first two Marks of Churchill, but a new version with a 6pr gun and redesigned turret, the Churchill III, appeared in March 1942. Other Marks and modifica-

Churchill I

78

tions followed, and the final type of Churchill, Marks VII-VIII, had six-inch frontal armour and a 75mm gun (Mk VII) or 95mm howitzer (Mk VIII, a close-support version). Many of the earlier Churchills were later re-worked to include improved features and extra "appliqué" armour. In North Africa, 120 Churchill IVs were modified to take the 75mm and 0.30in Browning co-axial mountings from Sherman tanks. These Churchills, known as "NA 75s" were used in the Italian campaign.

A total of 5,640 Churchills was produced during the War.

Churchills were first used in action in the Dieppe raid of August 1942, but these tanks, mostly Mark IIIs and Mark Is, had few opportunities to prove themselves as many of the landing craft were disabled off the beaches, and few of the tanks that got ashore were able to penetrate beyond the sea wall. A number of Churchill IIIs and earlier Marks were also supplied to the Russians in August 1942, and in October three Churchill IIIs were tested in battle at Alamein. The Churchill operated quite successfully in Tunisia, sometimes in mountainous country, and also in Italy to the end of the War. Several brigades of Churchills (up to a maximum of three, soon after D-Day) fought in the North West Europe campaign, where their heavy armour proved useful, particularly in actions like the assaults on the Channel ports, but their gun power fell a long way behind that of the later German tanks encountered.

Churchill III   [*Imperial War Museum*

79

Churchill V

[Imperial War Museum

Churchill VII

[War Office

Tank, Heavy, **TOG**

DATA FOR TOG II*

Weight:	80 tons
Length:	33ft 3in
Width:	10ft 3in
Height:	10ft 0in
Speed:	8.5mph
Armour:	2½in cemented to ½in mild steel
Armament:	1 × 17pr, 1 Besa mg
Engine:	Paxman Ricardo Diesel, 600hp
Crew:	6

Consideration was given in the early part of the Second World War to the need for a tank capable of breaking through the defences of the Siegfried Line. Sir Albert Stern, who played a leading part in tank production in World War I, was encouraged to gather together some of his old associates to produce an independent design to meet the following specification:

A tank capable of operating over shelled and waterlogged ground, armoured against 47mm and 37mm tank shells and 105mm gun-howitzer shells at 100 yards; the armament to be a gun of field calibre mounted low and able to pierce 7-foot reinforced concrete, one 2pr gun and one Besa in a sponson each side, one Besa to fire forward and another to fire to the rear; and four 2-inch smoke mortars.

The Committee under Sir Albert Stern included General Sir Ernest Swinton, Sir Eustace Tennyson d'Eyncourt and Mr H. Ricardo; and the detail design of the tank was drawn up by Mr W. Rigby and staff of William Foster and Co Ltd, of Lincoln, the firm responsible for the first tanks of World War I. The new tank was known whimsically as TOG, the initials standing for "The Old Gang".

T.O.G. I

[Imperial War Museum

The design of the TOG was begun in February 1940 and the tank first ran in October. TOG I as completed was rather similar to the French Char B; no sponsons were carried but a Matilda tank turret on top of the hull was utilised. The engine was a Paxman Ricardo Diesel and transmission and steering were by means of English Electric Co generators and motors. The tracks, like those of the World War I heavy tanks, were unsprung.

A new version, TOG II, was ready for running trials in March 1941, from a design begun in June 1940, after it was decided that the first model was too high and that the overall track configuration was no longer necessary. TOG II had a similar power unit and electrical transmission to TOG I but the armament was concentrated in the turret.

As finally developed and known as TOG II*, the tank had a 17pr gun and Besa in the turret and torsion spring suspension was fitted.

TOG I was later modified with an hydraulic transmission system designed by the Fluidrive Engineering Co, in place of the electrical transmission originally fitted and in this form was known as TOG IA.

A total of only two experimental TOG tanks was made (TOG I converted to IA and TOG II converted to II*) by William Foster and Co Ltd. Interesting research was made on forms of transmission and steering, but the high ratio of track length on the ground to the distance between track centres made these tanks very difficult to steer. The series was eventually abandoned because of excessive weight.

T.O.G. II*   [*RAC Tank Museum*

A.33 (with American type tracks)   *[War Office*

Tank, Heavy Assault, **A33**

Weight: 45 tons
Length: 22ft 8in
Width: 11ft 1½in
Height: 7ft 11in
Speed: 24mph
Armour: 114mm
Armament: 1 × 75mm, 1 Besa mg
Engine: Rolls-Royce Meteor, 600hp
Crew: 5

In 1942, although the policy of having two main classes of tank (infantry and cruiser) was still adhered to, it was decided to try and standardise, as far as possible, components for both classes. The A33, built by the English Electric Co and completed in 1943, was the only one of several infantry tank designs based on the Cromwell cruiser tank to reach completion. It had the Meteor engine and Merrit-Brown gearbox and the same armament as the Cromwell but, apart from the front view, bore little resemblance to the cruiser tank.

Two versions of the A33 were completed: one had tracks and side armoured skirting similar to those of the American M6 heavy tank; the other had British type tracks and armoured skirting covering the top run of the track.

The A33 never went into production and the Churchill infantry tank in its later versions continued to be produced up to the end of the war.

The Americans built to the same concept as the A33 an experimental assault version of the Sherman. This was known as T14; only two were made and the design was abandoned.

Valiant I

[War Office

Tank, Infantry, **Valiant (A38)**

Weight:	27 tons
Length:	17ft 7in
Width:	9ft 3in
Height:	7ft 0in
Armour:	114mm/10mm
Speed:	12mph
Armament:	1 × 6pr or 75mm, 1 Besa mg
Engine:	General Motors Diesel, 210hp
Crew:	4

Two features of the design of this tank were that it was to be heavily armoured but within certain weight limitations and that existing components should be used as far as possible.

The Valiant was a development of the Valentine, to which it bore a general resemblance. The armour was, however, much thicker and the nose plate was a sloping, angled casting. Unlike the Valentine, the road wheels of the suspension were all the same size. The rather tall turret mounted a 6pr or a 75mm gun with co-axial Besa mg. A General Motors 210hp engine was used, giving a speed of only 12mph. A later model was designed to use Meteorite 8-cylinder vee engine.

The parentage of this design devolved on Ruston and Hornsby Ltd., who completed the first prototype about 1944, but by that time the Valiant specification had been outclassed and so it never went into quantity production.

Tortoise

Tank, Heavy Assault, **Tortoise (A39)**

Weight:	78 tons
Length:	33ft 0in (23ft 9in excluding gun)
Width:	12ft 10in
Height:	10ft 0in
Speed:	12mph
Armour:	225mm/35mm
Armament:	1 × 32pr, 3 Besa mg
Engine:	Rolls-Royce Meteor, 600hp
Crew:	7

This massive vehicle may be regarded as the ultimate evolution of the British specialised infantry tank idea of heavy armour at the expense of mobility.

The Tortoise had armour protection up to an effective maximum of 9 inches, but the top speed was only 12mph. The gun, a 32pr (3.7-inch) with a muzzle velocity of 3,050 feet per second, was, however, the most powerful to be fitted in a British tank of World War II. The 32pr was mounted in the front of the hull with only a limited traverse (20 degrees each side), so the A39 was really more akin to an assault gun, on the lines of some of the German models on various Tiger chassis, than a tank. The secondary armament consisted of three Besa mgs: one in the hull front and two in a small rotating turret on the hull top.

Design of the A39 was begun in 1942, but the only vehicles to be completed, six prototypes built by the Nuffield organisation, were not finished until 1947.

Black Prince [*War Office*

Tank, Infantry, **Black Prince (A43)**

Weight:	50 tons
Length:	28ft 11in
Width:	11ft 3½in
Height:	9ft 0in
Speed:	11mph
Armour:	152mm/25mm
Armament:	1 × 17pr, 2 Besa mg
Engine:	Bedford, 350hp
Crew:	5

Vauxhall Motors Ltd undertook, towards the end of 1943, to develop an improved version of the Churchill infantry tank to mount a 17pr gun. The new tank, A43, named Black Prince, was wider than the Churchill because of the larger turret ring needed for the 17pr. The armour maximum (152mm) was the same as that of the Churchill VII, and so was the Bedford flat 12-cylinder engine, but the speed, due to the increased weight of 50 tons, was reduced to 11mph. A heavier version of the Churchill type suspension was used with wider, 24in tracks.

Six prototype vehicles were completed by 1945 and were under test when the war in Europe ended, so orders for the forthcoming production by Vauxhalls were cancelled.

Part 2

ARMOURED CARS

Austin Armoured Cars of 17th Bn., Tank Corps on reconnaissance, August, 1918

Development

A "MOTOR WAR CAR" designed by Frederick R. Simms was demonstrated for the first time to the Press on 4th April, 1902 at the Crystal Palace. This vehicle was the first British essay in what would, in modern terms, be recognised as an armoured car. Before this, in 1900, some steam-driven traction engines had been armoured and used in the South African War for hauling road trains. There were no successors to this type. An earlier design by F. R. Simms himself—a quadricycle, steered by handlebars and armed with one Maxim machine gun—was a significant event in the history of armoured fighting vehicles, but could scarcely itself be called armoured, as the only protection for the driver was a small shield attached to the machine gun. This little vehicle was first publicly demonstrated in June 1899.

Returning to the Simms War Car, the preliminary design was completed by the summer of 1898, and accepted by Vickers, Sons and Maxim, who at the same time agreed to supply the three automatic weapons and manufacture the 6mm steel armoured "skirt" for the chassis, which was to be built by Simms and Co. The engine finally decided upon was a 16hp 4 cylinder Daimler, able to run on either petrol or heavy oil—a facility recently reintroduced in modern tanks. This vehicle aroused considerable interest in the public in 1902, but not in the War Office, and the idea was abandoned. A motor railcar with the same hull form as the Motor War Car had, incidentally, been built by Vickers to Simms' designs and sent to Nairobi in 1900 for use in the South African War, but its subsequent fate is unknown.

There are few other British armoured cars known to have appeared before the outbreak of the First World War. One was built in 1906 by the firm of Sir W. G. Armstrong, Whitworth. The car was designed by W. G. Wilson (who later was closely connected with the design of the first tanks) using, it seems, the chassis of the Wilson-Pilcher car with 6 cylinder 18/24hp engine and four-speed epicyclic gearbox. The armament was a 1pr pom-pom, and the car was fitted with power take-off pulleys for use with a steel cable to enable it to pull itself out of difficulties. Later, there was an armoured version of the Ivel petrol-engined agricultural tractor and in 1913 another type of Armstrong-Whitworth armoured car—with a revolving turret—was supplied to the Imperial Russian Government.

A few experiments were made by the British Army in the years immediately preceding the War for the transport of machine guns by unarmoured motor vehicles. A few Autocarrier three-wheelers, for instance, were supplied for this purpose in 1910, and a few light touring cars were fitted up by a Territorial infantry battalion to carry Vickers-Maxim machine guns so that they could be fired from the vehicle. A number of foreign countries possessed experimental armoured cars in small numbers, but the British Army had no armoured cars at all on the outbreak of War in August 1914.

In September 1914 an aeroplane squadron of the Royal Naval Air Service under Commander C. R. Samson was sent to support the British naval force defending Antwerp. Touring cars belonging to this squadron were used for patrolling to protect the air bases, rescue the crews of crashed aircraft, and augment air reconnaissance. Early clashes with German cavalry indicated the value of armour protection and so a few of the cars and two lorries were fitted locally with mild steel plates. These vehicles, which were the first British armoured cars of World War I, were joined before the end of September by others sent out from England. All these early cars lacked overhead protection for the crew, but a fully enclosed armoured car with a revolving turret was designed by officers of the Admiralty Air Department (which controlled the RNAS armoured cars); at the same time experiments were made to determine the resistance of various thicknesses of armour plate to different types of bullets. A heavy armoured car, mounting a 3pr gun on a lorry chassis, was also designed to give support to the machine gun armed vehicles. Numbers of both the turreted armoured cars and the 3pr-equipped vehicles were received in France by early 1915 where, however, the opportunities for their employment became increasingly restricted as the opposing trench systems were developed.

The War Office contributed relatively little to armoured car development in the early part of the War. A few experimental vehicles were built, and a number of cavalry regiments were equipped (chiefly, it seems, on their own initiative) with a few armoured cars of different makes and designs. Support was given to the Army by armoured cars of the RNAS Armoured Car Force, which was expanded up to a total of 19 squadrons, some of which, however, were equipped with motor-cycle combinations. In addition, another RNAS squadron became solely concerned with experiments leading up to the design of the first tanks. The work of the Naval armoured car units with the Army in France was very useful, judging by the appreciative reports of several cavalry formation commanders. Armoured Car Squadrons were sent to other theatres of war, including Gallipoli, Egypt, East Africa and Russia, after mobile operations on the Western Front became impossible. In September 1915 what may well have seemed a logical step was taken, and most of the equipment and personnel of the RNAS Armoured Car Squadrons were transferred to the Army, whereupon many cars were stripped of their armour for use as staff cars or ambulances. The only new cars used in any quantity by the Army in the later War years were twin-turret Austins of the later type built originally for Russia.

The Simms Motor War Car being demonstrated to the press at the Crystal Palace, April 1902

Armstrong-Whitworth Armoured Car, 1906   [*Self-Changing Gears Ltd*

All the armoured cars built in Britain in World War I were based on conventional four-wheeled chassis with drive to the rear wheels only; the only mechanical innovation to appear being (in three types) the addition of a second steering wheel for driving in reverse. The chassis of touring cars of the more powerful type, or medium commercial chassis, were usually used for machine gun-armed armoured cars, and heavy commercial chassis with solid tyres were employed for cars equipped with heavier weapons. The only successful armoured car using a light car chassis was the Ford.

The chassis of the Rolls-Royce, which proved to be the most successful armoured car of World War I, was again selected in 1920 for the post-war equipment of the Army, which then had need of new armoured cars for use in Ireland. The Royal Air Force, which in 1921 was given the task of controlling Iraq, also took over a number of Rolls-Royce armoured cars, so that this model had then been employed by all three Services in turn. The RAF, being denied co-operation by the War Office in what was believed to be an Army function, undertook a policy of building or ordering its own vehicles with which to equip the RAF Armoured Car Companies. The Air Ministry tended to show greater interest in the more unconventional vehicles than did the Army. Armoured cars designed by Nicholas Straussler, for instance, which were in many respects in advance of contemporary British practice, were tested from 1933 onwards, and eventually a number of the latest type was purchased. An interesting Armstrong-Siddeley eight-wheeled armoured car was ordered in the late 1920s. This car probably used the Pavesi form of articulation about the horizontal axis that was experimented with by the Armstrong-Siddeley company at this time, although few details of this vehicle are now available. A rear-engined

91

six-wheel armoured car ordered by the Air Ministry from the same firm about ten years later is, however, shown here. This car had some features in advance of armoured cars used by the Army at that time (see page 96).

The Government of India also followed an independent policy in ordering, between 1921 and 1928, Rolls-Royce, Crossley and Guy armoured cars of different design from those used by the British Army, and more suited to local requirements.

The first attempt to improve on the limited cross country ability of the wartime and immediate post-war 4 × 2 armoured cars lay in experiments with rigid frame (as opposed to articulated) six-wheeled vehicles with drive to all four rear wheels. Lorries of this sort had been developed commercially in Britain from about 1924, and the first application to an armoured car was probably in India in 1927 or 1928 where the hull of a Crossley armoured car was tried out on the chassis of a Guy 6 × 4 lorry. Not long afterwards, however, the Army at home tested Scammell, Lanchester and Crossley 6 × 4 chassis and a 6 × 6 rear-engined chassis provided by FWD Motors Ltd. An Armstrong-Siddeley 8-wheeler and several models of Vickers-built armoured cars with auxiliary tracks for cross country use were also tried out at this time. The wheel cum track vehicles were not really satisfactory—they were complicated in design and rather unstable in operation. The Lanchester type was chosen for a production order. The Lanchester was a specially designed armoured car chassis but, like most commercial 6 × 4 vehicles, suffered in cross-country going through its relatively low ground clearance, coupled with the comparatively long distance between the front axle and the leading rear axle, bringing with it a tendency for the vehicle to "belly". Nevertheless, it was an improvement over earlier vehicles.

[B. T. White]
A Wolseley Armoured Car (first Admiralty pattern) entering Antwerp with the Naval Brigade in October, 1914

A small number of Crossley 6 × 4 armoured cars was also ordered for the Army, as well as a few others of different types for the RAF. Crossley and Morris Commercial six wheeled armoured cars, armoured by Vickers-Armstrongs were also sold to Iraq and Siam, respectively.

Between 1925 and 1927 the War Office ordered quite a number of lorries and tractors, mostly Burfords and Crossleys, with tracks instead of wheels at the rear, which gave them a somewhat better cross country performance than that of normal six-wheelers. Not much effort appears to have been made to design a British armoured car on these types of chassis, apart from two Burford machine gun carriers in 1928 and, it seems, an experiment with a Crossley-Kegresse in India, although as early as 1917 an Austin armoured car had been converted by the Russians into a half-track with Kegresse rubber tracks at the rear.

Armoured car development in Britain was, in general, overshadowed by interest in tanks. On the Continent, however, much greater attention had been given to the development of all-wheel-drive and to suspension systems suited to cross-country movement. Armoured cars designed by Nicholas Straussler and built in Hungary were, as previously mentioned, tested by the RAF. These cars embodied rear engines, four-wheel drive and transverse suspension, which permitted considerable independent wheel movement, and armoured hulls with few vertical surfaces. There were many points of merit in the design of these cars which were not found in British armoured cars of the same era.

The later Straussler armoured cars were built in the United Kingdom by Alvis Ltd, and this firm designed a small armoured scout car which was mechanically rather like a scaled-down version of the armoured cars. The Alvis Scout Car was entered in Army trials in 1938 against a similar type of vehicle designed by BSA. The BSA vehicle was eventually chosen, and led to the order for the first batch of a new and very successful class of vehicles in the British Army. The BSA Scout Car had a transmission system new to this country, although it had been used abroad. The drive was taken from the engine via a transfer box and differential through four shafts, one to each wheel. This system permitted a great deal more independent wheel movement than the conventional system for a 4 × 4 vehicle of a single shaft to a differential on the rear axle and another one to a differential on the front axle.

A Rolls-Royce Armoured Car stuck in a flooded shell hole, during the Battle of Arras in April, 1917. This car was fitted with a pivoted hook for dealing with barbed wire, and had an added cupola for the commander

At the outbreak of War in 1939, the three new types of wheeled armoured fighting vehicle in service, or about to be delivered, were the Scout Car (BSA), the Guy Armoured Car, and a Reconnaissance Armoured Car. The last named was built on a modified Morris 15 cwt 4 × 2 truck chassis, presumably for the sake of ease of production and cheapness, as its performance could not have been very much better than cars produced ten years earlier. Numbers of old vehicles were still in service alongside these new types. They included Rolls-Royce 1920 and 1924 Pattern Armoured Cars, some of which had been fitted with new turrets and re-armed to the same standard as the Morris Armoured Car. The RAF in the Middle East rejuvenated its old armoured cars soon after the start of the War by transferring the hulls and turrets to modern truck chassis, and the Indian Government effected a similar conversion with the old Rolls-Royce and Crossley vehicles. The new Guy Armoured Car was a rear-engined, short wheelbase, 4 × 4 vehicle, and these last qualities together with large tyres gave it good cross country ability. The early designation of "Tank, Light, Wheeled" (applied also to the prototypes of the later Daimler and Humber Armoured Cars) and the fact that the armament and armour protection were to the same standard as contemporary British light tanks, gave some idea of their intended employment as long range fighting reconnaissance vehicles. Perhaps the most important step forward introduced by Guy Motors in the Guy Armoured Car was the use of a system of welding the armoured plates of the hull and turret. This method was much quicker as well as offering more satisfactory protection than the riveted construction used hitherto, and was embodied in the Humber Armoured Cars which succeeded the Guy after a hundred of the latter were made, as well as in all subsequent armoured cars. The Humbers used the same hulls as the Guy, but employed chassis components which the Rootes Group could put into mass production: ultimately Humbers accounted for about 60 per cent of the total number of British-built armoured cars of World War II.

The evacuation of the British Expeditionary Force from Dunkirk in June 1940 with the loss of nearly all its vehicles led to the need for production of the greatest number of armoured vehicles for Home Defence in the shortest possible time. All types of wheeled chassis from private cars to furniture vans were pressed into service and armoured with what ever protection was available —even to concrete and boxes of pebbles. Some of these improvised vehicles were as primitive as any built in 1914, but certain of the better designs were later developed into successful Light Reconnaissance Cars. Various Home Guard units also made well-meaning attempts at armoured fighting vehicle design, but most of the products would have proved death traps had they ever come up against properly equipped enemy troops.

The Daimler Armoured Cars, which began to reach the troops in 1941 were perhaps the most advanced British wheeled fighting vehicles of World War II. They had all the mechanical sophistication of the BSA-Daimler Scout Cars, plus duplicate steering controls at the rear, as well as being the first cars to mount a 2pr gun.

Before modern armoured cars from the United Kingdom began to reach the Middle East, the brunt of the armoured car work in the Desert battles up to the autumn of 1941 was borne by South African-built armoured cars, of which a final total of 5,746 were manufactured. These cars used chassis components imported from North America, although most of the armament was supplied from the United Kingdom. Canadian-built armoured cars, scout cars and light reconnaissance cars (based on the British Humber, Daimler and Humber designs, respectively) were also used by British and other Commonwealth units as well as equipping the Canadian Army. India contributed over

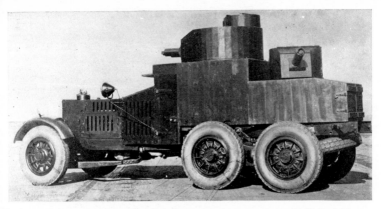

Scammell Experimental Armoured Car [*RAC Tank Museum*

FWD Experimental Armoured Car chassis

Wheel-cum-Track Armoured Car (Vickers)—D.3E1 (1928) [*B. T. White*

[*The Daimler Co Ltd*

Armstrong-Siddeley Armoured Car built for the Air Ministry about 1938

The chassis of a Daimler Armoured Car, showing engine at rear, independent coil spring suspension and duplicate steering gear

[*Imperial War Museum*

[*Imperial War Museum*

A Marmon-Herrington Mark III Armoured Car under shell fire in the desert, 1943

Lorries, 30cwt, Armoured, Anti-Tank, Bedford—on a Home Defence exercise in 1940

4,000 wheeled carriers to the Commonwealth war effort, in addition to armoured trucks and ambulances. These vehicles were built on chassis sent from Canada, and they were used in the Middle East and in the Far East campaigns. Most of the other principal British Commonwealth countries also built armoured cars, although these were in most cases used only locally. The contribution of the United States in armoured cars, and particularly in armoured trucks and half-tracks, to the equipment of British forces in World War II was very important, but the details are outside the scope of this book.

As the Second World War progressed, many different categories of specialised wheeled armoured vehicles came into being. Armoured Cars and Scout Cars were joined by Light Reconnaissance Cars, Armoured Command, Ammunition and Demolition Vehicles, Armoured Personnel Carriers, Flamethrower vehicles, and Anti-Aircraft, Rear Link, Observation Post and Command versions of standard armoured cars. There were also some self-propelled anti-tank guns on wheeled carriages, produced in the United Kingdom and in Canada. Many of these were inspired by the desert campaigns, where the country was on the whole favourable to the use of wheeled vehicles.

The need for heavier armament on British armoured cars was indicated during the desert campaigns by the numerous unofficial adaptations of Marmon-Herrington armoured cars to take captured enemy anti-tank weapons of between 20mm and 47mm calibre. The armament on British-built armoured cars progressed from the two machine guns (one medium and one heavy calibre) of the Guy and early Humber Armoured Cars to the 2pr of the Daimler and the comparable American 37mm gun of the Humber Mark IV, and ending up with the 6pr, and later, 75mm guns of the AEC Armoured Cars which was about the practicable limit for a mobile and reasonably well-protected vehicle.

The large variety of different categories of armoured vehicle in service by 1944 showed the need to standardise to some extent. Experiments were conducted towards this end in both the United Kingdom and Canada. The Canadians built a Universal Scout Car prototype which could combine the liaison function of a scout car with the duties of a light reconnaissance car. Different pilot models of a 4 × 4 armoured vehicle known as CAPLAD, and intended as a common basis for the Command, Armoured Personnel, Light Aid Detachment, Ambulance and Demolition functions, were built both sides of the Atlantic. Finally, the armoured car which was to have gone into mass production in Britain had the War not ended, was the Coventry, which combined features of both the Humber and Daimler Armoured Cars.

Nomenclature of British Wheeled Armoured Vehicles

NO STANDARD SYSTEM of naming British armoured cars seems to have been used during World War I, but they were usually known by the name of the manufacturer of the chassis.

The War Office after the War retained the manufacturer's name, followed by a Mark number and, where necessary, by the year of design—e.g. "Armoured Car, Rolls-Royce, 1914 Pattern, Mark I" (for wartime vehicles still in service) or "Armoured Car, Rolls-Royce, 1920 Pattern, Mark IA". The Air Ministry adopted a rather similar system, but used distinguishing letters—e.g. "Car, Armoured, Rolls-Royce, Type A".

By the outbreak of World War II, the War Office had adopted a type and Mark number system (similar to that used for tanks)—for the two new types built by Guy Motors Ltd, and the BSA Company representing the principal standard classifications of wheeled armoured vehicles—"Tank, Light, Wheeled, Mark I" and "Car, Scout, Mark I". Before long, however, with other manufacturers entering the field, the makers' names were reintroduced into the designations.

The new categories of wheeled armoured vehicles which came into prominence during the Second World War were usually given designations which were on the same basis as corresponding unarmoured chassis—e.g. "Car, 4 × 2, Light Reconnaissance, Standard Mark I" (known to the RAF as "Car, Armoured, Light, Standard, Type C") or "Lorry, 3 ton, 4 × 4, Armoured Command, AEC" (although this type was later re-designated "Armoured Command Vehicle, LP(AEC), 4 × 4, Mark I").

Special adaptations of normal vehicles were distinguished by a suffix denoting the purpose—e.g. "Armoured Car, Humber Mark III, RL" for a car fitted with special wireless equipment for Rear Link duties.

The above is only an outline of the method of nomenclature used: the systems were changed slightly from time to time and do not appear always to have been used consistently.

Early Royal Naval Air Service Armoured Cars

The Royal Naval Air Service squadron based at Dunkirk in early September 1914, under the command of Commander C. R. Samson, RN, was equipped with nine assorted aircraft and ground transport consisting of ten touring cars and a similar number of lorries. The cars were used for patrols to supplement air reconnaissance and, if necessary, to rescue the crews of aircraft shot down.

One of the cars of the unit, a 45–50hp Mercedes, was equipped with a Vickers-Maxim machine gun, and this vehicle, in company with other cars, became involved in action against German cavalry when reconnoitring near Cassel on 4th September. As a result, permission was granted by the Admiralty Air Department to the squadron for the shipyard Forges et Chantiers de France at Dunkirk to fit armour to the Mercedes. The armour, which was designed by Lieut Felix Samson, was in fact boiler plate, but was immune to rifle bullets at 500 yards, and gave reasonable protection to the crew and engine from front and rear, although the armour at the sides was lower. This RNAS first pattern of armour was also applied to another car, a 40–50hp Rolls-Royce. (In this context, "RNAS pattern" has been used to describe cars armoured in France, as opposed to "Admiralty pattern" for cars sent out from England with armour fitted). An Austro-Daimler and a Lancia were also armoured in France.

Lieut Felix Samson also designed armour for two "B" Type AEC chassis (former LGOC omnibuses), and this was also boiler plate, supplied and fitted by Forges et Chantiers de France. These armoured lorries could carry twelve riflemen to support the touring cars in action (and were in modern terms "armoured personnel carriers"), but proved too slow to keep up with the cars.

New armoured cars, built in England to the designs of the Admiralty Air Department, began to arrive by about the middle of September, and a force of 200 Royal Marines was sent to help man them. These Admiralty first pattern armoured cars were on Rolls-Royce, Talbot and Wolseley touring car chassis with strengthened springs and dual rear tyres. The three different makes were all armoured in roughly the same way—the engine being well protected, and the driver's head covered by an armoured hood, but the side armour was too low to give adequate protection to the rest of the crew, particularly in street fighting. One Vickers-Maxim machine gun was mounted on top of the driver's armoured hood. Some cars were later equipped with

Rolls-Royce Armoured Car—first Admiralty pattern

100

Talbot Armoured Car—a modified version of the first Admiralty pattern

Armoured AEC B-type chassis, RNAS

much higher armour, sloping inwards, which gave far more security to the crew. These cars were armed with two Vickers-Maxims on separate mountings. It is probable that these cars were Admiralty first pattern vehicles modified in France to the RNAS squadron's ideas.

A few cars, armoured in accordance with the experience gained by Commander Samson and his officers, were received from Forges et Chantiers de France in the early part of November. These cars of the RNAS second pattern were Talbots, with fully enclosed hulls and a small turret on top.

Other designs by Samson's unit before its withdrawal from France in February 1915 were a fully armoured 5 ton Mercedes lorry, armed with six machine guns; a wheeled carriage for a 3pr gun, with shield, towed by a special Rolls-Royce armoured car; an AEC lorry mounted with a 3pr Vickers semi-automatic gun; and an anti-aircraft mounting for a 3pr gun on a lorry.

The inadequacies of the first Admiralty pattern armoured cars were appreciated after visits to France by officers of the Air Department, and this led to the design of the fully armoured type with revolving turret. It is believed that all the earlier types of armoured car on Rolls-Royce chassis were rebuilt as turreted armoured cars, but that most of the Talbot and Wolseley cars with armour removed were subsequently used as tenders.

Early War Office Armoured Cars

The most successful armoured cars of World War I were those developed by the RNAS which built up a body of experienced officers for this work. The RNAS Armoured Car Squadrons together with their equipment were taken over by the Army in September 1915, but before that date the War Office had designed or sponsored a few experimental vehicles, some of which are described here.

An armoured car was built on an AEC "B" type chassis—a heavy commercial type with solid tyres, used for LGOC omnibuses—in 1915. This was probably the vehicle, constructed at Woolwich Arsenal, which was inspected at the request of the War Office by Flt-Cdr T. G. Hetherington, an officer of the RNAS Armoured Car force who was engaged in experimental work on the Naval armoured cars. Hetherington was astonished to learn that the vehicle would stop German bullets only at a range of 100 yards upwards. The general design of the armour of the AEC vehicle illustrated here was also used for an armoured car built on a Fiat chassis in India later in 1915.

One experimental light armoured car was built in 1915 for the War Office by the AC (Autocarrier) firm, which earlier had supplied a number of un-armoured three-wheeled vehicles to the Army for the transport of machine guns. This car used the AC chassis, with the 4 cylinder 1500cc Fivet engine and an unusual rear axle combined with the gearbox. The chassis and rear springs were strengthened to take the weight of the armour, which included a large circular turret. No further cars were built, probably because experiments proved that the armour was far heavier than the chassis could be expected to carry.

A number of armoured cars of different makes were also supplied to various Cavalry units, but as these, in most cases, appear to have been ordered on regi-mental, rather than War Office, initiative and in several instances paid for from private funds, they are described separately, as are the Leyland armoured cars of 1st AMB.

Armoured Car, AC (Autocarrier)   [*The Autocar*

Armoured Car, AEC B-type (War Office)   [*AEC Ltd*

Armoured Car,
Rolls-Royce (1914 Admiralty Turreted Pattern)

Weight:	3.5 tons	Armour:	8mm
Length:	16ft 7in	Armament:	1 Vickers-Maxim mg
Width:	6ft 3in	Engine:	Rolls-Royce 40–50hp
Height:	7ft 6in	Crew:	3
Speed:	50mph		

Early trials in action by Cdr Samson's RNAS crews had proved that the Rolls-Royce chassis was the most suitable for armoured cars and officers of the Admiralty Air Department were sent to see the Chairman of Rolls-Royce Ltd, with orders to requisition all chassis in the factory and in the hands of coach builders or agents and even cars completed with coachwork. The famous Admiralty pattern turreted armoured car was designed by Flight Commander T. G. Hetherington and Squadron Commander Briggs after conferences were held in the Air Department to determine a better form of vehicle than the first open type armoured cars. Ideas were translated from rough sketches into a plywood model before the detail design began. The first three production cars were completed by 3rd December, 1914 and six RNAS squadrons were equipped by mid-1915. An early experiment, on one car, was the mounting of a Vickers 1pr pom-pom in place of the turret. This was not continued, possibly because space was insufficient to permit handling of the gun inside the vehicle.

The Rolls-Royce was the most widely used armoured car of World War I, and after seeing action in France in 1915 was employed in Egypt, the Dardanelles, East Africa, Russia, in Lawrence's campaigns, and with Dunsterforce in 1918.

Some minor modifications were made at different times including, on some cars. a plate on the Vickers machine gun barrel to protect the aperture in the turret face; on other cars a pivoted hook was added to the front to engage and pull away barbed wire entanglements. A modification made in Egypt was the removal of the roof plates of the turret or the turret itself to make life more bearable for the crew in the heat of the desert. Some cars had cupolas for the commanders added on top of the turrets, but apart from this and other details, this design of armoured car remained in service unaltered for many years after the War. The RAF Armoured Car Company in Transjordan had a few in their original form as late as 1933. The War Office even referred to the Admiralty designs in preparing the drawings for the new 1920 pattern armoured car, which turned out to be very similar in appearance to the earlier vehicles.

Armoured Car, Rolls-Royce (Admiralty turreted pattern)   [*Imperial War Museum*

Armoured Car, **Lanchester (Admiralty Pattern)**

After the Rolls-Royce, the Lanchester was perhaps the most well known type of armoured car to be used by British forces in the First World War. The prototype was designed by the Admiralty Air Department and constructed on a Lanchester touring car chassis in December 1914. The production models followed in early 1915 and were very similar to the prototype in appearance, but Rudge Whitworth detachable wheels (double at the rear) were fitted; the springs

Armoured Car, Lanchester (Admiralty turreted pattern)   [*Imperial War Museum*

were reinforced and the chassis frame strengthened. The fighting body and turret of these cars were almost identical to the Admiralty turreted pattern Rolls-Royces and Talbots, but the unusual position of the engine beside the driver's feet in the Lanchester made possible a much more effective arrangement of the frontal armour.

Three squadrons of the RNAS Armoured Car force were equipped with Lanchesters and sent to France in 1915, and the Russians were also supplied with Lanchesters in the same year. The equivalent of about three squadrons of Lanchesters—about 36 cars—formed the nucleus of the large unit (although often referred to as a squadron), under the command of Commander Oliver Locker-Lampson, sent to the aid of the Russian Imperial Government. The expedition sailed at the end of 1915, bound for Archangel, but eventually became icebound and had instead to put into Alexandrovsk, near the North Cape. The cars were then found to be badly damaged, having broken loose in the hold during a storm *en route*, and as the radiators of many of them had not been drained they were cracked with the frost. The vehicles accordingly had to be sent back to the United Kingdom for repair.

The Lanchester armoured cars and other vehicles of Locker-Lampson's force were returned to Russia in the early summer of 1916, and the whole unit was then sent down to the Caucasus. A detachment went into North Persia, and the remainder of the force operated in the Caucasus itself, down as far as the Turkish border. The achievements of the unit in mastering the appalling mountain road conditions and keeping the vehicles in action were perhaps more noteworthy than the military effect of these operations. When the rainy season began in October the force was moved via the north shore of the Black

Sea into Rumania where, although too small to alter the final course of events, it had a considerable effect on the morale of its allies. The following June (1917) the unit was moved to Galicia in south Poland to support an unsuccessful Russian offensive. In November the Revolution broke out in Russia, putting a stop to offensive operations, and the squadron was evacuated through Archangel to England in January 1918. Some of the Lanchester armoured cars of this unit almost certainly operated farther on their wheels than any other vehicles of World War I.

The 38hp Lanchester chassis was used for these armoured cars, which weighed about 5 tons and were said to be capable of a speed of 50mph. The armament was one Vickers-Maxim machine gun mounted in the turret, and the armour was built up of 0.3in (8mm) plate.

Armoured Car, Delaunay-Belleville   [*Imperial War Museum*

Armoured Cars, **Talbot, Delaunay-Belleville and Sizaire-Berwick**

In addition to the Rolls-Royces and Lanchesters, which formed the bulk of the Admiralty pattern turreted armoured cars, a small number of similar vehicles on Talbot 25hp and Delaunay-Belleville chassis were built. The Talbot was very much like the Rolls-Royce in appearance, but had Warland rims, dual at the rear, with artillery type spokes, instead of wire spoke wheels. The fighting compartment and turret of the Talbot were identical to those of the Rolls-Royce, but the Delaunay-Belleville had a flat-topped circular turret without

Armoured Car, Sizaire-Berwick—"Wind Waggon"   [*RAC Tank Museum*

the bevels that characterised the other models, and the hull was rather larger. It was the armoured hull of a Delaunay-Belleville, incidentally, that was fitted on to a Killen-Strait caterpillar tractor in 1915, to test its possibilities as a light tank.

A Sizaire-Berwick 20hp chassis was used for an interesting experiment at the RNAS Armoured Car Division Headquarters at Wormwood Scrubs in the Summer of 1915. This was built as an armoured car intended for operation in desert conditions, and a 110hp Sunbeam aero engine was mounted at the rear, driving a four-bladed propeller, to provide propulsion over soft sand. This chassis was supplied by the F. W. Berwick Company, who also fitted the aero engine, but the armour was made by the Admiralty. One Vickers-Maxim machine gun was mounted beside the driver, and able to fire forwards only. This vehicle, known as "Wind Waggon", was never used in action, one probable reason being that the aero engine left very little space for the crew, armament or equipment.

The Talbot and Delaunay-Belleville Admiralty pattern turreted armoured cars were built only in small numbers—probably not more than the equivalent of one squadron—and they are not known to have been used in action.

Cavalry Armoured Cars, 1914-1915

The War Office showed only mild interest in armoured cars in the early stages of World War I, but this lack of enthusiasm was, to some extent, compensated for by the initiative shown at regimental level in a number of Territorial and volunteer cavalry regiments. It was not generally realised in 1914 that the days of the cavalry as an assault arm were already numbered by the machine gun and barbed wire, with trench warfare soon to come, but some commanding officers, at least, recognised the value of armoured cars for giving fire support to the horsed squadrons. Some of the armoured cars with which certain cavalry units equipped themselves are described here: these were probably not the only ones of their kind.

A fund to supply six armoured cars to the London Mounted Brigade (consisting of 1st County of London Yeomanry, 1st City of London Yeomanry and 3rd County of London Yeomanry) was instituted under the Lord Mayor of London. The sum collected may not have reached the necessary size, but two armoured cars, at any rate, were ordered on 24th November, 1914. These cars were built on Wolseley "CP" 30cwt lorry chassis with solid tyres, and were delivered in July of the following year. They were fully armoured vehicles with turrets. The London Mounted Brigade was sent out to Egypt in 1915, but there seems to be no record of armoured cars having accompanied them, although unarmoured Ford cars (said to have been donated by the City of London) were used in the subsequent campaign. The Wolseley "CP" chassis was used for another armoured car, incidentally, this time ordered by the War Office; but, although work on it was commenced at about the same time, it was not delivered until October 1915, so was presumably of different design from the London Mounted Brigade cars.

Two other types of armoured car were also built by the Wolseley Company, but on touring car chassis with pneumatic tyres. They were probably both built for cavalry units, although details are not known. One had an open top, whilst the other, a Mercedes, was enclosed and had a turret like that of the "CP" type cars built for the London Mounted Brigade.

The Westmorland and Cumberland Yeomanry was a Territorial unit which equipped itself with vehicles from private funds. One armoured car, completed in November 1914, had an open-top armoured body and was built on a 25hp Isotta-Fraschini chassis. A second car, built like the first, by Guy Lewin Ltd, was enclosed, and of unusual design, with sloping front and rear plates. This vehicle probably also used an Isotta-Fraschini chassis.

A Talbot 25hp Type 4 ST chassis was used as the basis of an armoured car delivered to the 2nd King Edward's Horse (a cavalry regiment raised from Colonial volunteers in London) in January 1915. This vehicle had an enclosed armoured hull built by the coachbuilding firm of Barker and Co Ltd. The turret was armed with one machine gun.

Armoured Car, Talbot (2nd King Edward's Horse)   [*The Autocar*

[*The Autocar*

Armoured Car, Isotta-Fraschini (1915) (Westmorland & Cumberland Yeomanry)

Armoured Car, Wolseley CP type   [*Nuffield Organisation*

Armoured Car, Seabrook

Armoured Car, **Seabrook**

This heavy armoured car equipped with a 3pr gun was designed to give support to the RNAS armoured cars armed only with machine guns. Built on the Seabrook 5 ton lorry chassis, of American origin, powered by a 4 cylinder, 32.2hp Continental engine, the first car was delivered on 5th February, 1915, by the Portholme Aerodrome Company, of Huntingdon. The 3pr Naval gun was mounted nearly over the back axle and had an all-round traverse. Shields were fitted to the 3prs in some cars. The armoured protection on these vehicles was 8mm plate, and that at the sides could be let down to form a platform for the crew serving the 3pr gun. Four Vickers-Maxim guns were carried, mountings being at the corners of the rear compartment.

Only about 25–30 of these cars were built and they were originally distributed three per squadron to the RNAS Armoured Car Squadrons equipped with Rolls-Royce or Lanchester armoured cars. Some of these heavy armoured cars were employed in action at Ypres where they impressed Sir John French, Commander-in-Chief of the British Expeditionary Force, who sent a request to the Admiralty for more of them. Their success was limited, however by their 10 ton weight which confined them to roads and prevented them crossing even slight ditches without the aid of the planks carried for the purpose. The springs, tyres, wheels and back axles often gave trouble due to the considerable loaded weight. In May 1915 the Seabrooks were organised into heavy squadrons of six cars each, but they were withdrawn from France towards the end of the year and some were sent to join the Western Frontier Force (Egypt) for use against the Senussi.

110

Armoured Cars, Peerless (2pr pom-pom)   *[Nuffield Organisation*

Pierce-Arrow and Peerless Armoured Cars (1915-1916)

Imported American Pierce-Arrow and Peerless heavy lorry chassis were used for a quantity of armoured cars built in Britain which appeared in several different forms.

Wolseley Motors Ltd, were responsible for the earliest work involving these chassis. The Admiralty ordered, on 30th December, 1914, 48 armoured cars to be built on Pierce-Arrow 14ft wheelbase chassis with 30hp 4 cylinder engines. These cars were for the Royal Marine Artillery Anti-Aircraft Brigade, which had an establishment of 16 Vickers 2pr automatic AA guns ("pom-poms"). These guns were mounted in 16 of the Pierce-Arrow armoured cars, the remainder of the vehicles being spares. The armament of the cars included one or more Vickers-Maxim machine guns, for which four mountings were provided. The armour consisted of Vickers 5mm plate on 32 of the cars and 8mm plate on the rest. The weight of these cars with guns mounted was over nine tons. All 48 of them were delivered between March and June, 1915.

During the time it had this equipment in France, between April 1915 and about the end of 1917, the RMA AA Brigade brought down about a score of enemy aircraft and, more important, gradually forced reconnaissance aircraft up to 10,000ft where they were far less effective.

The Peerless lorry chassis had chain drive to the rear wheels instead of the shaft drive of the Pierce-Arrow, but was of similar dimensions to that type, so that it was possible to use practically the same form of armour for the 16 armoured cars on Peerless chassis ordered from Wolseley Motors in January and February 1915 for the Russian Imperial Government. They were delivered in 1916. The armament of the Peerless cars was, like the Pierce-Arrows, a 2pr pom-pom and a Vickers-Maxim machine gun, although the Russians fitted some with a small turret in place of the pom-pom. A later and more well known model of armoured car on Peerless chassis—the twin turret type—is described separately on another page.

The Royal Naval Air Service Armoured Car Force commanded by Commander Locker-Lampson, serving with the Russians, was supplied in 1916 with a number of heavy armoured cars equipped with 3pr guns to give support to the Lanchester and other light armoured cars of the unit. Two Pierce-Arrow vehicles were armoured with ⅜in plate at W. G. Allen and Sons works at Tipton. The turntables for the 3pr gun turrets were made at the shipyard of John Shearman and Co at Newport, Monmouthshire, where the RNAS had a depot for the construction and repair of vehicles for the unit in Russia. The bonnet armour of these cars was identical to that of the Pierce-Arrows equipped with 2pr pom-poms, but the driver's cab was reduced to half the width to permit the gun to traverse forward. The driver's vision port was fitted with Triplex bullet-proof glass. In Russia the weight of these cars was found to be too much for the chassis and so they were modified by having the turrets removed and shields fitted to the 3pr guns and the hull sides filled in with flat plates.

Armoured Cars, Pierce-Arrow (3pr)　　　　　　　　　　　　　　　[*A.R. McIver*

112

Armoured Car, Leyland

Armoured Car, **Leyland**

Four Leyland heavy armoured cars formed the nucleus of 1st Armoured Motor Battery, Machine Gun Corps, which was raised at Bisley in the winter of 1915 and sent, the following year, to join the campaign in German East Africa. The chassis was a modified version of the famous "RAF Type" Leyland, with 4 cylinder engine developing between 30 and 40hp. A second steering wheel was fitted at the rear for driving in reverse in an emergency. The armament of these cars consisted of one Vickers-Maxim machine gun in the turret and one machine gun mounted at the rear of the hull, with only a limited traverse; the original equipment included a searchlight mounted on the turret. The armour was of $\frac{3}{16}$in and $\frac{1}{4}$in Beardmore plate.

These heavy vehicles each carried a crew of 6: this manpower was, doubtless, frequently found to be an asset during the campaign when the cars, which were fitted with narrow solid tyres, became bogged down in the bush. Some thought appears to have gone into the design of these cars, but the military effect achieved by them in German East Africa was slight, as the country was very unsuitable for vehicles of any kind.

Ford Light Armoured Car   [*RAC Tank Museum*

Armoured Car, **Ford**

Almost all the British armoured cars of World War I were built on the chassis of either powerful touring cars or heavy commercial vehicles. One outstanding exception was the Ford, used as the basis of some light armoured cars forming part of Commander Locker-Lampson's force in Russia.

The first vehicle was designed by CPO L. Gutteridge in early 1917 at the RNAS depot at Newport, Mon. This depot was where the vehicles of Locker-Lampson's unit were brought back from Russia in order to repair the damage sustained by storm and frost on their abortive first trip.

The Ford armoured car had an open top at the rear and was designed to carry a Vickers machine gun on its tripod. The tripod was locked to the floor of the vehicle by means of quick release catches so that the weapon could be quickly dismounted for ground use.

Nine cars were built. The chassis were first received at Newport and modified by the removal of all unnecessary fittings and then sent to Tipton, Staffs, to have the armour plate—5mm on the vehicle and 9mm on the shield attached to the machine gun—fitted at the yard of W. G. Allen & Sons. The cars were returned to Newport for camouflage painting and final fitting out.

The cars were sent to Russia in the early summer of 1917. They performed satisfactorily there and, amongst other things, it was discovered that they could run reasonably well for some distance with the tyres punctured. Towards the end of 1917 in Russia, CPO Gutteridge experimentally modified one car, by shortening the armoured body through the removal of one armour panel each side, and designed a mounting at the rear for a Lewis machine gun, so that the car could be operated by a crew of two. A casting for the mounting was made, but never fitted, as the Revolution broke out in November, thus curtailing, and eventually bringing to an end, the activities of Locker-Lampson's armoured car unit in Russia.

Ford cars with box bodies and equipped with machine guns were used fairly widely from 1915–1918 in Egypt, Palestine and in Lawrence's campaign. These vehicles were usually unarmoured, although one Ford with Dunsterforce in Mesopotamia in 1918 was built up as a dummy armoured car.

Armoured Cars built for Russia

The very limited output of motor vehicles in Russia in 1914 made it necessary for the Russian Imperial Government to place orders abroad for equipment for the army. A great deal of this equipment, some of it of dubious value under conditions in Russia, was supplied by Britain and France up to the time of the Revolution in 1917. The Russian army made increasing demands for armoured cars, which were often used in a dashing manner, although the crews usually lacked mechanical knowledge and were often helpless when their vehicles broke down. Considerable numbers of armoured cars were supplied by Britain. The majority were Austins (described here separately), but Lanchesters, of a pattern very similar to those of the RNAS, were also supplied and, in addition, designed and built specially to order, Isotta-Fraschini and Sheffield-Simplex cars.

The Isotta-Fraschini was designed by Charles Jarrott and built in England by his firm, Charles Jarrott Ltd, on an imported Italian 100–120hp chassis with solid tyres. It was a rather clumsy looking but well armoured vehicle, very similar to an armoured car built for the Italian Government in 1911 on

Armoured Car, Isotta-Fraschini built for Russia, 1914   [*The Autocar*

the same make of chassis. Mountings for Vickers-Maxim machine guns were provided in the turret and in the rear of the hull. The work on this vehicle was completed in a remarkably short space of time and the car was shipped to Russia in November 1914. As far as is known, only the prototype was built.

A batch of Sheffield-Simplex armoured cars was supplied to the Russian Imperial Government in 1916. This type was built on the Sheffield-Simplex 30hp chassis with a 6 cylinder engine of 4741cc. The armoured body was equipped with the twin turrets (with one Vickers-Maxim machine gun in each) favoured by the Russians. The car weighed 5 tons and was carried on Rubberine-filled self-sealing tyres.

Armoured Car, Sheffield-Simplex supplied to Russia, 1916   [*The Autocar*

Armoured Car, **Austin**

Weight:	4.14 tons	Armour:	8mm
Length:	16ft 0in	Armament:	2 Hotchkiss mg
Width:	6ft 7in	Engine:	Austin 50hp
Height:	7ft 10in	Crew:	5
Speed:	35mph	Range:	150 miles

The Austin armoured car was produced in greater numbers than any other make of British armoured car of World War I. The number built is uncertain, but the total ran into several hundreds. Nearly all the cars made were to the order of the Imperial Russian Government, influenced, no doubt, by the high regard in which British, and particularly Austin cars were held by the upper layer of Russian society.

The design of the Austin, with its twin cylindrical machine gun turrets side by side, remained basically the same throughout the war, although improvements in detail were made from time to time. The earliest type had solid studded rubber tyres, a rather tall cab with sloping sides for the driver, and the hull extended in a square armoured structure behind the turrets. Later vehicles had pneumatic tyres, and on some cars these were of the "KT" type with studded tread. Some of these cars were in service on the Polish front by the end of 1915. The second type of Austin armoured car had a different shaped driver's cab, with sloping front and vertical sides; the cab was also lower, permitting the machine guns a full arc of fire forwards. The armoured structure behind the turrets was shortened, leaving a small platform at the back of the vehicle. The final type of armoured car was generally similar to its predecessor, but several improvements were made. Dual rear wheels were usually fitted, for the first time, and a separate steering wheel for use in driving backwards was added, with modification to the rear armour to allow the second driver to see where he was going. (Some of the earlier cars, incidentally, had been modified by the Russians with duplicate steering gear.) Projecting armour plates were added to the turrets at either side of the machine gun aperture to protect the gun barrels.

Delivery of equipment to Russia was stopped when the Revolution broke out in November 1917, and several British Light Armoured Motor Batteries in Mesopotamia were equipped with Austin armoured cars. "Dunsterforce", operating in Persia in 1918, included three squadrons, each consisting of eight Austin armoured cars. Great difficulty was experienced in keeping the cars in action: the Rubberine-filled tyres wore out rapidly, and the back axles frequently gave trouble, in some cases apparently due to manufacturing faults.

Some spectacular work behind the enemy lines in August 1918, including an attack on a corps headquarters, was performed by the sixteen Austin armoured cars of the 17th Battalion, Tank Corps. The 17th Battalion was formed in April, after the opening of the big German offensive on the Western Front, and was equipped with Austins which were awaiting shipment to the Eastern theatre of war. The Tank Corps pattern of Hotchkiss machine guns in ball mountings were substituted for the Vickers-Maxim machine guns normally fitted in all the Austin cars, and the Battalion was sent to France, where it first saw action in company with the French on 11th June. Austin armoured cars of the 17th Battalion, Tank Corps eventually had the honour of leading the British Army into Germany after the Armistice. Not long afterwards, the Battalion with Austin cars was sent to Ireland to help deal with the troubles there.

Armoured Car, Austin-second type   [*Imperial War Museum*

117

Armoured Car, Peerless (twin turret type)   [*F. Mitchell*]

Armoured Car, **Peerless**, **(1919 Pattern)**

Weight:	5.8 tons	Armour:	8mm
Length:	14ft 6in	Armament:	2 Hotchkiss mg
Width:	7ft 0in	Engine:	Peerless 40hp
Height:	8ft 4in	Crew:	4
Speed:	18mph	Range:	96 miles

The immediate post-war era found Britain in urgent need of armoured cars—for internal security duties in India and in Ireland, for example—when most of the wartime vehicles were almost worn out. The Secretary of State for War (Winston Churchill) asked in July 1919 for 100 new armoured cars immediately, but considerable difficulty was encountered, firstly in finding suitable chassis to fit armoured bodies for which drawings were immediately available and secondly, a manufacturer willing to undertake war work now that the war had ended. Eventually it was decided to use Peerless lorry chassis that were held in store with a design of armoured hull that was a slight modification of that of the final pattern of the Austin armoured car. The Austin Motor Company was persuaded to undertake manufacture. The chassis were delivered to Birmingham between October 1919 and January 1920 and some of the completed armoured cars were ready to be sent to Ireland later in 1920.

The Peerless Armoured Cars were used for town patrols and the escort of motor convoys but were too slow for much of the work for which they were needed and were gradually replaced in Ireland from the beginning of 1921 by new Rolls-Royce Armoured Cars. With solid tyres and chain drive to the rear wheels, the Peerless Armoured Cars were sturdy vehicles however, and they were used for many years afterwards by Territorial Armoured Car Companies for training. The 1st Derbyshire Yeomanry still had one Peerless even as late as May 1940, after which it was relegated to aerodrome defence.

Armoured Car, Rolls-Royce, 1920 Pattern, Mark I　　　　　[*Imperial War Museum*

Armoured Cars, **Rolls-Royce, 1920 and 1924 Patterns**

	1920 PATTERN MK I	1924 PATTERN MK I
Weight:	3.8 tons	4.15 tons
Length:	16ft 7in	16ft 2in
Width:	6ft 3in	6ft 4in
Height:	7ft 7in	8ft 4in
Speed:	45mph	45mph
Armour:	9mm	9mm
Armament:	1 Vickers mg	1 Vickers mg
Engine:	Rolls-Royce 40-50hp	Rolls-Royce 40-50hp
Crew:	3	3
Range:	180 miles	180 miles

The Rolls-Royce Silver Ghost chassis was again used in the new type of armoured car to be built for the Army after World War I. The new vehicles were very similar in appearance to the Admiralty 1914 turreted pattern: the drawings of the 1914 cars were, in fact, supplied to the War Office by Admiral Sueter (former Director of the Admiralty Air Department) towards the end of 1920.

The Armoured Car, Rolls-Royce, 1920 Pattern, Mark I, as it was known, differed from the wartime cars only in detail. The wheels were of the disc type, instead of wire-spoked; the turret sides were slightly higher; and louvres were fitted to the armoured radiator doors. Some of the earlier pattern Rolls-Royces still in service after the War were modified to approximately the same standard as the 1920 Pattern, Mark I, although the early turrets were retained. The Air

Ministry, independently of the War Office, also built Rolls-Royce armoured cars—these were to equip the RAF Armoured Car Companies in Iraq and Egypt. They were armoured at No 1 Stores Depot, RAF, and bore the Air Ministry designation of "Car, Armoured, Rolls-Royce Type A". The armour was like that of the 1914 cars, but the wheels were of the disc type, although later changed to a heavier commercial vehicle pattern, with large section tyres for better performance on sand.

The next War Office model "Armoured Car, Rolls-Royce, 1924 Pattern, Mark I" was recognisably of the same family, but had a redesigned hull, and a new turret with a cupola for the commander. The Vickers machine gun was in a spherical mounting and many other detailed improvements were incorporated in the new cars. An improved version of the 1920 Pattern car, known as the 1920 Pattern, Mark IA, was also produced. This approximated to the standard of the 1924 Pattern cars, and like them had a commander's cupola and a spherical gun mounting. (The earlier cars had had a fork mounting for the machine gun, with the barrel projecting through an open port: a plate was often added to the barrel to protect this point.)

At various times Rolls-Royce armoured cars were supplied to the Irish Government (13 in 1922), and to various Colonies. These were mostly of the 1920 Pattern, but at the outbreak of World War II, the British Army still had 24 cars of the 1924 Pattern, Mark I, ten of the 1920 Pattern, Mark IA, and 42 of the 1920 Pattern, Mark I. Most of these were used for training in the United Kingdom, but the 11th Hussars in Egypt were equipped with cars that had been modernised by the substitution of open-top turrets armed with a Boys anti-tank rifle, a Bren light machine gun and a smoke discharger. These cars were used in action in 1940–1941 in the early Libyan campaign.

[*Imperial War Museum*

Armoured Car, Rolls-Royce, 1924 Pattern, Mark I, with modified turret, in 1940

Armoured Car, Lancia

Armoured Car, Lancia, turreted pattern

Armoured Cars, **Lancia**

Lancias were among the first armoured cars to be ordered by the Air Ministry after the decision had been taken by Trenchard that the RAF should make its own armoured cars for the support of aircraft in the maintenance of security in Iraq.

Lancia armoured cars were first used by the police in the Irish disturbances up to and during 1922. These were open top vehicles with loopholes all round to enable the crew to use their weapons. An internal partition divided the driver's compartment from the rear part. On some cars in Ireland the frontal armour was increased in height and a V-shaped wire netting roof was added to keep out brickbats and bombs. Sixty-four Lancia armoured cars were handed over to the Irish Government in 1922, and these cars later had armoured roofs added to them and were normally equipped with two Lewis machine guns. The Royal Ulster Constabulary had 135 Lancia armoured cars in 1923.

Some of the vehicles supplied to the RAF were similar to the cars with heightened frontal armour used in Ireland, although they had more modern lighting equipment and a small searchlight was added at the front. These cars, like the Irish vehicles, were really armoured personnel carriers rather than true armoured cars.

The other RAF Lancia was a fully enclosed armoured vehicle, although the same type of 4 × 2 chassis with dual tyres at the rear, using a 4 cylinder engine, was used. It was equipped with a small multi-sided turret mounting one Lewis machine gun.

Lancia armoured cars were in use with the RAF in the Middle East by 1923. They seem to have lasted only a few years, as by the early 1930s Rolls-Royce armoured cars appear to have formed the main equipment of the RAF Armoured Car Companies, by then reduced in number.

Armoured Car, Guy (Ind-
ian Pattern)

Armoured Cars, **Indian Pattern**

Shortly after the outbreak of the Great War, arrangements were made in India to form armoured car units for internal security duties and for work on the NW Frontier. The first armoured cars to equip these units were ready in 1915. They were built at Railway workshops on various motor car chassis of the more powerful makes, including Rolls-Royce, Minerva, Standard, Mercedes and Daimler. Fiat lorry chassis were also used.

Later in the War, armoured cars on American Jeffery-Quad chassis were sent to India, and some, together with 1914 Pattern Rolls-Royces, and a number of the locally built armoured vehicles were still in use in 1920, when the Government of India decided to order cars to its own specifications from England, to be manned by the Royal Tank Corps in India.

The first of these—known as "Armoured Cars, Rolls-Royce, 1921 Indian Pattern"—were built on the 40/50hp Silver Ghost chassis. The armour design was entirely different from previous Rolls-Royce armoured cars, however. The hull was more roomy, taking up all the space occupied by the rear platform on the 1914 and 1920 models, and was lined with asbestos to make the interior more bearable in the Indian climate. The turret was dome shaped and fitted with 4 ball mountings for Vickers machine guns, two of which were normally carried. The tyres were solid rubber, but with a sort of deep honeycomb tread to make them more resilient.

Some cars of this type were built for Persia in addition to sixteen—the complement of one armoured car company with reserves—supplied to the Government of India.

The next batch of armoured cars—the "Armoured Cars, Crossley 1923 Indian Pattern"—were armoured in an identical fashion to the 1921 Pattern, but the Crossley chassis was selected, in all probability, as a somewhat cheaper alternative to the Rolls-Royce. These had a 50hp 6 cylinder engine and on some of them a device, facilitated by the internal insulation, for electrifying the hull exterior was introduced. This was considered a useful asset in close fighting. Various modifications were introduced in different batches of these armoured cars: some had worm elevating gear for the machine guns, whilst in others it was shoulder operated. The arrangement of the engine air louvres also varied and in the 1925 Pattern the unditching planks were carried flat, as running boards. Two cars of similar type were supplied to South Africa.

The four-wheeled armoured cars with solid tyres had an unsatisfactory performance off roads, so about 1927 a Guy six-wheeled lorry chassis was experimentally fitted with the hull of a Crossley Armoured Car. The cross country ability of this vehicle was tested on the Frontier, and proved very good, so a quantity of Guy chassis were ordered so that the existing armoured car hulls could be transferred to them. A much heavier Guy chassis, complete with armoured body was supplied instead, however. The "Armoured Car, Guy, Indian Pattern", was quite an efficient vehicle, but proved to be too large and heavy for many of the roads and bridges in the frontier district, and the sixteen or so that were supplied in 1928 were withdrawn from use in 1934 and converted to artillery tractors. These armoured cars weighed about 9 tons and had a 6 cylinder engine of 120bhp which gave them a top speed of 45mph.

The Indian Pattern Rolls-Royce and Crossley armoured cars were nearly worn out by 1939, so the armoured hulls were removed from most of them and fitted to Chevrolet truck chassis with pneumatic tyres, dual at the rear. Some of these "Armoured Cars, Chevrolet, IP", as they were designated, later saw service with the Indian Army in the campaigns in Iraq, Syria and Persia in 1941–1942, and were eventually handed over to the Persian Army in 1942. The South African Crossleys were similarly modified, but on Ford chassis.

A few of the Rolls-Royce cars that had not been converted were used for training by the Auxiliary Force in Burma, and these fell into the hands of the Japanese in 1942. Japan, incidentally, had taken delivery in the later 1920's of a number of Crossley armoured cars, similar to the Indian Pattern vehicles but with pneumatic tyres. These were used in Manchuria in 1931 and were still in service when the Japanese entered the War in 1941.

Armoured Car, Chevrolet (Indian Pattern)   [*Imperial War Museum*

Armoured Car, Lanchester, Mark I   *[The Daimler Co.*

Armoured Cars, **Lanchester, Marks I, IA, II and IIA**

Weight:	7.5 tons (Mks I-IA)	Armour:	9mm
	6.95 tons (Mks II-IIA)		
Length:	20ft 0in	Armament:	1 Vickers 0.5in, 1 Vickers 0.303
			in, 1 Vickers 0.303in (in hull)
Width:	6ft 7½in	Engine:	Lanchester 88bhp
Height:	9ft 3in	Crew:	4
Speed:	45mph		

(Dimensions apply to Mk IIA—typical for other models)

The Lanchesters were the first armoured cars ordered in quantity by the British Army to utilise the rigid six-wheel chassis with drive to all four rear wheels, which offered a better cross-country performance than that of the earlier conventional 4 × 2 vehicles.

The chassis were supplied by the Lanchester Motor Company. They were specially designed for armoured car bodies (unlike most other contemporary British six-wheel armoured cars), the first two prototypes being ordered in 1927. The prototypes differed in a number of ways, including the shape of the bonnets and turrets, from the later vehicles, but the second one, D1E2, had duplicate steering gear at the rear, and this arrangement was continued in the production series.

The armour layout of the Lanchesters was similar to that of the Rolls-Royce armoured cars, with rotating turret and a platform at the rear, but provision was made in the front of the hull at the left hand side for either an extra machine gun mounting or a No 9 WT set.

The four variants of the Lanchester Armoured Car were much the same in appearance, but the Marks II and IIA had single tyres all round, whereas the earlier Marks had dual rear wheels. The Marks I and IA had circular turret cupolas with flat tops, but the Marks II and IIA had a different type with sloping sides. Wireless sets were fitted in the Mark IA and Mark IIA vehicles, and these consequently lacked the hull machine gun. Most of the cars had a 6 cylinder engine, rated at 40hp and developing 88bhp at 2,200rpm, but a few cars were fitted with a more powerful version, rated at 60hp.

A total of 39 six-wheel Lanchester Armoured Cars were built, made up of 4 prototypes, 18 Mark I's 4 Mark IA's, 7 Mark II's, and 6 Mark IIA's. The 12th Lancers were equipped with these cars from 1931 until just before the outbreak of World War II. A number of Lanchester Armoured Cars were sent to various Volunteer Forces in Malaya, where they were eventually lost to the Japanese in 1941–1942. One interesting conversion of a Lanchester to a passenger carrying vehicle was made about the end of 1940. This car was used for the transport of Cabinet Ministers and other VIPs.

Armoured Car, Crossley (30/70hp chassis)   [Crossley Motors Ltd

Crossley Six-wheeled Armoured Cars

	Crossley (30/70hp chassis)	Crossley Mk I
Weight:	7.12 tons	5.43 tons
Length:	20ft 7in	15ft 3in
Width:	7ft 10in	6ft 2in
Height:	9ft 5in	8ft 7½in
Speed:	50mph	45mph
Armament:	2 Vickers mg	2 Vickers mg
Engine:	Crossley 70bhp	Crossley
Crew:	4	4

Crossley six-wheeled chassis of different models formed the basis of several types of armoured cars supplied to the Royal Air Force as well as the British Army and other countries in the 1930s.

One of the earliest of these armoured cars was a rather large vehicle built by Vickers-Armstrongs on the Crossley 30/70hp medium chassis with 4 cylinder engine. This vehicle had a hull, with dome-shaped turret, on similar lines to those of the Indian Pattern armoured cars of the same period. Four alternative mountings for Vickers machine guns were provided in the turret, although only two guns were normally carried. The six-wheel chassis had dual tyres at the rear, and these could be fitted with tracks to improve performance in bad going. An interesting feature was the method of mounting the spare wheels at either side. These projected below the level of the chassis frame and were free to revolve, and so prevent the vehicle "bellying", a weakness in long-wheel-base 6 × 4 vehicles. One of these Crossleys was in service with No 2 Armoured Car Company, RAF in Transjordan from about 1928 to 1934, or later. Vickers-Armstrongs published, about 1930, a drawing of another similar vehicle, but with the turret replaced by a 40mm automatic gun on an open mounting. This version may never have been built, however.

Another six-wheel armoured car, supplied to the RAF in 1930, used a more powerful chassis—the 38/110hp Crossley IGA4 series 1 with a 6 cylinder engine. The hull and turret design was similar to that of the Lanchester Mark I cars supplied to the Army, but the turret had only one Vickers machine gun, and the spare wheels were mounted free to revolve. This car, like the 30/70hp vehicle, had ground/air wireless equipment, with a frame aerial.

Armoured Car, Crossley (38/110hp chassis)   [*Vickers-Armstrong*

Armoured Car, Crossley, Mark I   [*B. T. White*

The Crossley 20/60hp light six-wheel chassis with a 4 cylinder engine was used as the basis of yet another armoured car, similar in general layout to the previous car, but with single tyres all round. This vehicle was offered for sale commercially to foreign governments by Vickers-Armstrongs. A few armoured cars of a similar type were purchased by Iraq. These vehicles differed in having movable radiator doors and special turrets, and had some characteristics of the Crossley Mark I supplied to the British Army. Some were captured from the Iraqi army by British forces during the fighting in 1941.

The first Crossley six-wheel armoured car tested by the British Army was ordered from the Royal Ordnance Factory in 1928. It was an experimental vehicle known as D2E1 and used a light six-wheeled chassis with dual tyres at the rear. The armament was two Vickers machine guns, one in the turret and one in the front of the hull. The turret, following War Office practice at the time, was the same as those on the contemporary light tanks (Mark I). This vehicle later had the turret removed, and was fitted with two Vickers 0.5in machine guns on an open anti-aircraft mounting.

A second experimental vehicle, D2E2, ordered in 1929, was similar in layout to the first one, but had a lower bonnet and single tyres all round and the turret, at first like that of D2E1, was later changed to one of the Light Tank Mark III pattern. D2E2 was followed by a small production order for five similar vehicles, known as "Armoured Cars, Crossley Mark I". These were built in 1931 at the Royal Ordnance Factory on chassis supplied by Crossley Motors Ltd. They supplemented the larger number of Lanchester Armoured Cars already in service, and remained in use until after the outbreak of World War II, although only for training purposes in the later years.

Cars, Armoured, Fordson   [Imperial War Museum

Car, Armoured, **Fordson**

The Rolls-Royce armoured cars with which the RAF Armoured Car Companies in the Middle East had been equipped since the 1920s were nearly worn out by the beginning of the Second World War, so arrangements were made for the armoured hulls and turrets to be removed and fitted on to modern truck type chassis.

The Rolls-Royces of No 2 Armoured Car Company were sent in batches to Cairo between January and August 1940, where a total of twenty armoured cars, which included four reserves, was built for this unit on Fordson chassis by September 1940.

The Fordson Armoured Cars bore a strong external resemblance, as might be expected, to the Rolls-Royces from which they had inherited their outer shells, but the wheelbase of the Fordson chassis was longer than that of the Rolls-Royce (although one new short wheelbase chassis was used) and had characteristic truck-type wheels. The hull armour was extended over the platform behind the turret, and this extra space was used to house the wireless equipment which was carried in most cars. As originally modified, the Fordsons carried the same armament as the Rolls-Royce armoured cars—one Vickers machine gun in the turret mounting and one Lewis machine gun on a ring mounting on top of the turret—but as a concession to modern warfare a Boys anti-tank rifle was later added in the turret to the right of the Vickers mounting. Later still, the single Lewis gun was replaced on the ring mounting by twin Vickers "K" or Browning air-cooled machine guns.

Fordson Armoured Cars of No 2 Armoured Car Company were in action in the Western Desert from September 1940 to April 1941, and then in Iraq against Rashid Ali's forces, followed by operations in Syria in June. In October 1941 the Company served temporarily as part of the 11th Hussars (an armoured car regiment of the Eighth Army), afterwards being engaged in aerodrome defence and reconnaissance before the Fordsons were eventually replaced by modern armoured cars.

Car, Armoured, Alvis-Straussler, Type A   [*Imperial War Museum*]

Car, Armoured, **Alvis-Straussler, Type A**

Twelve cars of this type, bearing the Air Ministry designation shown above, were supplied to the Royal Air Force near the beginning of World War II and some of these were in service with the RAF Armoured Car unit at Aden by the end of 1940. These vehicles were the latest of a series of armoured cars designed by Nicholas Straussler, an engineer of Hungarian origin. The first type was built by the firm of Manfred Weiss, of Budapest, in 1933. A second prototype, much the same as the first, was made in 1935 and tested by the RAF in Iraq. This car had a specification much in advance of contemporary British armoured cars, including four-wheel drive, rear-mounted engine, transverse leaf spring suspension at front and rear, and a curvilinear armoured body which could easily be removed for the vehicle to be serviced. A duplicate set of driving controls was fitted at the rear. The 1935 vehicle had a 100bhp engine, but a later development tested by the War Office in 1938 had instead two Ford V-8 engines of 88.5bhp each, side by side, complete with gearboxes, which were interconnected. One engine drove the nearside wheels, and the other engine the offside wheels although, in an emergency, either engine could drive the vehicle. The armoured car showed a very good cross country performance on trials, but was not adopted for the Army because engine cooling was considered to be inadequate. The next type, known to the designer as Alvis-Straussler AC3 D, was the one which, in a slightly modified form, was supplied to the RAF about 1939. Built by Alvis Ltd, it was generally similar in layout to the 1935 model but the armour was angled instead of curved and a number of mechanical changes were incorporated, including four-wheel steering. The drive to the front wheels and the steering on the rear wheels could, however, be disengaged for normal road work by a single lever. The engine was

129

a 6-cylinder Alvis of 120bhp, and cooling was by means of radiators at either side. Twelve cars were also built for the Dutch East Indies Government and these, unlike the RAF version, had a machine gun position in the front of the hull in addition to that in the turret. It is interesting to note that some Straussler armoured cars, built in Hungary but generally similar to the RAF type, were used by the German Army during World War II.

Armoured Car, Reconnaissance, Morris Model CS9 (LAC)   [*Imperial War Museum*

Armoured Car, Reconnaissance, **Morris (Model CS9/LAC)**

Weight:	4.2 tons	Armour:	7mm
Length:	15ft 7½in	Armament:	1 Boys atr, 1 Bren mg
Width:	6ft 8½in	Engine:	Morris Commercial 96.2bhp
Height:	7ft 3in	Crew:	4
Speed:	45mph	Range:	240 miles

In 1935–1936 several types of armoured cars were built on the chassis of the Morris Commercial 15cwt truck, then the standard vehicle of its class in the Army. One prototype was fitted with a fully enclosed turret (rather like that of the Mark VI series light tanks) with commander's cupola and armed with one Vickers 0.5in machine gun. This vehicle and another prototype on the same type of chassis were both designed and built at the Royal Ordnance Factory, Woolwich; neither went into production. The third type, in which the wheelbase, to improve stability, was lengthened by about 18 inches, and the engine power increased, was equipped with an open-top turret armed with

130

a Boys anti-tank rifle and a Bren light machine gun, with a smoke discharger in the middle. This vehicle, which was a light reconnaissance car rather than a proper armoured car, was chosen for production and a total of 100 (including the prototype) were built. The production vehicles differed from the first one in having vertical-sided rather than slightly conical turrets, and other minor details. Some, however, were later converted to armoured command vehicles.

Thirty-eight Morris armoured cars were taken to France in 1939 by the 12th Lancers, the only armoured car regiment with the BEF. The 11th Hussars, the other original cavalry armoured car regiment of the British Army, were equipped with some Morris armoured cars at the beginning of the Libyan campaign and used them up to the Spring of 1941. Fitted with wireless, they were employed as troop leaders' cars and at squadron and regimental head-quarters. The Morris armoured cars had only conventional drive to the rear wheels, but the 11th Hussars found that, compared with the Rolls-Royce ar-moured cars also used by the regiment, the Morris vehicles performed better on soft sand, but the springs and steering did not stand up so well to hard going.

Armoured Car, Guy, Mark I   [*Imperial War Museum*

Armoured Cars, **Guy, Marks I and IA**

Weight:	5.2 tons		Armour:	15mm
Length:	13ft 6 in		Armament:	1 Vickers 0.5in mg, 1 Vickers 0.303in mg, (Mk I); 1 Besa 15mm, 1 Besa 7.92mm mg (Mk IA)
Width:	6ft 9in			
Height:	7ft 6in			
Speed:	40mph		Engine:	Meadows 53bhp
			Crew:	3
			Range:	210 miles

The Guy Mark I was the first all-welded armoured fighting vehicle to go into production for the British Army. Known officially at first as "Tank, Light, Wheeled Mark I", it was also the first short wheelbased 4 × 4 armoured car to enter service with the Army. The Tank, Light, Wheeled designation was dropped later, but the Guy had the same armament and armour as the contemporary Mark VI series of Light Tanks and also a cross country performance not greatly inferior.

The original design for an armoured car based on the Guy Quad-Ant field artillery tractor chassis was drawn up at Woolwich Arsenal. This involved the repositioning of the engine at the rear and modification of the suspension to take the weight of the armoured hull. Five mild steel prototypes were built by Guy Motors Ltd, in 1938, and these vehicles had hulls and turrets of riveted construction. However, after satisfactory tests of the prototypes, when Guy Motors were asked to produce a run of these armoured cars the firm made the suggestion, which was accepted by the War Office, that a welding process should be used for the fabrication of the armoured hulls and turrets. A rotary manipulator and jigs were designed by the Company for welding the hulls, and production began in 1939. Excluding the various riveted and welded prototypes, 101 Guy Armoured Cars were built, of which the first fifty had Vickers machine guns and the remainder Besa machine guns, and were designated Mark IA.

Incidentally, a rival design to the Guy Tank, Light, Wheeled was tested in 1938—this was an Austrian Steyr-Daimler-Puch chassis with a Morris Commercial engine and fitted with a similar sort of hull and turret to the Guy's. This vehicle was not adopted because its performance did not come up to requirements.

A few Guy Armoured Cars were in France in the early part of the War —two troops, each of three cars, formed part of the unit known then as "No 3 Air Mission", and later as GHQ Liaison Regiment or "Phantom".

After the evacuation of France in 1940, Guy Armoured Cars were used for defence in the United Kingdom, including one troop of cars of the 12th Lancers used for the escort of VIPs. The Dutch, Belgians and Canadians used a number of Guy Armoured Cars for training in Britain.

Owing to heavy commitments for the production of lorries and gun tractors, Guy Motors were not in a position to make the large numbers of armoured cars that were required, so they handed over the design and technique to the Rootes Group, although continuing to supply hulls for Humber Armoured Car chassis.

Armoured Cars, **Humber, Marks I, II, III and IV**

	MARK I	MARK II	MARK III	MARK IV
Weight:	6.85 tons	7.1 tons	7.1 tons	7.1 tons
Length:	15ft 0in	15ft 0in	15ft 0in	15ft 0in
Width:	7ft 2in	7ft 2in	7ft 2in	7ft 2in
Height:	7ft 10in	7ft 10in	7ft 10in	7ft 10in
Speed:	45mph	45mph	45mph	45mph
Armour:	15mm	15mm	15mm	15mm
Armament:	1 Besa 15mm	1 Besa 15mm	1 Besa 15mm	1 37mm gun
	1 Besa 7.92mm	1 Besa 7.92mm	1 Besa 7.92mm	1 Besa 7.92mm mg
Engine:	Rootes 90bhp	Rootes 90bhp	Rootes 90bhp	Rootes 90bhp
Crew:	3	3	4	3
Range:	250 miles	250 miles	250 miles	250 miles

Armoured Car, Humber, Mark II   [*Rootes Ltd*

The Rootes Group built over sixty per cent of the total British production of armoured cars in World War II. Most of these were Humbers, which served in nearly all the main theatres of war from 1941 onwards.

The chassis of the Armoured Car, Humber Mark I was based on that of the Karrier KT4 field artillery tractor, supplied to the Government of India just before the War. The engine, repositioned at the rear, was the 6 cylinder, 4 litre Rootes type, widely used in Humber, Commer and Karrier cars and lorries. The hull and turret were identical to those of the Guy Mark IA armoured car, and were indeed produced by Guy Motors after that firm had ceased to build chassis for armoured cars. The Guy IA and Humber I armoured cars were almost identical externally, the most apparent differences being the horizontal rear mudguards and longer front shock absorbers on the Humber.

The later Marks of Humber Armoured Car had the same chassis as the Mark I, but successive improvements were made in the hull, turret and armament. Mark II had a redesigned hull, with the driver's cab built into the face of a sloping glacis plate, and the radiator armour at the rear was altered to a louvred pattern. This type of hull was continued in subsequent Marks. Mark III, which came into production early in 1942, had a more roomy turret than Marks I-II, with the roof sloping to the rear, and a crew increased to four men. The Humber

Mark IV armoured car had an American 37mm gun as main armament—the first British vehicle to be so equipped.

For driving in reverse, the engine cover at the rear could be raised on the Humber Armoured Cars so that the driver could see through a special aperture.

Humber Armoured Cars of the earlier Marks were used extensively in the Middle East campaigns from autumn 1941 onwards, with the Mark IV coming generally into service during the Italian campaign and in North West Europe. Some of these cars were sold to foreign countries after the War, and one was noted in use by the Portuguese in Goa as late as December 1961.

A counterpart of the Humber was built in Canada—"Armoured Car, General Motors Mark I, Fox I". About 200 of these cars were made: they closely resembled the Humber III but were armed with Browning (0.5in and 0.3in) machine guns and used the GM 104bhp engine and automotive parts. The Fox was claimed to have a better performance than the Humber's.

Armoured Car, Daimler, Mark II

[Imperial War Museum

Armoured Cars, **Daimler, Marks I and II**

Weight:	7.5 tons	Armour:	16mm
Length:	13ft 0in	Armament:	1 2pr gun, 1 Besa mg
Width:	8ft 0in	Engine:	Daimler 95bhp
Height:	7ft 4in	Crew:	3
Speed:	50mph	Range:	205 miles (with auxiliary tank)

Design work on the Daimler Armoured Car started in April 1939, shortly before the BSA-Daimler Scout Car went into production. The armoured car—originally ordered as "Tank, Light, Wheeled, BSA", before the BSA company was absorbed by the Daimler Company Ltd—was in most mechanical respects a larger version of the Scout Car, and probably had more advanced design features than any other wheeled AFV of World War II. Like the Scout Car, the Daimler Armoured Car had a rear engine layout, the transmission being taken forwards to a transfer box containing a single differential, and thence, via four parallel driving shafts and Tracta universal joints, to each wheel. The hubs contained final reduction gears. Four-wheel steering was also fitted in the prototype armoured car although, unlike the Scout Car, this was omitted from production vehicles. The transmission arrangement, together with independent coil spring suspension at front and rear, permitted any one wheel to be raised up to 16 inches without the others losing contact with the ground. A rear steering wheel was fitted to enable the commander to take over for rapid driving in reverse, for which all five gears were available. Disc brakes, then uncommon, were used.

The Daimler Armoured Car had no conventional chassis, the automotive components being attached direct to the lower part of the armoured hull, which had a pot-shaped fighting compartment, of polygonal form. The armament was originally intended to have been two Besa machine guns but production vehicles had a turret almost the same as that of the Tetrarch light tank, equipped with a 2pr gun and co-axial Besa machine gun. This was the first British armoured car to be fitted with a 2pr gun. Towards the end of the war, the Littlejohn conversion was sometimes fitted to the 2prs on Daimler Armoured Cars, reducing the calibre at the muzzle and greatly increasing the penetrative power of the projectile. A 3in Howitzer was experimentally fitted for close support work, in place of the 2pr, but few vehicles, as far as is known, were so modified. Some cars in the NW Europe campaign used as regimental command vehicles had the turrets removed completely.

Total production of Daimler Armoured Cars amounted to 2,694 vehicles including Mark IIs, which succeeded the Mark I. The new Mark of car was very similar to the Daimler Mark I, but a number of improvements were incorporated, including a two-speed dynamo, an escape hatch in the roof of the driver's compartment, modified gun mounting, and a different type of radiator and armoured grille.

Daimler Armoured Cars came into service in 1941 in the United Kingdom, and were in action in the North African campaign in the following year. They were used also in Italy, North West Europe and in South East Asia Command.

Armoured Cars, AEC, Marks I-III

	MARK I	MARK II	MARK III
Weight:	11 tons	12.7 tons	12.7 tons
Length:	17ft 0in	17ft 10in	18ft 5in
Width:	9ft 0in	8ft 10½in	8ft 10½in
Height:	8ft 4½in	8ft 10in	8ft 10in
Speed:	36mph	41mph	41mph
Armour:	30mm	30mm	30mm
Armament:	1 2pr 1 Besa mg	1 6pr 1 Besa mg	1 75mm gun 1 Besa mg
Engine:	AEC Diesel 105bhp	AEC Diesel 158bhp	AEC Diesel 158bhp
Crew:	3	4	4
Range:	250 miles	250 miles	250 miles

The AEC Armoured Car was designed as a private venture. It was felt by the Associated Equipment Company Ltd that there was a need for an armoured car with both armament and armour equal to that of a tank and accordingly a mock-up was built, painted in conspicuous colours, and unofficially introduced into a demonstration of vehicles at Horse Guards Parade in 1941. It attracted the attention of the Prime Minister and led to a production order.

The Armoured Car, AEC, Mark I was a four-wheel drive vehicle using many components of the "Matador" tractor. A 7.58 litre diesel (the first oil engine to be used in a British production armoured car) was at the rear, inclined in line with the driving shaft to the front wheels, which were the pair driven under normal conditions. Drive to the rear wheels (for use in bad going) was via a transfer box in the middle of the vehicle, the shaft being beside the engine, thus permitting a lower height for the hull. The armoured hull was of simple design, and the turret, equipped with a 2pr gun and co-axial Besa machine gun, was the same as that of the Valentine tank. A number of cars in the Middle East were later converted to take a 6pr-equipped turret, however. The maximum armour protection of the AEC armoured car was 30mm—nearly double that of the Daimler and Humber armoured cars. The driver drove by means of periscopes only when in the closed down position, but in the prototype vehicles a direct vision port was provided, and this was the main feature that distinguished them from production cars.

The AEC Mark II was mechanically on the same lines as the Mark I, but a more powerful engine, similar to that of the Valentine tank, was used and the hull design was revised to give better frontal protection and eliminate

Armoured Car, AEC Mark I—prototype   [*AEC Ltd*

projecting angles likely to catch on obstacles. A different turret, armed with a 6pr and a Besa machine gun, was provided. The Mark III was externally almost the same as the Mark II but a 75mm gun replaced the 6pr in the turret, which had various improvements, notably two, instead of one, electric fans in the roof.

A total of 629 AEC Armoured Cars was built, of which 122 were of the Mark I type. The Mark Is were in action in the North African theatre from 1942 onwards, and the later Marks were in service in the North West Europe campaign. They were usually employed in the Heavy Troops of armoured car regiments in support of the lighter armoured vehicles. A number of AEC Armoured Cars was also supplied to the Yugoslav partisans in 1944.

Armoured Car, AEC Mark III   [*AEC Ltd*

Armoured Cars, **Coventry, Marks I and II**

DATA FOR MARK I

Weight:	11.5 tons
Length:	15ft 6½in (excluding gun)
Width:	8ft 9in
Height:	7ft 9in
Speed:	41mph
Armour:	14mm
Armament:	1 2pr gun, 1 Besa mg
Engine:	Hercules 175bhp
Crew:	4
Range:	250 miles

The Coventry Armoured Car was a combined effort by Humber Ltd, Commer Cars Ltd, and the Daimler Company Ltd and was intended to take the place in production of both the Humber and Daimler Armoured Cars.

The overall design was co-ordinated by Humbers, who also undertook the detailed work connected with the hull, turret, armament, stowage and engine; Commer worked on the design of the axles, gearbox, and transmission generally; and Daimler did the design work on the steering and suspension. Both Humber and Daimler produced and tested prototype vehicles.

The first prototypes were ready in 1944. As might be expected, the Coventry had many features of the Humber and Daimler Armoured Cars, although its general appearance more closely resembled the latter. The four-wheel drive transmission was more conventional than the Daimler's, however, with driving shafts to differentials on the front and rear axles. The engine was an American Hercules RXLD 6 cylinder petrol type, of 175bhp. Like the Daimler Armoured Cars, a second steering wheel and duplicate controls were provided at the back of the fighting compartment. The armament was a 2pr gun and co-axial Besa machine gun in the turret. The Mark II version had a 75mm gun instead of the 2pr, and the crew was reduced from four to three men.

Large contracts for production of Coventry Armoured Cars by the Rootes Group and the Daimler Company were issued, but only a few vehicles had come off the production line by the time the War ended, and the contracts were cancelled. The Coventry was never used in action by British forces, but a number were supplied to the French Army, which employed them in the fighting in Vietnam not long after the end of World War II.

Armoured Car, Coventry Mark I   [*Imperial War Museum*

[*Imperial War Museum*

Armoured Cars, Marmon-Herrington Mark II. The nearest car had been modified to take a captured Italian Breda 20mm gun

South African Armoured Cars

	MARK II	MARK III	MARK IVF
Weight:	6 tons	6 tons	6.64 tons
Length:	(wheelbase 11ft 2in)	(wheelbase 9ft 9in)	18ft 1½in
			(wheelbase 9ft 10in)
Width:			7ft 0in
Height:			7ft 6in
Speed:	50mph	50mph	50mph
Armour:	12mm	12mm	12mm
Armament:	1 Boys atr	1 Boys atr	1 2pr gun
	1 Bren mg	1 Bren mg	1 o.30in Browning mg
Engine:	Ford	Ford	Ford 95bhp
Crew:	4	3	3
Range:	200 miles	200 miles	200 miles

Armoured cars designed and built in South Africa were used by United Kingdom as well as South African armoured car units, and they played a very useful part in the various African campaigns. They were of particular importance in the Western Desert in 1941, when few armoured cars had been received from Britain.

These vehicles were designated "South African Reconnaissance Cars" by the Union Defence Force (as it then was); whilst those that were in service with United Kingdom units were known as "Armoured Car, Marmon-Herrington". The chassis which formed the basis of these cars were imported from North America, the armament, in most cases, was supplied from the United Kingdom, whilst the hulls (at first riveted, but later welded) were manufactured in South Africa.

The Mark I car used only by the UDF was built on a Ford 3 ton, 4 × 2 chassis. The Mark II had the same hull as Mark I, but used a 134in wheelbase Ford chassis with Marmon-Herrington conversion to four-wheel drive; and Mark III was generally similar, but with a 117in wheelbase chassis and no rear doors were fitted—unlike Mark II, which had double doors at the back. In the course of production of Mark III, however, various improvements were made, including solid instead of louvred radiator armour, and in later vehicles a single rear door was included in response to adverse crew comments. All these vehicles had a Vickers machine gun in the turret and another in the rear left side of the hull in the original design, but when supplied to the Middle East Forces were equipped instead with a Bren light machine gun and a Boys anti-tank rifle in the turret, with another machine gun for anti-aircraft use. Once in service, however, many field modifications were made to improve fire power. Various captured weapons were mounted, usually in place of the turret, and these included, on Mark IIs, the Italian 47mm Breda the French 25mm anti-tank gun, the 20mm Breda AA/anti-tank gun (mounted either with a large shield or in the existing turret) and the German 37mm anti-tank gun. Four Bren guns, on a single anti-aircraft mounting, or twin Brownings were also used. Mark IIIs were fitted with the 47mm and 25mm guns, and also with the German 28/20mm tapered bore anti-tank gun. There were probably many other unofficial armament variations on Mark II and Mark III cars besides these.

The Mark IV armoured car was an entirely different design from its predecessors. It was rear-engined and had no chassis, the components being attached direct to the all-welded armoured hull. A 2pr gun on a field mounting (as the turret was considered too light for a tank-type mounting) was the main armament. A Browning air-cooled machine gun was added beside the 2pr in later models. The Mark IVF was similar in appearance to the Mark IV but used, instead of Marmon-Herrington automotive units, the components of Canadian-built Ford F60L lorry chassis.

Armoured Car, Marmon-Herrington Mark IVF   [*Imperial War Museum*

Other experimental vehicles, not produced in quantity, were the Mark VI, an eight-wheeler, with either 2pr or 6pr main armament, intended for Desert operations; the Mark IIIA and the Mark VII, two generally similar vehicles fitted with Vickers machine guns on anti-aircraft mountings, otherwise on the same lines as the Mark III; and the Mark VIII, a conventional front-engined vehicle with a 2pr gun in a long turret.

Mark II and Mark III cars saw action chiefly in the North African campaigns; the former with Mark Is were employed also in Abyssinia, whilst Mark IIIs also saw action in Madagascar, and were used for training in the East and West African colonies. Some were also sent to Malaya and the Dutch East Indies, where they fell into the hands of the Japanese. The Mark IV, which did not appear in quantity until 1943, was used in the Mediterranean theatre, and was supplied also to the Arab Legion.

Armoured Car, Humber, AA, Mark I   [*Imperial War Museum*

Anti-Aircraft Armoured Cars

The Pierce-Arrow and Peerless vehicles of 1915–1916 equipped with 2pr pom-poms have already been described but, apart from these, the only British vehicle known to have been built as a specialised anti-aircraft armoured car before World War II was a version of the Crossley experimental six-wheel armoured car (D2E1) which appeared about 1930. This car had an open ring mounting with two Vickers 0.5in machine guns in place of the turret normally fitted. Drawings of another Crossley—the 30/70hp armoured car chassis fitted with a

40mm automatic gun (similar to the 2pr pom-pom) in place of the turret—were issued by Vickers-Armstrongs, also about 1930, but it is uncertain whether this vehicle was actually built in this form.

The importance of AA protection for armoured units against low-flying aircraft was more readily appreciated after the events of 1940, and an anti-aircraft machine gun was provided for all British armoured fighting vehicles. A special version of the Humber Mark I armoured car appeared about 1942. The normal turret in this type was removed and replaced with a turret, designed by Stothert and Pitt Ltd, equipped with four Besa machine guns and an AA ring sight. This vehicle was known as Armoured Car, Humber, AA Mark I.

As described elsewhere, Marmon-Herrington armoured cars were modified in the Middle East to receive a variety of captured German and Italian weapons, some of which were suitable for anti-aircraft use. In the Middle East also, a Daimler Armoured Car was experimentally modified to permit very high elevation of the main armament, but this design was not pursued. American Staghound AA armoured cars equipped with two 0.5in Browning machine guns and a special naval sight were used in Italy and in North West Europe by British units.

The final British development in the period under review was an AEC Anti-Aircraft Armoured Car, of which a prototype was produced about 1944. This vehicle consisted of an Armoured Car, AEC Mark II fitted with a large turret like that of the Crusader AA II tank. This turret was equipped with two 20mm Oerlikon cannon. The Armoured Car, AEC, AA was not put into production as the almost complete elimination of the Luftwaffe by the Allied air forces after the Normandy landings made this type of specialised vehicle unnecessary.

Alvis Dingo Scout Car

[*RAC Tank Museum*

Car, Scout, Daimler Mark II   [*Imperial War Museum*

Scout Cars

	DAIMLER MKS. I-III	HUMBER MKS I-II	LYNX I-II
Weight:	2.8 tons (Mks I-IB), 3 tons (Mk II), 3.15 tons (Mk III)	3.39 tons	4 tons
Length:	10ft 5in	12ft 7in	12ft 1½in
Width:	5ft 7½in	6ft 2½in	6ft 1in
Height:	4ft 11in	6ft 11¼in	5ft 10in
Speed:	55mph	60mph	57mph
Armour:	30mm	14mm	30mm
Armament:	1 Bren mg	1 Bren mg	1 Bren mg
Engine:	Daimler 55bhp	Humber 87bhp	Ford 95bhp
Crew:	2	2–3	2
Range:	200 miles	200 miles	200 miles

The Scout Car, in the form developed and used by the British Army, was a unique and highly successful military vehicle. Designed as a small two-seater armoured vehicle with good cross-country performance for liaison and reconnaissance duties in the battle area, two types of Scout Car were tested by the Army in 1938. Both prototypes were rear engined vehicles, unarmoured at the back. One of them, submitted by Alvis Ltd, and known as Dingo, was in some respects—notably the transverse dual leaf-spring suspension—a smaller version of the interesting Alvis-Straussler armoured car. The other vehicle, designed by BSA was externally not dissimilar to the Alvis Dingo, but had

143

an interesting and effective form of transmission. Drive from the engine at the rear passed forward to a transfer box, containing forward and reverse gears and a differential. Four propeller shafts, carried within the side frame channels, conveyed the drive via bevel reduction gears and Tracta-jointed shafts to each wheel. This arrangement in conjunction with independent coil suspension permitted any one wheel to be raised eight inches without the others losing contact with the ground. The vehicle steered on all four wheels.

The BSA design was accepted for the Army and, after some modifications had been made, put into production. The hull was redesigned as an octagon with sloping plates (including rear protection), and was fitted with a sliding roof. The driver's seat faced slightly inwards to enable him to have a better view through the rear flap in the armour when driving in reverse. This vehicle was known as Car, Scout, Mark I at first, and later as Car, Scout, Daimler Mark I after the BSA Company had been absorbed by the Daimler Company Ltd, and other makes of scout car were taken into service.

The Daimler Scout Car went through several modifications during the course of production, which amounted in total to 6,626 vehicles by the end of World War II. The Mark IA was fitted with a folding (instead of sliding) roof; and the fan draught of the engine was reversed in Mark IB. All these early vehicles had provision for four-wheel steering, although conversion was made later to normal steering in many cars as it had proved a liability in the hands of unskilled drivers. Mark IIs were built without provision for steering the rear wheels; they also had revised radiator grilles at the rear. The Car,

Car, Scout, Humber, Mark I [Rootes Ltd

144

Car, Scout, Ford Mark I, Lynx I

Scout, Daimler Mark III dispensed with the armoured roof altogether (earlier cars were, in any case, nearly always operated with the roof open) and had built-in waterproofed engine ignition equipment.

The Ford Motor Company of Canada undertook production of the "Car, Scout, Ford I, Lynx I", using armoured hulls (of similar design to those of the Daimler Scout Cars) manufactured by the International Harvester Company. This vehicle used existing Canadian automotive units and was heavier than the Daimlers and, with central driving shafts to front and rear axles, also higher. A new version, Lynx II, was designed to incorporate a number of necessary improvements. This had the same 95bhp V-8 engine but with modified cooling arrangements, strengthened chassis components, no armoured roof, and could be identified by the sand channels mounted across the rear instead of the front of the vehicle. During the War, 3,255 Lynx Scout Cars were manufactured in Canada.

The great demand for Scout Cars by several arms of the Service could not be met by existing production alone, which led to the Rootes Group being asked to design and produce a Scout Car. The resultant vehicle, "Car, Scout, Humber Mark I", was based on the same 87bhp engine and many of the components of the other Humber four-wheel drive military vehicles, but rearranged for a rear engine layout. This car was larger than the Daimler Scouts, and could accommodate three men. The roof was fixed, with two sliding hatches, and this arrangement permitted the operation of a Bren light machine gun mounted on the roof, sighted and fired by remote control linkage from inside. The suspension consisted of semi-elliptic leaf springs, transverse at the front. Coil suspension was tested, but not put into production vehicles. The Mark II was similar to Mark I, but had synchromesh on the 2nd gear in addition to the 3rd and top gears. Production of Humber Scout Cars, from about the end of 1942 to the end of the War, amounted to 4,300 vehicles.

145

The specifications of vehicles designed as Scout Cars and as Light Reconnaissance Cars tended to converge towards the end of the War. A Daimler Scout Car was experimentally fitted with a turret ring, and by the cessation of hostilities a prototype Universal Scout Car had been built in Canada. These experimental vehicles led eventually to the post-war Ferret series of liaison and reconnaissance vehicles.

Scout Cars were used in action with British and Commonwealth forces everywhere during World War II. Their main employment was in tank units or armoured car regiments, but they were used also in many other types of unit. Daimler Scout Cars were seen on all the main War fronts; Humbers mainly in North West Europe; whilst Lynxes were employed in South East Asia Command and with Canadian formations in Italy and 21st Army Group.

[*Imperial War Museum*

Car, 4x2, Light Reconnaissance, Beaverette I, followed by a Beaverette II

Light Reconnaissance Cars

	BEAVER-ETTE I-II	BEAVER-ETTE III-IV	HUMBER MK I	HUMBER MK II	HUMBER MKS III-IIIA	OTTER	MORRIS MK I-II
Weight:	2 tons	2.6 tons	2.8 tons	2.98 tons	3.5 tons	4.8 tons	3.7 tons
Length:	13ft 6in	10ft 2½in	14ft 4in	14ft 4in	14ft 4in	14ft 9in	13ft 3½in
Width:	5ft 3in	5ft 10in	6ft 2in	6ft 2in	6ft 2in	7ft 0in	6ft 8in
Height:	5ft 0in	7ft 1in	6ft 10in	6ft 11in	7ft 1in	8ft 0in	6ft 2in
Speed:	40mph	24mph	45mph	45mph	50mph	45mph	50mph
Armour:	11mm (MS) and 3in wood	10mm	12mm	10mm	10mm	12mm	14mm

	BEAVER-ETTE I-II	BEAVER-ETTE III-IV	HUMBER MK I	HUMBER MK II	HUMBER MKS III-IIIA	OTTER	MORRIS MK I-II
Armament:	1 Bren mg (or 1 Boys atr)	1 Bren mg (or 2 Vickers "K")	1 Boys atr 1 Bren mg	1 Boys atr 1 Bren mg	1 Boys atr 1 Bren mg	1 Boys atr 1 Bren mg	1 Boys atr 1 Bren mg
Engine:	Standard 45bhp	Standard 45bhp	Humber 80bhp	Humber 80bhp	Humber 87bhp	GM, 104 bhp	Morris 71.8 bhp
Crew:	3	3	3	3	3	3	3

The earliest vehicles in this category, originally classified as Light Armoured Cars by the Army, were the Humberette and Beaverette, built on normal Humber Super Snipe and Standard 14hp passenger car chassis. These were rushed into production for Home Defence after the Dunkirk evacuation.

The "Car, 4 × 2, Light Reconnaissance, Standard Mark I, Beaverette I" (or "Car, Armoured, Light, Standard Type C, Beaverette I", as it was known to the RAF) was produced originally at the instigation of Lord Beaverbrook, after whom it was named, for the defence of aircraft factories. A total of 2,800 Beaverettes of all Marks was eventually built and used by the RAF for airfield protection, as well as by the Army. The armour consisted of $\frac{3}{8}$in or $\frac{7}{16}$in mild steel at the front and sides, with 3in oak planks reinforcing the frontal protection. Beaverette II was similar, but also had plates at the rear.

The Beaverette III (known at first to the RAF as "Beaverbug I—Car, Armoured, Light, Standard Type D") was built when supplies of proper armour plate had become available. This was totally enclosed, and had a small turret. Mark IV was much the same as Beaverette III, but the hull front was stepped back, the upper half being angled to give better protection and observation facilities.

Car, 4x2, Light Reconnaissance, Standard Mark III, Beaverette III   [B.T. White

The Beaverettes were usually equipped with a Bren light machine gun but the later turreted cars, when used by the RAF, often had twin Vickers "K" aircraft-type machine guns. Sometimes a complete perspex aircraft turret was substituted.

"Car, 4 × 2, Light Reconnaissance, Humber Mark I, Ironside I", followed the Humberette (referred to above) to which it was generally similar, but WD pattern rims with Runflat tyres were fitted and other minor changes to improve protection were made. Interesting variants of this model were the "Special Ironside Saloons" built for the conveyance of the Royal Family and Cabinet Ministers during air raids or possible invasion. About three of these cars were made, all slightly different from each other, and fitted out to saloon car standards inside.

Car, 4x2, Light Reconnaissance, Humber Mark I, Ironside I   [*Rootes Ltd*

The Humber Mark II Light Reconnaissance Car was similar to Ironside I. and also built on the Super Snipe chassis, but was fitted with a small turret, The "Car, 4 × 4, Light Reconnaissance, Humber Mark III", first produced at the end of 1941, had a similar arrangement of armour protection and turret to its predecessor, but used a specially designed four-wheel drive chassis. The Mark IIIA had a slightly modified hull, with extra observation ports at the front corner angles. During World War II 3,600 Humber Light Reconnaissance cars of all Marks were built by the Rootes Group. The Marks III and IIIA, in particular, were widely used on the Mediterranean fronts and in the North West Europe campaign in the Reconnaissance Regiments of infantry divisions, and by the RAF Regiment for airfield protection work.

The "Car, Light Reconnaissance, Canadian GM Mark I, Otter I" was a vehicle which consisted basically of Canadian components adapted to meet the same specification as the Humber Mark III Light Reconnaissance Car. The engine was a General Motors 6 cylinder type, of 104bhp. A total of 1,761

Car, 4x4, Light Reconnaissance, Humber, Mark III

[*Rootes Ltd*

[*Imperial War Museum*

Car, 4x4, Light Reconnaissance, Canadian GM Mark I, Otter I

149

Light Reconnaissance Cars was built in Canada between 1942 and the end of the War: they were used mainly by Canadian forces in Italy and 21st Army Group, but were supplied also to British units. Some cars used by the RAF Regiment had a 20mm cannon mounted in the front of the hull and, in addition, twin Browning machine guns on an AA mounting on the turret.

Another British light armoured vehicle built in large numbers was the "Car, 4 × 2, Light Reconnaissance, Morris Mark I" (or "Car, Armoured, Morris Type E" to the RAF). This was a rear-engined, rear wheel drive vehicle, with a smooth enclosed underbelly which helped to give it a quite good cross-country performance for a car without all-wheel drive. The driver was in the centre at the front, the gunner and turret behind him at the right, with the third man at the left. Hatches in the roof of the hull permitted the operation of a Boys anti-tank rifle from this position. Suspension was semi-elliptic at the rear, with independent coil springs at the front. On the Mark II version, four-wheel drive was introduced, and the suspension was changed to leaf springs all round. About 2,200 Morris Light Reconnaissance Cars, Marks I and II, were made, including a turretless OP version.

The Hillman Gnat was conceived as a replacement for the unarmoured motor-cycle combinations equipped with Bren guns that were in service in considerable numbers with the Army in 1940–1941. Components of the Hillman Light Utility Car, then in mass production, were used so that this little two-man armoured car could be built readily in large quantities. A rear engine layout was adopted, which meant the addition of a transfer box to take the drive back to the rear axle, but all the other main mechanical components were the same as those of the Hillman Utility. Three prototypes (later classified

Car, 4x4, Light Reconnaissance, Morris Mark II   *[Nuffield Organisation*

150

Hillman Gnat

[*Rootes Ltd*

[*Nuffield Organisation*

Morris single-seat armoured car with Morris Mark I Light Recce Car

as Light Reconnaissance Cars) were built in 1942, but cross-country performance turned out to be poor owing to the low power-weight ratio. The project lapsed after Major-General V. V. Pope, its chief sponsor, was killed towards the end of 1941.

The Morris Salamander was a similar type of vehicle to the Hillman Gnat, but using Morris components. The Salamander followed an earlier interesting Morris prototype—a small single-seat armoured car, equipped with two machine guns firing forwards and aimed with the car itself. Neither of these two Morris types, like the Gnat, were put into production, as official opinion turned in favour of larger vehicles capable of carrying three men.

At the other end of the scale to the Gnat and the Salamander was the Armoured Car, Dodge, which weighed about 8 tons. Seventy were built in the Summer of 1940 by Briggs Motor Bodies Ltd to the design of Sir Malcolm Campbell.

They were later classified as Light Reconnaissance Cars.

Morris Salamander   [*Nuffield Organisation*

152

Armoured Carrier, Wheeled, IP Mark IIA, equipped with Boys anti-tank rifle and Vickers-Berthier on AA mounting

Wheeled Carriers

DATA FOR ARMOURED CARRIER, WHEELED, I.P. MARK IIA

Weight:	5.7 tons	Speed:	50mph
Length:	15ft 6in	Armament:	1 Boys atr, 1 Bren or Vickers-Berthier mg
Width:	7ft 6in	Engine:	Ford 95bhp
Height:	6ft 6in	Crew:	3–4

A prototype "Carrier, Wheeled" was ordered from Guy Motors Ltd towards the end of 1939 but, apart from this experimental vehicle, production of armoured carriers in the United Kingdom was concentrated on tracked vehicles of the Universal Carrier type. When, however, it was decided in 1940 to commence the production of armoured vehicles in India, a wheeled carrier suitable for service in the Middle East was chosen. Armour plate was made at first experimentally and then in quantity by the Tata Iron and Steel Company, and the chassis used for the first vehicles was a front-engined Ford 113½in wheelbase type with Marmon-Herrington conversion to four-wheel drive. The first type of vehicle was known as "Armoured Carrier, Wheeled, IP Mark I", the IP standing for "Indian Pattern".

The "Armoured Carrier, Wheeled, IP Mark II" and all subsequent models were built on Ford 4 × 4 rear-engined chassis, supplied from Canada in "completely knocked down" condition and assembled on arrival. Over 9,000 of these rear-engined chassis for India were produced by the Ford Motor Company of Canada, although the total number of carriers completed in India during the War was only 4,655 (the bulk of them built by The Tata Iron and Steel Company and the East Indian Railway Workshops)—the difference in numbers probably being accounted for partly by losses incurred in transit through enemy action and partly by the diminished need by 1944 for production of armoured vehicles in India. Four models of the Mark II Carrier were built: the Mark IIA had larger tyres than the Mark II, but was otherwise the same; Mark IIB had a slight extension of the hinged roof plate; and Mark IIC had a number of improvements, including wider track at front and rear, heavier front axles and springs, slightly larger tyres, and a 12-gallon auxiliary petrol tank. An Armoured Observation Vehicle version of Mark IIC, with a small turret, was also built.

The Mark III vehicle was really equivalent in specification to a Light Reconnaissance Car and was, in fact, usually known as "Armoured Car, IP Mark III"; 276 of these were built. The roof was enclosed and a turret, mounting a Boys anti-tank rifle and a Bren light machine gun, was fitted but the other main details of appearance and specification were the same as the Mark IIC Carriers.

The "Armoured Carrier, Wheeled, IP Mark IV", the final version, was, like the earlier Indian Pattern Carriers, a rear-engined vehicle with open top, but it did not have the sloping glacis plate of the Mark II-III series; the driver had a vertical steering column and sat in a small centrally-placed cab.

The Indian Wheeled Armoured Carriers were used for many of the same functions as were the tracked Universal Carrier types, namely as reconnaissance or artillery officers' vehicles, or to carry the crews of infantry weapons, such as mortars or Bren light machine guns. The Indian Carriers saw their most useful service in action with the British-Indian Divisions in the Middle East. They were also used in the Italian campaign and in the Far East theatre of War.

Self-propelled Guns

Few armoured self-propelled mountings on wheeled carriages were built in Britain in World War II—tracked carriages, which offered a steadier platform, were generally favoured. The terrain in North Africa gave the greatest scope for the employment of wheeled vehicles, and a number of prototype wheeled SP guns were designed in 1942 and one type—the Deacon—went into production on a limited scale.

Carrier, AEC, 6pr Gun, Mark I (Deacon). One hundred and seventy-five of these vehicles were built in 1942 and sent out to the Middle East. A number of anti-tank batteries were re-equipped with Deacons to help increase their mobility in combating tanks. They served until the end of the North African campaign in the spring of 1943 and were then handed over to the Turkish Government. The AEC Matador 4 × 4 chassis with a 6 cylinder 95bhp diesel engine was used for this vehicle, which weighed 12 tons and had a speed of 19mph. A somewhat similar 2pr mounting was built in India on a Ford chassis.

SP 17pr Gun—Thornycroft. The design of this vehicle, using a Thornycroft six-wheeled chassis fitted with a 6-cylinder engine, was commenced early in 1942: one prototype was built. It was completely enclosed with 50mm armour plate, and the 17pr anti-tank gun was mounted at the rear, with a limited traverse. The firing trials were very satisfactory but, due to the loaded weight of 13¾ tons, the cross-country performance was below the desired standard and, as no existing Thornycroft components were suitable for a more highly powered version, the project was dropped.

Other experimental vehicles. Another SP 17pr carriage was one designed by Nicholas Straussler. This was an ingenious device which amounted, more or less, to the addition of two extra wheels to a 17pr field carriage, a motive unit built up from Bedford lorry components and a small lightly armoured cab for the driver. The result was a very inconspicuous SP mounting, but the crew

[*AEC Ltd*

Carrier, AEC, 6pr Gun,
Mark I (Deacon)

[*Transport Equipment
(Thornycroft) Ltd*

S-P 17pr Gun—Thornycroft

S-P 17pr Gun—Straussler

155

were very exposed and the idea was dropped. A similar adaptation of a 6pr field carriage using Standard automotive components was also not proceeded with.

Three types of self-propelled gun mountings were built on adaptations of existing armoured chassis: a 2pr mounted on a Ford Lynx Scout Car, and a 6pr on a General Motors Fox Armoured Car (both designed in Canada), and a 6pr mounted low in the front of a Morris Mark II light Reconnaissance Car and known as Firefly. The weapons in each case were anti-tank guns on field mountings, mounted to fire forwards, with only a limited traverse. None of these designs went into production, in all probability because they were made unnecessary by the appearance in quantity of conventional armoured cars with similar weapons mounted in fully rotating turrets.

Armoured Command Vehicle, Guy Lizard   [*Guy Motors*

Armoured Command Vehicles

The purpose of Armoured Command Vehicles is to provide senior officers commanding armoured formations, their staff and brigade commanders with mobile headquarters vehicles in the field. Wireless equipment, to maintain forward contact with armoured units and senior headquarters to the rear, is essential; also sufficient space for the staff and their equipment, including maps and map tables.

The first Armoured Command Vehicle designed as such for the British Army was an armoured office body on a Morris 15cwt truck chassis, and this type was issued to 1st Tank Brigade Headquarters about 1937. A number of Morris Armoured Cars, Reconnaissance, were later converted to approximately the same standard as this vehicle, but the accommodation offered by the 15cwt 4 × 2 chassis was rather cramped, and the cross-country performance was not particularly good.

The Headquarters staff of 1st Armoured Division in France in May-June 1940 were carried in mild steel prototype and plywood mock-up armoured command vehicles, but a proper armoured command vehicle, built on the Guy Lizard 4 × 4 chassis, powered by a Gardner 5 cylinder diesel engine, was available in small numbers later in the year. Guy Lizard Armoured Command Vehicles were, by early 1941, issued to Headquarters, 7th Armoured Division in the Western Desert and some formations in the United Kingdom, but continued production by Guy Motors of the numbers required was not possible, and a new design, suitable for the AEC Matador chassis, was prepared.

The "Armoured Command Vehicle, AEC, 4 × 4," appeared in two versions—HP (High Power), with an RCA receiver and a No 19 Wireless set, and LP (Low Power) with one No 19 and one No 19 HP set. The LP Mark II had an internal partition dividing the wireless and staff compartments. The HP vehicles differed externally from the LP versions in that many of them had a square projection on the bonnet to facilitate camouflage as a lorry. All the AEC 4 × 4 ACVs were engined with the 95bhp AEC diesel.

A new design of Armoured Command Vehicle with a more spacious interior, but reduced overall height, was produced towards the end of World

Armoured Command Vehicle, LP (AEC) 4x4, Mark I   [AEC Ltd

157

War II on an AEC 6 × 6 chassis, with 6 cylinder 150bhp diesel engine. There was again an HP version and an LP version, the former equipped with one No 19 and one No 53 wireless set, and the latter with one No 19 and one No 19 HP set.

The 4 × 4 AEC Armoured Command Vehicles were used by armoured formation headquarters on the North African, Italian and North West Europe fronts from 1941 onwards. Three armoured command vehicles of this type were captured by the Afrika Korps in the Desert in April 1941 and two of these, christened "Mammoths", were subsequently used by Rommel's headquarters, and the third by the GOC 5th Light Division to the end of the North African campaign—a tribute to their design and workmanship.

Armoured Command Vehicle, HP (AEC) 6x6, Mark I

[*AEC Ltd*

Improvised Armoured Vehicles

The expected invasion of Britain after the withdrawal of the British Expeditionary Force from France in June 1940 with the loss of most of its equipment led to the production, with the greatest urgency, of large numbers of improvised armoured vehicles. These included the Beaverette and Humberette Light Armoured Cars, which are dealt with elsewhere in this book, and a wide variety of lorries, armoured in various ways.

Armadillos were a large group of vehicles designed and built by the London, Midland and Scottish Railway workshops at Wolverton. Mock-ups of various designs for armouring lorries with boiler plate were made, but rejected in favour of a type utilising a wooden structure. This consisted of an open top wooden box, with external dimensions of 5ft 10in long, 5ft 4in wide and 4ft 6in high, with another box inside, leaving a space of 6in between the inner and outer skins. The space between was closely packed with small pebbles. This structure, which was capable of withstanding machine gun fire at close range, had weapon apertures on all sides plus a bar across the top for a machine gun mounting, and was mounted on the platform of the lorry. The driver's cab of the vehicle had light steel protection. A total of 312 vehicles, mostly requisitioned lorries and vans, were fitted with protection in this form, and designated Armadillo Mark I.

Armadillo Mark II was the name applied to 295 Bedford 3 ton and 30cwt lorries fitted with a longer pebble-lined box, and protection for the radiator and petrol tank was added in later vehicles of this series. A 1½pr COW gun was mounted to the rear of a pebble-lined box of reduced length in 55 Bedford 3 ton lorries, and this version was called Armadillo Mark III.

Concrete was another unusual material used for the protection of a further group of vehicles intended, like the first Armadillos, for aerodrome defence. Old commercial lorries of the heavier type (both four-wheelers and six-wheelers) had built on to them concrete pillboxes of various shapes and sizes adapted to the type of vehicle used. These lorries were fitted with their concrete armour (which was proof against armour-piercing bullets) by Messrs Concrete Ltd, to the design of Mr C. B. Matthews, MBE, MICE, then Managing Director. They were called "Bisons", after the trade mark of the company.

The Beaver-Eel was one of the types of armoured car produced to the orders of Lord Beaverbrook for the protection of aircraft factories. Known officially to the RAF as "Tender, Armoured, Leyland Type C", the Beaver-Eel consisted of an open-top steel armoured body on a Leyland Retriever 3 ton 6 × 4 lorry. The prototype was built by Leyland Motors Ltd, in June 1940 and delivery—to a total of 250 vehicles by the Leyland factory—began in the same month. A further 86 were built by the LMSR. Some vehicles were armed with four Lewis machine guns and a 20mm cannon; others had a 1½pr COW gun instead of the 20mm; whilst others had machine guns only. After the invasion emergency was over the majority of Beaver-Eels had their armour removed and were rebuilt as ordinary lorries.

"Lorry, 30cwt, Armoured Anti-Tank, Bedford" was the official name for the Bedford type OXA lorries supplied to mobile units of the Home Defence Forces in 1940. A steel armoured structure replaced the lorry cab and body, and protection was also fitted to the radiator and petrol tanks. Loopholes were provided for the operation of weapons which usually included a Boys anti-tank rifle and a Bren light machine gun. This vehicle, illustrated on page 97, weighed about eight tons and was powered by the Bedford 6 cylinder engine of 72bhp. One was experimentally armoured with plastic armour; a number of Bedford civilian type lorries were also armoured in a generally similar way to the OXA type, and allocated for aerodrome defence.

Many Home Guard units produced their own armoured vehicles. Some of these appeared to be quite well designed, but others would have been certain death traps to their users, had they ever seen action. The use of armoured cars without proper support was unsuited to the role of the Home Guard, and these unofficial armoured cars were discouraged by the authorities in most cases. It is known that various Home Guard units in the following counties had armoured cars of one sort or another: Hertfordshire, Bedfordshire, Norfolk, Lancashire, Berkshire, London, Gloucestershire, Kent, Cheshire, Somerset, Middlesex and Hampshire. There were probably others. It is only possible to describe two of the more successful types here. Twelve ex-Tilling AEC type ST buses were stripped down to the chassis and armoured with mild steelplates by an LPTB Home Guard unit at the London Chiswick depot. These weighed about 12 tons and looked rather like armoured command vehicles. No fixed armament was carried, but slits and loopholes were provided in the sides to enable the rifles of the crew to be used.

159

The 28th Bn Hampshire Home Guard constructed what was, for its time, a well armed armoured car. An existing Dodge Armoured Car (one of the type designed by Sir Malcolm Campbell) was modified—the height of the armour being reduced and a short-barreled 6pr gun, of the type used in World War I tanks, mounted. The gun had an all-round traverse and was supplied with a quota of semi-armour-piercing ammunition.

[*Imperial War Museum*

Armadillos, Mark I. The nearest vehicle is a Bedford and behind is another Bedford between two different Fordsons

Bison Armoured Lorries with concrete armour   [*Concrete Ltd*

Miscellaneous Wheeled Armoured Vehicles

Some of the special purpose vehicles not already dealt with are described briefly here.

Armoured Personnel Carriers and Armoured Ambulances

No vehicles in either of these categories were produced in numbers in Britain during World War II, although about 1920 some Crossley tenders were experimentally fitted with armour and, about 1935, there was a version of the "Dragon Portée" Morris 15cwt truck with some frontal armour protection. Canadian General Motors vehicles (rather like Otter Light Reconnaissance Cars without turrets) and American White Scout Cars, classified as "Trucks, 15cwt 4 × 4 Armoured Personnel", as well as US half-track vehicles were, however, used in considerable numbers by British and Commonwealth forces. As well as personnel carriers for infantry in armoured divisions, these vehicles were adapted as armoured ambulances and command vehicles. In India a few hundred Canadian Ford 15cwt 4 × 4 trucks were built as armoured ambulances and as armoured personnel carriers and used in the Burma campaign in 1944–1945. In an effort to achieve a suitable design for a chassis for the main functions that armoured trucks were required for prototypes were built in the United Kingdom and in Canada towards the end of the War of a vehicle known as CAPLAD. The initials stood for Command, Armoured Personnel, Light Aid Detachment, Ambulance and Demolition—the functions which, with suitable fittings, it was designed to undertake. The British prototype used Ford 3 ton 4 × 4 components, and the Canadian version was an adaptation of the General Motors Fox Armoured Car, but work in both countries on the CAPLAD was ceased at the end of the War.

Flamethrowers

These vehicles on wheeled chassis were, with the exception of the Basilisk, built principally for aerodrome or coastal defence.

Commer Flamethrower. The first experimental vehicle built by the Lagonda Company. It was on a Commer 4 × 2 chassis and had an annular flamethrower in a small turret.

Cockatrice. Sixty were built on Bedford QL 4 × 4 chassis for Royal Naval airfield defence. Armed with flame projector in turret and two Lewis machine guns on an AA mounting at the rear end of the hull.

Cockatrice (Heavy). A vehicle similar in arrangement to the Bedford Cockatrice, but using an AEC 6 × 6 chassis. The armoured hull was offset to the right. Six were built and used for the defence of RAF airfields.

Heavy Pump Unit. A pump-driven flame projector powered by an auxiliary engine and mounted in an armoured AEC 6 × 6 chassis. Only one experimental vehicle was built.

Basilisk. A prototype flamethrower vehicle intended to accompany armoured units in the field. The flame projector in a small turret was mounted on an armoured hull and chassis generally similar to that of the Armoured Car, AEC Mark II, although, in fact, designed earlier.

Armoured Demolition Vehicles

A number of vehicles to carry demolition equipment were built on AEC Matador 4 × 4 chassis. Externally they were almost identical to the Armoured Command Vehicle, without the side rollers for the tent extension, but a hatch was provided in the roof for the operation of a pile driver (used for preparing

161

holes for demolition charges). The other equipment carried included a compressor for driving pneumatic tools. Tracked vehicles were later more generally used for the functions for which these vehicles were built, and so some of them were subsequently converted to Armoured Command Vehicles.

Armoured Ammunition Carriers

This type, known officially as "Lorry, 3 ton, 4 × 4, Armoured Ammunition, AEC", was also built on the Matador chassis. This specialised role was, when required, rnore usually performed by tracked vehicles.

Armoured Artillery Tractors

Only two types of armoured wheeled vehicles are known to have been designed as artillery tractors for the British Army. One was a modified version of the Tractor, 6 × 4, Field Artillery, Morris, built about 1935, and the other was a 6 × 6 AEC vehicle built in 1944. In both cases only the front portion of the tractor was armoured. Only prototypes of the Morris and AEC vehicles were built. In World War II, towing vehicles for British field artillery and heavier weapons were usually unarmoured lorries, but when for a special operation armoured vehicles were considered essential, modified tanks were usually employed.

Armoured Trailers

A type of four-wheeled trailer, known as Scorpion and armoured with plastic armour, was used for the defence of Royal Naval airfields in World War II—100 were built for this purpose. They were armed with two Browning machine guns in a small open-top turret. Beaverfrog was a trailer for aircraft factory defence and a four-wheeled Armoured Observation Trailer was built by Garner Motors in about 1942.

Basilisk flamethrower armoured car   [*AEC Ltd*

162

Part 3

SPECIALISED ARMOUR

Churchill AVRE followed by a Churchill Crocodile in Geilenkirchen, Germany, 1945

[Imperial War Museum]

Development

THE SAYING that necessity is the mother of invention has as much truth in the battlefield as elsewhere, and the static warfare on the Western Front created by unflankable trench systems resulted in the appearance in action of British tanks in September 1916. By the end of World War I, experience, both of the British users of the tank and their allies and of the enemy in devising methods of combating it, had prompted the development of a number of types of British tracked armoured vehicles which joined the fighting tank itself on the battlefield.

Firstly were the service vehicles—supply tanks carrying stores for both the battle tanks themselves and for the other arms they supported; signals tanks to maintain communications between tank formations; and salvage tanks for recovery and repair work.

Secondly were the obstacle crossing aids—at first added to the standard tanks in the form of fascines or cribs and later in the form of specialised bridge-laying tanks. Also to be crossed by tanks were minefields, for which the first methods of clearance by tanks began to be tried just after the War ended. The first experiments with amphibious tanks began at about the same time.

Thirdly were the devices to aid the tank in the offensive such as searchlights—first suggested, although not built, in World War I—or special variants in its armament, such as flamethrowers. The Pedrail Machine, whose ancestry actually ante-dated "Mother" by some six months, was finally completed as a tracked flamethrower.

Once the War was over both the impetus and much of the financial support for development of tanks and other armoured vehicles was lost, but experiments continued slowly on the same lines, most of the basic requirements of armour remaining, although the emphasis changed from time to time.

The outbreak of World War II saw the United Kingdom with drawing board designs or, in some cases, prototype tracked armoured vehicles on tank chassis for some specialised functions, but very few special tanks were in service.

The trenching machine intended by Winston Churchill (again First Lord of the Admiralty and once more ready to devote energy to land, as well as sea, battles) to take assaulting infantry and tanks right up to the Siegfried Line was one of the earliest and certainly the most magnificent forms of special device of World War II. The German conquest of France in 1940 made it unnecessary for the time being to consider assaulting the Siegfried Line and attention was turned instead to other forms of special armour suitable for defence as well as attack—such as flamethrowers. By 1942 study of the needs of support in an assault landing was more important.

Taking each group in turn, of the service vehicles no exact equivalent was developed after World War I to the Supply Tanks or Tank Mark IX, although in 1944 Armoured Personnel Carriers were hastily improvised on tank chassis to meet a need which did not seem to have been fully appreciated earlier. Provision was made for wireless in all modern British tanks (although not always fitted) at the beginning of World War II, but some tanks were fitted with long range sets to enable commanders to maintain contact with formation headquarters. Armoured Recovery Vehicles had been largely neglected during the inter-war years and it was not until early 1942, after the German success in this field began to be appreciated, that steps were taken to provide ARVs on the same chassis as contemporary cruiser and infantry tanks. Beach Armoured Recovery Vehicles were developed following the Dieppe raid and in anticipation of a full scale invasion of France.

The Dieppe Raid of 19th August 1942, in which some 30 Churchill tanks were sent to support the landing of infantry of the 4th Canadian Division, underlined the need for specialised armour to support amphibious landings. Both flamethrowers and bobbin carpets carried by Churchill tanks were sent to Dieppe, but from 1942 onwards much more intensive study was made of the problems of an opposed amphibious operation and many forms of specialised armour were developed and put to good use in the Normandy landings nearly two years later.

An amphibious tank was built in 1919 by the addition of air drums to a Tank Mark IX and some of the immediate post-war experimental tanks were designed to float. Vickers-Armstrongs produced a few amphibious light tanks during the inter-war period. Devices for floating heavier tanks tended to be clumsy, however, but the light, compact and effective "Duplex Drive" equipment invented by Nicholas Straussler made it practicable to convert 30-ton tanks into amphibious vehicles without loss of fighting power or mobility once ashore.

War Office policy on the development of mobile flamethrowers veered between the choice of carriers or tanks. Eventually, after experiments and trials to find out the best form of flamethrower equipment, the Wasp was applied to both Carriers and—as the Crocodile—to Churchill tanks.

The story of the tank-armoured searchlights is mainly one of an unsure policy as to their use, since, technically, the idea which had its origin in World War I was developed to a stage where effective equipment might have been used at least by 1941.

A fairly effective tank bridge was produced in 1918 and improved in the next year or so. A change to lighter types of tank by the Army made the heavy bridges redundant, but by 1939 various forms of bridging for medium tanks were

[*Imperial War Museum*

Tanks, Mark V carrying Cribs moving up to the Hindenburg Line, 1918

Churchill IIIs of the Calgary Regiment after the Dieppe Raid, August 1942

available in prototype or design form although production in numbers did not come until later in the War. One lesson of the Dieppe operation was the need for a means of making a rapid exit for tanks from the beaches over sea walls and other obstructions, and AVRE—carried Small Box Girder bridges were used for this purpose at D-Day (and subsequently, for crossing other obstacles). The Ark was developed for the same purpose although also, in practice, had a much wider application, particularly in Italy where several rivers were crossed by means of Arks in series and deep trenches overcome by Arks on top of each other. For tactical use by armoured formation commanders a few scissors type tank bridges were included in the headquarters squadron of each armoured brigade. For placing much larger bridges under fire the pushing system by tanks—first devised in 1918—was adapted in World War II for built-up Inglis and, later, Bailey bridges.

The "RE Tank" of 1919 was, in effect, revived in the Churchill AVRE. The need for a general purpose assault engineer vehicle of this type was yet another lesson of the Dieppe operation and work on the AVRE was begun in late 1942. At D-Day and onwards, AVREs besides laying, as mentioned, bridges for exit from the beaches, performed a variety of useful jobs, including carpet-laying over soft ground, demolition of strong points and obstacles and some mine clearance tasks.

Mine clearance was one of the functions of the "RE Tank", but, following extensive experiments with different tank operated devices, including ploughs, rollers and explosives, between the Wars and during World War II, eventually armoured units equipped with flail tanks became the main means of dealing with this problem. The flail device appears to have been first suggested by Major Galpin of the Mechanisation Board (the officer who designed the scissors tank and who, although little known, deserves mention with Lt-Gen Sir G. le Q. Martel and Nicholas Straussler as an original thinker in the field of specialised

167

armour) in early 1939. The idea was shelved at the time and was, like many other inventions, proposed quite independently by Major A. S. J. du Toit in 1941 following the extensive use of minefields in the desert campaign. Development of the flail tank was carried out both in the United Kingdom and in the Middle East, at first separately because of the difficulty of communications at the time, although, later, ideas were exchanged. It reached its peak in the Sherman Crab, which was used with considerable success in North West Europe from the invasion beaches onwards, although the Middle East designed Sherman Scorpion flail tank (improved from the earlier designs used in North Africa) was the type employed contemporaneously in Italy. Experiments with ploughs, rollers and explosive for mine clearance by tanks persisted until 1944. It was then generally recognised that the flail tank was the most certain way of clearing anti-tank mines but it was more complicated, expensive to manufacture and slower in operation than the relatively simple rollers and ploughs. However, it was the most certain in its effect, although the best type of roller—the CIRD—and the best plough—the Bullshorn—together with the Snake mineclearing explosive device were all taken to France in 1944 in limited quantities for use in special circumstances. Smaller versions of both rollers and ploughs existed for use against anti-personnel mines, for which they were fairly effective.

Tank bulldozers appeared for the first time in World War II. Bulldozer or angledozer blades for clearance of earth or rubble obstacles to make way for the passage of armour could be fitted to practically any type of tank (British-used Shermans were, for example, so fitted in the Mediterranean theatre) but for the North West Europe campaign obsolescent cruiser tanks were de-turreted and permanently modified as tank dozers. Some Caterpillar dozers were armoured for work under fire but these lacked mobility compared with the tank dozers.

An AVRE with SBG bridge moving up for the assault on Le Havre, September 1944

The organisation of special armour in formations must be mentioned here. In the earlier part of World War II such special armour as existed was operated at regimental level or by smaller units: the Scorpion Regiment equipped with the early Middle East flail tanks is an example. However, it was felt expedient to place the special armour (excluding vehicles such as ARVs and bridgelayers normally controlled at unit or formation level) for the invasion of Europe under unified command and the 79th Armoured Division, under its energetic commander Major-General Sir Percy Hobart, was given operational control and responsibility for development of all the special equipment to be used in the D-Day assault and in the subsequent campaign. The Division took over this function in April 1943; by the time of the Rhine Crossing in March 1945 it was the largest Division in the British Army, with more than 1,500 tanks and other tracked vehicles alone. The formations controlled by the 79th Armoured Division (although not all at once) included an Armoured Brigade of flail tanks (three regiments); a Brigade of CDL tanks; a Brigade of Crocodiles (three regiments at maximum strength); an Armoured Engineer Brigade (three regiments of AVREs, etc.); five British tank regiments, two Canadian regiments and three United States tank battalions all trained in DD tanks for the D-Day landings, and one different British regiment and one United States' tank company for the Rhine crossing. There were also two regiments (one British, one Canadian) with Kangaroos and six regiments with Buffaloes, some of which were converted from existing units in the Division. The system worked very well, because the specialist advice of the staff of the 79th Armoured Division was available to Army Commanders planning an operation; units could then be allocated as appropriate although still under their regimental or brigade commanders, so ensuring that the equipment was used to its best advantage. Units of the Division, particularly the tank flamethrowers, were often in demand by the United States Army commanders since the American Army at that time had no comparable organisation.

In Italy, during the winter of 1944/5, a formation corresponding in some ways to the 79th Armoured Division in miniature was formed—the 25th Armoured Engineer Brigade, comprising the 51st Royal Tank Regiment (with two squadrons of Crocodiles and one squadron of flail tanks) and Nos 1 and 2 Armoured Engineer Regiments—both equipped with AVREs, Arks and other engineering devices. In addition, although not under unified command, the 9th Armoured Brigade was reorganised at about the same time to control the training and operation of DD tanks and, later, Sherman Kangaroos and American-built Landing Vehicles Tracked were placed under control of this Armoured Brigade.

At unit level, although there was no hard and fast division, equipment which carried out an original function of the Sappers was operated by the Royal Engineers and other special armour such as Crocodile flamethrowers was the responsibility of units of the Royal Armoured Corps.

Nomenclature of British Specialised Armour

THE SPECIAL vehicles and devices described in this book fall into two categories for nomenclature. One consists of modifications to the basic tank itself (by means of removal of parts of the main structure, such as turrets) and/or the addition of more or less permanently attached apparatus, flail equipment for instance. The other consists of equipment which fairly readily was attached to normal tanks or tanks modified only slightly for the purpose.

Special vehicles in the first category bore the name of the equipment added as a suffix to the name of the basic chassis, although the full basic type designation (e.g. Tank, Cruiser . . . .) was generally omitted. Mark numbers of both equipment and/or chassis name were also included in the full title where necessary for identification purposes—for example "Sherman V Crab Mark II".

Tanks in the second category bore the designation of the tank to which the equipment was attached followed by "with"—preceding the designation of the device, as "Matilda II with AMRA Mark IA".

Where a modified vehicle carried special equipment in addition this was shown, where necessary, in full as, for example, "Churchill III AVRE with SBG Bridge".

It will be noted from the examples in the book that the form of nomenclature was usually dictated not necessarily by the amount of modification but by the intended degree of its permanency.

The examples above all relate to World War II, when by far the greatest number of special armoured vehicles of the period under review was produced. However, the same system was generally applied also to earlier vehicles.

Tanks, Mark IV (Supply) moving up   [*Imperial War Museum*

Tank, Mark IV towing a
sledge carrying supplies

Special Tanks, World War I

Armour in specialised roles did not appear to any great degree in World War I, although some of the requirements of the future were envisaged towards the end of the conflict. The bridging tanks designed just before and just after the Armistice are described separately, but the fascines carried by standard tanks to enable them to cross wide trenches were introduced for the tank attack at Cambrai in November 1917 and should be mentioned here. The Tank Mark IV could cross a 10ft-wide trench, but parts of the Hindenburg Line trenches were known to be 12ft wide and so the fascine, 4ft 6in in diameter and 10ft wide, made up from smaller bundles of brushwood was devised. These fascines were carried on top of the tanks, over the front horns and could be dropped into the trench to be crossed, so decreasing its effective width. Later, to serve the same purpose, the crib, a hollow cylinder 5ft in diameter and 10ft wide, consisting of timbers bolted on to a metal framework was introduced. This was lighter and handier than the fascine (12cwt compared with the 30cwt fascine) and cribs were used in the big attack on the Hindenburg Line in September-October 1918. As an aid to the infantry in this attack, some tanks also towed light bridges for crossing trenches.

Another form of bridging device was devised for an amphibious raid planned for August 1917 on the Belgian coast behind the enemy lines. It consisted of hinged ramps fitted to the fronts of a few Tanks, Mark IV to enable them to surmount the sea wall. However, the operation was cancelled.

Adaptation of the basic vehicle for other special functions were few, but numbers of Tanks Marks I, II, III, and IV with the guns removed were used as Supply Carriers, both for the Tank Corps and other arms. The Supply Tanks Mark I converted in May 1916 could, for instance, carry sufficient ammunition and fuel to replenish five fighting tanks. Further stores could be carried on sledges which could be towed by any kind of tank. The Gun Carrier, Mark I was also used as a supply vehicle: it was, in fact, more often used in this role than for transporting artillery. A gun carrier could carry up to 200 six-inch shells.

Following these conversions, the Tank, Mark IX was designed specially as an infantry or supply carrier and a total of 35 was completed by the end of the war, although too late to be used in action. One of these tanks, known as Mark IX Duck, was turned into an experimental amphibious tank after the War by means of "camels" or long air-filled drums attached to the sides.

A Signals' adaptation of Tanks Mark I with armament removed and fitted with wireless equipment appeared in 1917 and three of these tanks were attached to each of the three tank Brigades which took part in the battle of Cambrai in November. The signal tank had a wireless mast some 15 feet high mounted on the driver's/commander's cab.

For tank repair work, old Tanks, Mark IV of the Tank Salvage Companies were fitted with a jib and pulley block. Gun Carriers were also modified, but with a power-driven crane at the front.

Tank, Mark V** (RE Tank) with 20ft tank bridge

RE Tank

After the Battle of Cambrai in November 1917 the Tank Corps General Staff foresaw the need in the future, and in particular in an advance into Germany, for a bridging device to enable tanks to cross small rivers and canals, some of which would be defended as obstacles against tanks. In February 1918, an experimental bridge that could be laid over a gap up to 20 feet by a tank under fire was designed and was proved in trials to be a practicable proposition. However, the Tank Corps Headquarters in France had insufficient resources for its manufacture in quantity. Accordingly, the Director of Fortifications and Works, War Office, sent Major C. E. Inglis, RE, to France to discuss the question of tank bridges with Tank Corps HQ and then to carry out the neccessary design work. In addition to the 20ft tank bridge it was decided that a special bridge, capable of taking 35-ton tanks over a 100ft gap, and a heavy pontoon, which could be built up into rafts for tanks or used with bridge sections to make a floating bridge for gaps in excess of 100 feet, would be required. Major Inglis designed a bridge made up of tubular girders which successfully met the latter conditions and also redesigned the 20-foot tank bridge. Experiments were also started on a girder bridge mounted on idle tracks which could be pushed by a tank straight over a gap.

Three Tank Bridging Battalions, RE were raised at Christchurch, Hampshire in October 1918 and were to be equipped with forty-eight tanks fitted with 20ft tank bridge and 12 of the Inglis Tubular girder bridges. It was hoped that the Battalions would be equipped and trained in time to be sent to France by about February of the following year. The Armistice intervened, however, and two of the Battalions were disbanded and the third reduced to an experimental unit only, under the command of (then) Major G. le Q. Martel and known as the Experimental Bridging Company, RE.

172

Now that the War was over, more time could be spent on experimental work and the existing equipment, which had had to be designed in haste, was tested and redesigned where necessary by the Experimental Bridging Coy and new experiments, aimed at making the power of a tank available in a variety of military engineering tasks, were started.

The tank used as the basis of these experiments and which became known as the "RE Tank", was the standard heavy tank which had just started coming into use at the end of the War, the Tank, Mark V**. This type of tank, in fact, had already been used for the 20ft tank bridge which would have been the equipment of the three Tank Bridging Battalions. In the wartime design the bridge was picked up and lowered by means of a mechanical winch, but a hydraulic ram was fitted in the new model, both for this purpose and a variety of other tasks that the tank was intended to perform. The hydraulic ram mounted on top of the tank was worked by a Janney Pump driven off the tank main engine. The ram operated a jib permanently carried on the tank and hinged at the front. By means of this jib the tank could pick up the 20-foot bridge, advance with it under fire and in less than a minute lay it over a gap without exposing the crew.

It was also found that the Inglis Tubular Girder Bridge mounted on idle tracks could by means of the tank and its jib be manœuvred into position and in less than a minute from time of arrival be pushed forwards across gaps of up to 70 feet. The tank could also be used for minefield clearance. A heavy steel roller in two parts, each weighing more than a ton, was towed in front of the tank by means of chains attached to the jib projecting in front and was found to be capable of exploding on contact mines containing up to 9lb of high explosive without damaging the tank or injuring the crew. (Rollers, incidentally, were also tested with a Tank, Mark IV, mounted on castors attached to twin beams projecting in front). The tank-mounted jib was also of more general use in field engineering and could raise a load of 10 tons 12 feet in two minutes or up to 15 tons at a slower speed.

Tank, Mark V** (RE Tank) with anti-mine roller

Further trials were made with these tanks on clearing barbed wire entanglements by means of grapnels on the end of steel cables—a method that had been used in the Battle of Cambrai after the main assault to allow the cavalry through.

The laying of buried signal cable was another function that could be performed by means of the RE Tank when towing a specially modified mole draining plough. This type of plough has a thin vertical cutting blade to the bottom of which is attached a cigar shaped cylinder. When operating, the cylinder was towed along about two to three feet below the surface, leaving a small tunnel at this depth. For cable laying, the cable was led down the blade through a tube to the cylinder, which was hollow. As many as 30 cables together could be laid in this way.

Finally, it was found that trenches 3ft deep could be cut in two runs at a speed of 2mph by means of a Fowler-designed plough towed by the Tank Mark V**. The trenches were only 3ft wide, tapering to 2ft at the bottom, but a great deal of manual labour was saved by this method. Apart from all these mechanical functions the RE Tank could, of course, also be used for carrying RE demolition parties forward under fire and in many cases provide a measure of protection for them while they worked outside the tank.

The RE Tank was finally abandoned after all these experiments had been completed, because the heavy tank itself was given up by the Army, which from 1921 onwards was gradually re-equipped with the Vickers tank of around 12 tons in replacement for the wartime tanks. The main equipment designed for the Tank Mark V**—bridging for tanks of 35 tons—was no longer suitable therefore and attention was given to the requirements of much smaller and lighter tanks in the more mobile conditions anticipated in future warfare.

NLE Trenching Machine   ("White Rabbit No 6")

In a memorandum written in November 1916 dealing with mechanical power in the offensive, Winston Churchill visualised an attack in which a force of tanks and tracked artillery was accompanied by machines which would cut or roll fairly deep tracks across the enemy trench systems. The infantry, followed by supply tractors, would then be able to advance across the enemy lines relatively unscathed. He also proposed that armoured trench cutters should be employed for consolidating the trackways and for constructing lateral communications.

It seems likely that Churchill must have had these ideas in his mind when in 1939, in the early months of World War II, with the opposing Maginot and Siegfried lines likely to lead to the same sort of stalemate created by the trenches in 1914–1918, he gave thought to a means of cutting through enemy positions. Churchill was then First Lord of the Admiralty but, as in the first war, he was even then thinking in wider terms of the prosecution of the war than by his department alone. In November he asked the Director of Naval Construction, Sir Stanley Goodall, to experiment on the lines of a machine to cut a trench across no man's land and right up to the enemy lines along which infantry and tanks could advance to the assault. It was necessary that such machines should be able to cover the necessary distance between the opposing lines during the hours of darkness to increase the element of surprise.

A sum of £100,000 was allocated for experiments; C. J. W. Hopkins, MBE, an Assistant Director of Naval Constructions, was given charge of the project and he chose W. F. Spanner, a naval architect on his staff, to undertake the preliminary design work at Bath. Some of Sir William Tritton's drawings of early tanks were found of service in planning the drive layout and the design of track for the machine and six alternative proposals were roughed out. The most likely of these was handed to the Bassett-Lowke model train firm, who built from the drawings a working model about 3ft long. The model was demonstrated by Churchill during December 1939 to General Ironside the Chief of the Imperial General Staff, the Prime Minister (Neville Chamberlain) and other senior officers and Cabinet Ministers in the basement of the Admiralty, where it cut its way through simulated soil in a highly satisfactory way. The model was also taken to France in January and shown to General Gamelin, who did not express an opinion, and to General Georges who was enthusiastic.

In February 1940 Cabinet approval was given for the construction of 240 machines, known then under the code name of "White Rabbit No 6", although this was later changed to "Cultivator" to avoid any possible suggestion of a surprise weapon. The "Department of Naval Land Equipment" headed by C. J. W. Hopkins was formed under the Ministry of Supply in March to superintend the project, and production "parentage" was placed with Ruston-Bucyrus Ltd of Lincoln, well known as manufacturers of civilian earth-moving equipment, whose chief engineer, William Savage, was given prime responsibility for this work. A large number of firms was awarded contracts to supply components, for which great secrecy had to be maintained and, with the same object, a part of the Rushton-Bucyrus works was completely screened off for assembly of the machines The contract for the 240 trench cutting machines was allocated as to 200 of the normal infantry type and 40 of a wider pattern to cut a passage for tanks. An early snag in production arose in April because it had originally been proposed to use a single marine type of Merlin engine but all Rolls-Royce engine production was needed for the Royal Air Force and so Davey-Paxman diesels were introduced instead and the work proceeded. At the same time, analysis of the soil in different parts of Northern France and Belgium was taken so that suitable areas for the employment of the "Cultivators" could be selected.

[*Imperial War Museum*

NLE Trenching Machine Mark I—prototype ("Nellie I"). Note rotary cutters under the plough blade.

175

The German attack in the West in May 1940, however, brought about an entirely different state of affairs and the major part of the "Cultivator" production plans was shelved, although permission was given for a few machines of each type to be completed for experimental purposes or for some special tactical use, or even the emergency digging of anti-tank ditches in the event of an invasion of the United Kingdom.

The design work was continued under strict security precautions at the Anchor Street, Lincoln premises of Ruston-Bucyrus. Many problems were involved in what to a large extent was new territory; in particular the design of a gearbox to cope with the enormous load and a satisfactory means of disposing of the tons of earth displaced by the cutters. Trials of the cylindrical cutting device— rather like scaled up lawn mower blades—took place in the early spring of 1940. A proposal that the machine should cut a curved path to give more cover to the attacking infantry had to be abandoned as too difficult to achieve but otherwise the work went as planned, although because of the various difficulties and reduced priorities the completed prototype, now known as NLE Trenching Machine Mark I, or more familiarly as "Nellie I", was not ready for trials until July 1941 and was demonstrated to Churchill (then Prime Minister) in November.

In general appearance Nellie I betrayed the use that had been made of drawings of World War I tanks, particularly in the wide-pitch overall tracks and downward sloping rear end, but the whole front section containing the trench cutting apparatus was hinged in the vertical plane and had at the front a large V-shaped plough blade (equivalent to the mould board of an agricultural digging plough) incorporating a form of coulter for the leading cut. Behind the mould board was the cutting cylinder equipped with hardened steel blades. When going into operation, the rotary cutters were lowered and cut into the surface of the ground as the machine advanced at ½mph and lowered itself into the depression which had been cut until the point of the plough entered the earth. From this stage the plough took the first cut at the front of the vehicle (and also sheered through or turned aside any obstacles such as wire entanglements or trench revetments) just ahead of the rotary cutting cylinders. The cylinders ejected the

"Nellie I"—a close up of the front section containing the cutting device. Note one of the side conveyors

"Nellie I" at full depth at the end of a run. Note drivers' cab with hatches open

"Nellie I"—looking back over the rear of the hull along the trench that has just been cut

earth removed through transverse conveyer belts and deposited it either side of the trench. The maximum depth of trench that could be cut in loam was five feet, although the removed soil thrown on the parapets increased the protection for assaulting troops by about another three feet. The width of the trench was 7ft 6in. The vehicle was not itself armoured, since in digging-in it created its own protection as it advanced, but an armoured cab was provided for the driver who sat in a position on top near the front of the main part of the machine, just behind the cutting section. Nellie I weighed nearly 130 tons, was 77ft 6in long, 18ft 6in wide overall and 10ft 2in high. Power was provided by two Davey-Paxman diesel engines, model 666R, one to propel the machine forward and the other to drive the cutters. These engines, built by an associated firm of Ruston-Bucyrus, were designed by Harry Ricardo, who had had considerable experience in work of this nature dating back to the engines for the Tank Mark V of World War I. They had hydro coolers and radiators were situated on the top of the vehicle and at the rear.

The original order for 240 trenching machines was drastically curtailed in May 1940 when the immediate need for this equipment no longer existed and production resources were needed for other more urgent supplies. Three years later, in addition to the pilot model, four narrow infantry machines had been made and five wide "officer" machines (for tank trenches) were actually under manufacture. Four of the latter were cancelled, but the remaining six machines were kept in store until the summer of 1945 when, the Siegfried line having been breached by more conventional means, no use remained for them and all but one were broken up.

Winston Churchill watching a demonstration of "Nellie I" on 6th November, 1941

178

Dragon, Mark I with 30ft Bridge   [*Imperial War Museum*

Carrier and Pusher Bridging Tanks

The first post-war tank bridging experiments using heavy Tanks, Mark V**
of wartime design were followed by experiments using as bridge carriers the
contemporary much lighter tracked vehicles of the new generation. The earliest
of these was Dragon Mark I—a field artillery tractor with a chassis rather
similar to that of the Vickers Tanks then coming into service—mounting a
30ft bridge, intended to cross gaps of up to 26ft. This equipment, designed
about 1923 by Major H. H. Bateman of the Royal Engineers Experimental
Bridging Establishment at Christchurch, Hampshire, consisted of a girder bridge
carried on rollers mounted on top of a superstructure built over the Dragon. The
bridge was launched straight forwards over the gap. In the launching process
two light steel guide ways (normally carried on the bridge itself) were pushed
across the gap first, and then the bridge was propelled over them into position.
Although the Dragon was not armoured, the main disadvantage of this experimental design was that during the launching of the bridge several members of
the crew had to work in the open.

A simple light girder bridge, 18ft long for a span of 16ft, was designed
about 1925 for carriage by Vickers Medium Tanks and was fitted experimentally
to a Tank, Medium, Mark II. This design does not appear to have been successful, possibly because the span was too short to be of great practical use, and in
the Army manœuvres of the late 1920s and the 1930s the passage of tanks over
water obstacles was effected by Royal Engineers using standard bridging or
rafting equipment, although a "stepping stone" device for tracked vehicles
crossing shallow rivers was tried out. This consisted of hollow timber crates
spaced by ropes at intervals across the river—the tank pushing each in turn down
to the river bed as it crossed.

Another bridging device, although not a bridge, experimented with in
April 1940, was the Roller Fascine. This was comprised of two 6ft 9in diameter

cable drums mounted side by side on an axle to which was fixed a pair of short ramps. The structure, pushed into a ditch, could take the weight of tanks up to 25 tons crossing it. The early experiments were conducted with a Dragon, Medium Mark IV as the pusher vehicle, but the device was intended for use with Matildas and Valentines.

A 1918 invention, the Mobile Inglis Bridge—a complete Inglis Tubular Girder Bridge on idle tracks—was revived in the early part of World War II, a Matilda tank being used as the pusher. A very much smaller equipment carried on idle tracks, the mobile tracked ramp—used for overcoming certain types of vertical obstacles—also employed the Matilda as a pusher. Exactly the same principle was used for the Mobile Bailey Bridge, introduced later in the war. A Churchill tank or Churchill AVRE was used to push the bridge, which was built up from standard Bailey panels and could be used for gaps of up to 80 feet. The Skid Bailey Bridge was similar but ran on skids instead of tracks.

Another use of Bailey Bridge components was known as the Plymouth Bridge. In this, the made-up Bailey Bridge was launched by two tanks—the fore part of the bridge carried on a specially adapted turretless Sherman and the rear end supported and propelled by another Sherman. This rather specialised type of Bridge was first used in the Italian campaign (in May 1944) in which Mobile Bailey Bridges were also employed. In the experimental Dachshund Bridge—rather similar to the Plymouth Bridge—the Shermans retained their turrets and in the Brown Bridge (another type) the lead tank did not have to go into the water. Skid Bailey Bridges (referred to above) were first used in North-Western Europe in January 1945 operated by AVREs of 79th Armoured Division.

Mobile Inglis Bridge being pushed by Matilda tank   [*Imperial War Museum*

[*Imperial War Museum*

Covenanter II Bridgelayer—bridge, still folded, being raised for laying

Scissors Bridging Tanks

In 1936, Lt-Col G. le Q. Martel, who had been in charge of the tank bridging experiments after World War I, again turned his attention to this problem and designed a bridge which could be laid quickly by a tank under fire. The bridge could span a gap of up to 30ft and carry the standard medium tanks then in use. Although the design itself worked satisfactorily, the hydraulic gear gave trouble and the device was subsequently redesigned by Major Galpin of the Mechanisation Board for operation by a screw jack and at the same time incorporating a folding type of bridge.

The "scissors bridge" as it became known, was carried in the folded position over the back of a turretless tank, with the bridge hinge at the rear of the vehicle. When the bridge was laid, the weight was brought down on to three steel rollers incorporated in the launching gear in the front of the tank and on this pivot the folded bridge was swung through a 180deg arc, the hinged part uppermost. When just past the vertical position the bridge began to open out to its full width, being fully opened when reaching the horizontal position to be finally placed across the gap. The bridgelayer tank then disengaged the bridge from the launching gear and backed away. The bridge—"Scissors Bridge, 30 foot, No 1"—was adapted for laying by either Covenanter or Valentine tanks. It could bridge a span of 30ft and carry tanks of up to 30 tons and when production quantities allowed, scissors tanks were issued on a scale of six to each armoured brigade or tank brigade equipped with cruiser tanks or Valentine infantry tanks. Of the two types, the Valentine Bridgelayer was the more widely used and saw service overseas in the Mediterranean theatre, in the Burma campaign 1944/5 and in North West Europe. Twenty-five were supplied to the USSR. The basic Covenanter tank was somewhat unreliable and for this reason Covenanter Bridgelayers were issued mainly for training and home defence formations in the United Kingdom, although the Australian Armoured Corps received a few towards the end of the War.

When the 38-ton Churchill Infantry Tank came into service a much heavier tank bridge was needed for tank brigades equipped with this tank and a form of scissors bridge with a rigid span for 30ft and capable of taking loads up to 80 tons was produced. The mode of operation was much the same as that of the earlier scissors bridges but the bridge span itself remained horizontal throughout the laying process. The bridge was attached at its central point of balance to a launching girder, pivoted at the front of the tank and with rollers at its lower end, to take the weight of the bridge when launched. During the launching the girder went through an arc of approximately 180deg, carrying the bridge span balanced in a horizontal position.

The Churchill Bridgelayer with "Bridge, Tank, 30 foot, No 3 Mark 2" (as its final version was known) was issued to brigades equipped with Churchill tanks—the heaviest tanks used by British forces during the War—and saw service in Italy and North Western Europe.

Covenanter II Bridgelayer—bridge, now supported on rollers, almost opened out just before touching opposite bank

Valentine I Bridgelayer—vehicle facing left

[*RAC Tank Museum*

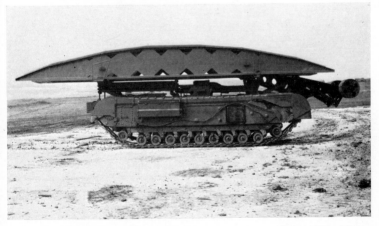

Churchill IV Bridgelayer—vehicle facing right

[*Imperial War Museum*

183

Churchill Ark I, with a Churchill gun-tank crossing to surmount a sea wall

Ramp type Bridging Tanks

An experimental device known as "Octupus" for crossing minefields consisted of a turretless tank fitted with ramps fore and aft. Used in series—the second tank of this type crossing the first, followed by a third crossing the two others by means of their ramps and so on—even a large minefield could be crossed, given luck and a sufficient supply of ramp tanks. More economical methods of traversing minefields were devised, but Octupus, renamed Ark (short for *Ark Royal*—the shape rather suggested an aircraft carrier) was retained as a means for tracked vehicles to cross obstacles such as trenches, ditches or rivers, steep banks, or other vertical obstructions such as sea walls. Both Sherman and Churchill tanks were used for conversion to Arks and development took place in Italy as well as the United Kingdom. The Sherman Ark had a trackway built over its sloping hull deck. Only about half a dozen Sherman Arks were built and although used in Italy they were less satisfactory than the Churchill type, which had a longer hull and a horizontal top line, features better adapted for conversion to this type of vehicle. A Sherman-Bailey Ark, with 20ft, Bailey bridge ramps was built experimentally in Italy.

The Churchill Ark I had top decking over the tracks and the maximum span it could cover was 28ft. The later and more widely used Churchill Ark could cover a much greater span in both versions—Churchill Ark II (UK Pattern) and Churchill Ark II (Italian Pattern). The Italian Pattern vehicle could be distinguished from the others by the absence of a separate trackway over the tank hull, the Ark's own tracks forming the trackway for tracked vehicles crossing it. The ramps were standard US Pattern M1 or M2 bridging ramps modified for the purpose and were raised or lowered through tall king posts at front and rear. The maximum span this vehicle could cover with M1 ramps was 54ft 4in and with M2 ramps, 48ft 5in. Churchill Ark II (UK Pattern) developed by the 79th Armoured Division in July 1944 could span up to 47ft 6in and was generally similar to the pattern designed in Italy but for a separate raised trackway over the hull which could take wheeled as well as tracked vehicles. Only the front ramps were operated by means of a king post, the rear ramps being held in the upright position by rods secured to the sides of the tank. A welded conning tower was included in the plate which blanked off the turret aperture. The front hull Besa machine gun could be retained in all patterns of Ark.

A total of 50 Ark Is was built, assembly by REME workshops and the MG Car Co Ltd beginning in early 1944. After successful trials of the Ark II (UK Pattern) arrangements were made for conversion sets to be made so that REME workshops could convert all Ark Is to the new model. Experiments with 20ft ramps for Ark II, which would have increased the span by a further 15ft were carried out in 1944/5 but the work was eventually cancelled because wider trackways were needed for the new tanks coming into service at the end of the War.

Arks were used in both the North West Europe and Italian campaigns. They were particularly useful in Italy where they were used (sometimes in series) to make causeways for crossing flooded ground or rivers—both the Savio and the Senio were crossed in this way—and to bridge ditches or small ravines. For the deeper gaps two Arks were used, one on top of the other.

An experimental type of Ark not used in action was invented by Major T. A. Lakeman and was designed as an attachment to a standard Churchill. With the turret and main armament retained, the tank had the advantage over normal Arks of remaining a fighting vehicle. However, the trackway of the Lakeman Ark, as it was known, was consequently high and the rear ramp long and rather steep. It was difficult for tanks to surmount successfully and after trials it was decided that it was impracticable for tanks with turrets to be used for this class of vehicle.

[*Imperial War Museum*

Churchill Ark II (Italian Pattern). Two Arks, one on top of another, filling a deep ditch

The Churchill Great Eastern was a ramp tank designed to overcome much greater horizontal or vertical obstacles than the comparatively simple Arks could overcome. The tank carried on a girder superstructure a long ramp sloping upwards from the rear deck to a height of some 20 feet at the front. The second part of the ramp was hinged at this point and was normally carried folded back over the lower part of the ramp. A hinged extension of the lower ramp which reached to the ground was normally held in raised position at the back of the tank. To provide a passage for tracked vehicles across a vertical obstacle the Great Eastern would be driven up to the obstacle as close as possible. The second part of the ramp (lying on the lower part) was then propelled by means of two groups each side of 3in electrically fired rockets upwards and over so that the complete ramp (including its rear extension, when lowered) formed an inverted V over the obstruction. When launched the span was 60ft, and a wall 12ft high and 5ft thick could be crossed.

The idea for the Great Eastern emanated from MD1, the versatile experimental establishment at Whitchurch, Bucks, headed by Colonel Millis Jefferis, and a prototype was built there on a Churchill I chassis and tested in May 1944. (During the early trials, incidentally, too many rockets were used to propel the bridge span so that the tank was blown over on its side). As the trials proved the design to be fairly satisfactory a further 10 Great Eastern ramp tanks were built on Churchill IV chassis, modified with the heavier Churchill VII suspension units to take the weight of some 48 tons. Two of these vehicles were received by the 79th Armoured Division in Holland early in 1945, where, although not employed in action, one was used to give a demonstration of its spectacular rocketry to an appreciative, newly-liberated Dutch audience.

Three Ark-type bridging vehicles which incorporated some of the same features as the Great Eastern were the Churchill Woodlark, the Churchill Foldupus and a lighter vehicle derived from it, designed for use in the South East Asia Command, and known as Valentine Burmark. In all three types the ramps were positioned by means of rockets. None of these designs went beyond the experimental stage.

[*Imperial War Museum*

Sherman Ark in Italy, 1945. This tank is fitted with "Platypus Grousers" on the tracks for better adhesion

[*RAC Tank Museum*

Churchill Lakeman Ark positioned to enable a Churchill tank to surmount a high concrete wall

[*Imperial War Museum*

Churchill Great Eastern—three quarter rear view of standard vehicle

Churchill AVRE Carpetlayer, Type C Mark II   [*Imperial War Museum*

Assault Vehicle Royal Engineers

The Dieppe Raid of August 1942 showed the difficulties of engineers working under fire to try to prepare demolition charges to destroy obstacles. It was accordingly suggested by Lieut J. J. Denovan of the Royal Canadian Engineers that a tank should be adapted to carry engineer parties and their equipment so they could carry out work under fire, either from the tank or outside it, but protected by the positioning of the vehicle. A spigot mortar could be mounted to fire heavy demolition projectiles for destroying concrete obstacles. Instructions were given for a unit of the Royal Canadian Engineers to build a prototype vehicle, using a Churchill II tank as a basis, on the lines suggested and this work was completed by December 1942. Much of the standard tank interior stowage was removed together with the main armament and new compartments were provided for stowage of engineer stores. A dummy spigot mortar was fitted in the turret. In the meantime, a prototype spigot mortar was mounted in a Covenanter tank; following tests with this weapon a contract for the design and supply of further prototypes suitable for mounting in Churchills was awarded to Colonel L. V. S. Blacker's firm and one of these, when completed by February 1943, was mounted in the Churchill II prototype engineer vehicle referred to above.

A second prototype of the Assault Vehicle Royal Engineers (AVRE), as the vehicle became known, was constructed on a 6pr Churchill, the type which later became standardised for conversion to AVREs. This second prototype was stowed in a similar manner to the first, although the Petard spigot mortar was not fitted. When demonstrated together the two prototypes between them successfully showed the capabilities of the AVRE for demolition of concrete obstacles by charges hand-placed by the crew under the protection of the vehicle; destroying obstacles with the Petard and clearance of minefields by means of the same projectiles, and orders were given to make plans for production. In

December 1943, after further trials and modifications by 79th Armoured Division and construction of a final prototype, MG Cars Ltd at Abingdon were given the main contract for conversion of Churchill IIIs and IVs to AVREs. In the meantime, the first 108 vehicles were produced in REME workshops. The final total of AVREs built, including these was about 700.

The main feature of the AVRE (although not fitted in all vehicles) was the Petard spigot mortar which fired the 40lb "Flying Dustbin" with a 26lb charge up to a range of about 230 yards, although the effective range was much less than this—up to about 80 yards. Twenty-six Flying Dustbins were carried and loading took place from a special sliding hatch constructed in the roof of the co-drivers compartment. AVREs also had, as a special feature, brackets on the front plate and mounting plates on the hull sides for the attachment of various devices, as required. These devices included the Small Box Girder bridge (SBG) for a 40-ton load over a span of 30 feet; various carpetlayer attachments; the CIRD anti-mine roller, mechanical demolition charge-placing devices, such as Onion or Goat; and the Fascine, a bundle of wooden stakes 8ft in diameter and 12 to 14 feet wide used for crossing trenches, which was carried on the top of the hull in front of the turret. The AVRE was also commonly used as the pusher for Mobile Bailey Bridges or Skid Bailey Bridges although Arks or other tanks were sometimes employed.

The carpetlaying devices, used for crossing soft patches on beaches or other terrain in which tanks would become bogged, came in different forms, including Bobbin Carpet—the most common—consisting of hessian matting reinforced by scaffold tubing; Roly Poly and Log Carpet. In laying, the carpet unwound itself in front of the tank which ran over it, leaving a path for following armour.

[*Imperial War Museum*

Churchill AVRE with Goat for demolishing concrete sea wall: the upper part of the framework straddles the wall

189

A carpetlaying device was first tried out experimentally on a Tank, Cruiser Mark I in March 1939 and in the following year a design was approved for fitment to Infantry Mark II (Matilda) tanks. In 1941 a similar device for Universal Carriers was put into production. One of the earliest carpetlaying devices for Infantry Mark IV tanks was attached to a standard Churchill III of the Calgary Regiment used in the Dieppe Raid. This consisted of a small bobbin mounted at upper track level on brackets attached between the front horns of the tank. A Churchill II at about the same time was fitted with an experimental carpet device supported by curved side girders. One of the earlier models for AVREs, Carpetlayer Type A, was similar in size to the Dieppe model, but attachment to the Churchill AVRE (like all later types) was by means of side arms. Carpetlayer Type B used two bobbins on the same spindle, laying two narrow carpets, one in front of each track. A larger bobbin mounted on vertical side arms above the level of the top turret was used in Type C; and Carpetlayer Type D had an even larger bobbin mounted in a similar way, although the supporting structure differed. The last two types were those chiefly employed in action—a number of Bobbin Carpets were used on the D-Day beaches.

Experiment with mechanical placers for demolition charges operated by AVREs culminated in the Goat, but Carrot was one of the earlier of these devices, tried out with Matilda and Churchill tanks. Small charges up to 25lb could be pushed straight against the obstacle and fired immediately, but heavier charges were attached to the front of an Anti-Mine Reconnaissance Caster Roller device which was pushed up to the obstacle and then detached from the tank, from which the charge was fired by remote control after the tank had backed away. Carrot was also intended for minefield clearance by detonating mines by its own explosion. Onion was a later development, tried out with AVREs, consisting of charges attached to a vertical framework which could be placed against an obstacle, released and the charges fired electrically from the AVRE at a distance.

Goat was similar in operation to Onion, but in this device the framework carrying the charges was carried horizontally; on meeting the obstacle the structure was pivoted from its front end downwards and forwards so that it was left standing vertically against the obstacle, supported by two legs which sprang into position. The charges were then fired electrically from the AVRE after it had retired. In an experimental form of Goat the frameworks to which the charges were attached could be carried at both the lower and upper ends of a tall girder structure. This girder was attached to the AVRE between the front horns and was hinged in such a way that it could be pushed up the face of an obstacle, such as a concrete wall, so that it could straddle it, leaving the two sets of charges on opposite sides.

Returning to the basic AVRE and its equipment, it was decided in late 1943 to develop if possible an alternative to the Petard with a greater range. The resulting weapon, known as Ardeer Aggie, was mounted in a Churchill III tank. It was a recoilless gun which fired a dummy charge of sand to the rear to offset the effect of the projectile fired forwards. After experiment, however, it was felt that the weapon did not offer sufficient advantages in range and performance to offset the considerable drawbacks of an inadequately protected mounting, the undesirability of firing a charge of sand to the rear to the possible detriment of both supporting troops and the vehicle's own engine, and the problem of both stowing and loading the dummy charges in addition to the actual demolition projectiles.

At an early stage in the development of the AVRE it was decided to investigate the alternative possibility of converting the Sherman tank, by then beginning to arrive in quantity from the USA, to this role and by the end of

[*Imperial War Museum*

Churchill AVRE with
Onion. The explosive
charges are attached
to the vertical frame-
work

[*Imperial War Museum*

Churchill IV AVRE
being loaded with
Fascine. Note bolts
on side of hull for
attachment of special
devices

1943 a prototype Sherman V AVRE was completed. A Petard, redesigned for the Sherman mounting, was carried and interior stowage was on the same lines as the Churchill AVRE, although the absence of side doors necessitated modification of the co-driver's escape hatch in the hull floor to provide a sliding door for the loading and unloading of explosive stores. However, it was later decided that Shermans could not be spared for the AVRE task and experiment and much of the design work was transferred to the generally similar Canadian Ram tanks. Two Ram AVRE prototypes were converted early in 1944 but it was decided that, although the Rams that were fitted with side doors had some advantages over the Sherman, the lighter armour, lesser interior space and inferior obstacle crossing ability made both Ram and Sherman less suitable than the Churchill for use as AVREs.

Churchill AVREs were first used in action in the Normandy landings in 1944 where, right from the start of the assault, they proved their value in laying carpets on the beaches, providing exits over sea walls with SBG bridges, and demolishing obstacles. Three Assault Regiments, Royal Engineers, each with an establishment of about 60 AVREs came under command of 79th Armoured Division and continued to play a useful part in the North West European campaign until the end. AVREs were also employed in the Italian Campaign, in a somewhat different regimental organisation in which the two Armoured Engineer Regiments each had a nominal strength of 18 AVREs employed in squadrons containing Arks and other specialised armour.

Churchill Ardeer Aggie

[*Imperial War Museum*

Matilda with AMRA Mark IA   [*Imperial War Museum*

Anti-Mine Rollers

The use of heavy rollers for the mechanical clearance, by detonation, of buried mines was one of the earliest and indeed the most obvious of anti-mine devices and the experiments in this direction with Tanks Mark IV & V** between 1919 and 1926 have already been described. Interest in the need for an effective means for the mechanical clearance of minefields was revived in 1937 when a roller device was ordered from John Fowler & Co Ltd and tried out on a Dragon, Medium Mark III. Development continued so that by early 1942 a device known as Anti-Mine Roller Attachment had been produced and issued in versions adapted for attachment to the main types of tank then in production—one pattern for the early Cruiser Tanks Marks I to IV; AMRA Mark IA for the Matilda; Mark IB for Valentine, Mark IC for Covenanter and Mark ID for Crusader. The Mark IIE for Churchill tanks was produced later. The device consisted of a girder frame projecting in front of the tank carried on four heavy rollers which trailed before the tank's tracks, two to each side. In the earlier models the rollers were smooth and of either solid or hollow construction in appearance but the later ones were ridged, being made of a number of discs bolted together. This device could be used as necessary by attachment to ordinary tanks of armoured regiments on an *ad hoc* basis, before specialised armoured formations had appeared on the scene. The Matilda with AMRA was used operationally for mine clearance in the Middle East.

In the Middle East also, concrete rollers with projecting spikes, one roller to each track, but otherwise similar in principle to AMRA, were tested experimentally with Valentine tanks as well as being attached to specially protected lorries and AEC Mark I Armoured Cars. A further spiked roller device (one to each track), known as Porcupine, attached to a Sherman tank was tested in the UK in 1943 but as it survived only two German Teller mines was soon discarded.

B.T.F.V.—G

Another anti-mine device of revolutionary design was proposed in 1943 by Humber Ltd of Coventry. This design, known as Katok, consisted of one enormous self-propelled roller, 10ft in diameter and 12ft wide and estimated to weigh 40 tons. The power plant was carried in a cradle inside the roller; the device was to be controlled through electric cables by a tank following behind. Experiments however indicated that 4in-thick steel would be necessary for the outer cylinder and the estimated weight would be greatly exceeded, and this interesting idea was not proceeded with.

By 1943, although experiments with anti-mine rollers continued, the emphasis began to be placed more on their use for quick and simple detection of anti-tank mine fields rather than actual clearance, for which it became widely realised that flail devices offered the best solution. Nevertheless rollers were still useful against anti-personnel mines. The rollers were uncertain in use because even a small bump in the ground or a stone could keep the roller off a mine and leave it unexploded. This revised function was reflected in the name of the Anti-Mine Reconnaissance Castor Roller, developed by the Obstacle Assault Centre, Aldershot which appeared in 1943 in two versions—No 1 Mark I for Churchill tanks and No 1A Mark I for the Sherman V. This device was very much the same in layout as the earlier Fowler roller, or AMRA, but the ground contact of the four rollers was improved by means of leaf springs.

What was probably the most effective British anti-mine roller device of World War II was suggested by Major General Worthington, General Officer Commanding the 4th Canadian Division and was known as the Canadian Indestructible Roller Device. Development was undertaken by the Canadian Army in conjunction with the War Office Obstacle Assault Centre. The device consisted in its prototype form of two solid armour plate rollers of 26in diameter and 16in width, each weighing one ton and trailed from a girder frame in front of each track. They were pivoted from a bar at the front of the frame and when

Sherman with **AMRCR No 1A Mark I** *[Imperial War Museum*

Churchill AVRE with 18in CIRD   [*RAC Tank Museum*

a mine was detonated either or both rollers were swung upwards and forwards over the pivot bar so that a spade incorporated in the trailing arm dug in the ground and, with the forward movement of the tank, returned the roller to its original position. After experiment, the width of the rollers was decreased to 15½in and a new 18in wide, 28in diameter, roller was also produced (for Churchill tanks only) in 1944. These rollers in light soils, at any rate, were found in trials capable of exploding 93 per cent of mines buried 2in deep and 71per cent where the mines were 4in deep.

The Canadian Indestructible Roller Device (CIRD) was designed for operation by Churchill or Sherman tanks. The girder frame was attached to the hull sides at two points either side. In 1945 prototypes of a CIRD were made for use with Cromwell and Comet tanks—in this version the rollers were pivoted outside the frame which was attached to the front glacis plate of the tank.

Canadian Indestructible Roller devices were held available for attachment to the Churchill AVREs of the 79th Armoured Division in North Western Europe, although there is no record that they were used in action. A troop of Shermans equipped with the CIRD was included in each squadron of the three regiments of Sherman Crab tanks of the 30th Armoured Brigade and were taken to Normandy. They were never used in action, however, because casualties in the D-Day landings made it necessary to abolish the roller troops in order to provide replacements for flail tank crews.

Rollers continued to be used to some extent as an alternative to the laborious and dangerous process of clearing anti-personnel mines by hand. A device called Centipede, consisting of a frame with two dozen closely spaced small rollers, was designed to be towed behind the Valentine Scorpion flail and later the Crab and other tracked vehicles. A somewhat similar apparatus, developed by the 79th Armoured Division and known as Rodent, could be pushed in front of a Weasel (US-built light amphibious tracked vehicle) and was effective in exploding various types of German anti-personnel mines.

The rollers described above were intended to locate and destroy mines by detonation through ground pressure exerted by the roller. The Lulu detector was, however, a roller device designed only to locate the presence of buried mines by means of electrical detector coils linked to an amplifier carried in the Sherman tank which operated the apparatus. The detector coils were carried suspended from the axles inside the 4ft diameter rollers—one pushed in front of each track and one towed behind the tank—which were of wooden construction.

The front parts of the lattice girders, which trailed the rollers about 11ft in front of the tank were also of wood; counterbalance weights ensured that the rollers were only in light contact with the ground. A buried mine produced a signal through the tank's intercommunication system and a linked warning light showed which roller was over the mine. The device was first tried out at the end of 1943 and was finally abandoned in 1945, being considered insufficiently reliable and also too fragile for use in the field. The Lulu was at first known as Zulu; the ethnically associated Bantu was the same equipment carried by a Staghound armoured car.

Sherman with Lulu Detector   [*Imperial War Museum*

Anti-Mine Ploughs

In 1937 some attention was being paid to the problem of anti-tank mines by both the War Office and, in the field, by the 1st Tank Brigade. In March the War Office placed a contract with John Fowler & Co (Leeds) Ltd for an anti-mine coulter plough. This device, which was fitted experimentally to a Dragon, Medium, Mark IIIc, consisted of a girder structure extending in front of the vehicle and carrying two rollers, one in front of each track. In front of each roller were attached five coulters (the knife-edged blades preceding the tines in an agricultural plough) in a V arrangement. The coulters could be pushed at a depth of 2½–3in at an operating speed of 3mph. This equipment, which was at the time believed to be effective, was also applied in a modified form to an Infantry Tank Mark I in 1939.

196

Fresh work on anti-mine ploughs was started in April 1943 when Samuel Butler Ltd of Leeds produced the Farmer Front device, to the order of the War Office Obstacle Assault Centre, Aldershot. This equipment, fitted to a Churchill IV, was in essence a development of the Fowler Coulter device and consisted of a frame pivoted to the sides of the tank and supported at the optimum height above ground by three 3ft diameter rollers. Attached to the front of the frame at its centre point was a sub-frame fitted with 19 plough tines in arrow formation. This arrangement, when propelled by the tank, "combed" mines out of the ground. It had a tendency to dig in and buckle the main frame, however, and was abandoned after trials.

Farmer Track was then built, also by Samuel Butler Ltd, later in 1943. This device consisted of a similar pivoted frame to that of Farmer Front, this time supported on two 5ft diameter narrow rollers. Attached to the frame in front of each roller in V formation were six forward-curving tines. The disadvantage which led to its abandonment after trials was that uprooted mines tended to fall between the tines, which, if placed closer together to obviate this, tended to clog up.

The third "Farmer" device of the Obstacle Assault Centre was Farmer Deck which was built by Ransomes, Sims & Jefferies Ltd at Ipswich and was tested concurrently with the other two during 1943. Although, like the others, finally abandoned (in the Spring of 1944) Farmer Deck showed more promise and several different experimental models were built followed by a production run of some 200. The main feature of this apparatus was the counterbalancing of the structure to which the two large ploughshares (one in front of each track) preceded by rollers or skids intended to support them were attached. The idea of this was to relieve the load on the front rollers or skids so that they should not explode mines but pass over them, to be dug out and turned aside by the ploughshares.

One of the earliest Farmer Decks, attached to a Churchill II, had two skids between the ploughshares and the side girders carrying the counterbalance weights at the rear were of lattice construction. A later model (known also as OAC Mark I Plough), fitted to a Churchill IV, had a modified lattice girder structure and the skids were replaced by a pair of plough furrow wheels projecting in front of each ploughshare.

The Farmer Deck version known as OAC Mark II Plough (also on the Churchill IV) eliminated the cumbersome lattice girders, counterbalanced pivoted side beams being connected by vertical links to a separate front framework carrying the ploughshares and preceded by two smooth cylindrical rollers of the pattern used in the AMRA anti-mine roller device. The final version of Farmer Deck (again on a Churchill IV) had two separate assemblies of rollers and ploughshares (instead of being attached to a single frame) and this allowed them considerable vertical movement independently of each other.

Another plough device, tested by 79th Armoured Division on a Churchill IV during the latter part of 1943, was the antithesis of the complicated Farmer Deck series. This consisted only of two ploughshares (one in front of each track) attached to a short girder frame pivoted to the tank sides just to the rear of the front idler wheel. The height of the frame, and hence the cut of the ploughshare, was adjusted by means of Atherton lifting equipment (a simple block and tackle to enable tank crews to remove engines etc) mounted on the tank turret.

In addition to the model mentioned above, several types of anti-mine ploughs were tested by the 79th Armoured Division at their training area in Suffolk concurrently with the ploughs developed by the Obstacle Assault Centre. One of these was the device known as the MD1 Plough or Jefferis Plough after the experimental establishment, run by Colonel Millis Jefferis, at which it was designed. This appeared in two main versions, one for the Churchill and the other for the Sherman tank. It was a relatively simple girder structure, attached to the front of the tank, on which was mounted a V-shaped ploughshare with fork tines in front of each track (seven to each ploughshare on the Churchill version, five in the Sherman type). A broad skid to maintain the plough depth projected in front of each ploughshare. Changes in details of the design were introduced during trials.

The most successful series of anti-mine ploughs developed by the 79th Armoured Division were the Bullshorns, a name associated with the well-known bulls head divisional sign. They were, indeed, in their latest version, the only anti-mine ploughs to be taken with the division when it took part in the North West Europe campaign. The design of these ploughs, which were broadly on the same lines as the Jefferis Plough, went through several stages, Bullshorn Mark II, for instance, (fitted experimentally to the Churchill IV) having a single wide skid (to maintain optimum ploughing depth) in the centre, completely filling the space between the wide and deep plough blades in front of each track. The Bullshorn Mark IIIc, as fitted again to the Churchill IV, had a cruciform frame attached to the front of the tank so as to permit movement about the horizontal axis and to which was fitted in front of each track a blade (resembling an angle-dozer blade) with inward curving tines. In front of each of these were skids to maintain the correct depth for the plough. A similar pattern was also designed for Sherman tanks. The ploughing speed for the Bullshorn was about 4mph and it was judged to be the best anti-mine plough device to be developed before D-Day.

Another contribution to the extensive list of anti-mine devices was in effect a form of rake, rather than a plough, but has been included here for

Tank, Infantry Mark I with Coulter Plough

Churchill IV Farmer Front [*RAC Tank Museum*

Churchill IV Farmer Track [*RAC Tank Museum*

[*Imperial War Museum*

Churchill II Farmer Deck—an early version with front skids

convenience. This apparatus, believed to have been designed by Nicholas Straussler, inventor of the DD tank, consisted of eight backward-curving tines, four in front of each track, on two pivot bars mounted at the ends of four long leaf springs attached to a frame extended in front of the tank. The tines were mounted to allow pivotal movement independently of each other, although downward pressure on all of them was maintained by the leaf springs. When the tank advanced, the tines were calculated to maintain sufficient ground pressure to explode any mine encountered. The shock would, however, be lessened by the upward and backward movement of the tine on its pivot bar. When the tine was activated in this way it threw upwards a weighted horizontal arm attached to it at the pivot. The weight of this arm slowed down the movement of the tine and also returned it to its normal position afterwards. The distal ends of the weighted arms (one to each tine) were supported in brackets attached to the frame and their upward movement was limited by two horizontal bars, one over each group of four weighted arms.

Finally, a light mine clearing plough for attachment to a Weasel (a United States-built light amphibious carrier) developed by an experimental wing of the 79th Armoured Division in Belgium, should be mentioned. This was very much like a miniature version of the Bullshorn plough described above.

Experiments with mine clearing devices of all sorts before D-Day had shown that the flail was undoubtedly the best. However, the cratering caused by the detonation of mines by flails in the soft clay soil in certain sections of the Normandy beaches would have made the beaches impassable. Accordingly, a number of Bullshorn equipments for attachment to AVREs were taken to France by the 79th Armoured Division and these were used to plough up and sweep aside mines (for clearance later by RE parties on foot) in these soft clay areas of the D-Day beaches.

Sherman with Jefferis (MDI) Plough in the raised position   [*Imperial War Museum*

Sherman with Bullshorn Mark III

[*Imperial War Museum*

Valentine III or V with anti-mine device

Churchill Gun Carrier with Snake projectors   [*Imperial War Museum*

Anti-Mine Explosive Devices

Clearance of a lane through a minefield by exploding the mines from a distance would be a quick and simple means, if practicable, and some effort was put into the development of a tank-operated method of this nature. A device known as Snake, which consisted of a long cylinder of explosive made up from a number of sections, could be towed by a tank to near the minefield. The tank then moved to the rear end of the Snake and pushed it forward into the minefield, the tank itself stopping at the edge. The Snake, when detonated by remote control, could clear a lane suitable for infantry use about 2ft 6in wide in a minefield; it could also be used to blow up barbed wire. Any tank could be used to operate Snake, which was experimented with both in the United Kingdom from October 1941 onwards, and in the Middle East.

Later, electrically-fired rocket-propelled Snakes were tried out by the 79th Armoured Division in 1943/4. These were carried in multiple tubes about 20ft long on Churchill tanks and the rockets were fired into the minefield from its edge and exploded. Two versions of this device appeared, one on a Churchill IV with a total of ten Snake tubes, five mounted over each track, and the other on a Churchill Gun Carrier (less 3in gun) with 50 tubes—25 on each track guard. This device was not very successful and the vehicles were used in later trials of Snake simply to carry Snake sections forward where they could be assembled into a long unit for normal pull and push operation by a tank. Snakes were carried in the stores of the 1st Armoured Engineer Brigade, RE of the 79th Armoured Division and operated by AVREs were used in conjunction with flail tanks in clearing minefields in the assault on Le Havre in 1944. The AVRE's Petard projectiles could also be used for exploding mines. In Italy, 48 400ft-long Snakes were manufactured in 1944, but were never used in action.

Tapeworm was an explosive device operated by a tank (usually a flail) towing across a minefield a flexible hose which then had liquid explosive pumped into it and exploded.

Another attempted method of clearing minefields (although not by explosive) which may be mentioned here was by flame with Crocodile flame-throwers. This was tried out by an experimental wing of the 79th Armoured Division in Belgium between December 1944 and early 1945, but was not highly successful.

Matilda Baron Mark IIIA flailing

Early United Kingdom Types of Flail Tank

Major A. S. J. du Toit arrived in Europe towards the end of 1941 to assist in the development of his proposals for a "flail" type of mine clearance device and began work in conjunction with the special research and experimental department of AEC Ltd at Southall, Middlesex. The earliest flail device built in the United Kingdom was known at first by the code name of "Tank Winch" but later as Baron, from an earlier exponent of the use of the flail in war and was applied to a Matilda II tank.

The first model, Baron Mark I, which was completed by the end of 1941, consisted of the Matilda II tank (which retained its turret, with 2pr gun and coaxial Besa mg) on which a revolving rotor, some 10ft in front of the tank was mounted by means of arms attached to the sides of the hull. The rotor from which the flail chains were suspended was driven by a 60bhp Chrysler 6-cyl engine, mounted with its radiator at the side of the tank. The power was taken through propeller shafts to a final chain drive at the rotor. The normal height of the rotor above ground level was about 6ft, but hydraulic rams, one either side, powered by the tank's turret traverse pump, could raise or lower the side arms so as to maintain a constant height over irregular ground. This did not work very well, however, and since the auxiliary engine was found to be not powerful enough and other points needed improvement this prototype was sent back to AEC Ltd to be rebuilt.

Baron Mark II, as the rebuilt flail tank was designated, was completed by April 1942. A Bedford 6-cyl engine of 73bhp replaced the Chrysler unit and transmission of the flail drive was by means of universal-jointed shafts to a worm reduction gear at the rotor end of the side arm. A separate radiator for the Bedford engine was dispensed with and some of the coolant for the main engines of the tank was by-passed to cool it. Provision for cutting barbed wire was included in the Baron Mark II rotor (various forms were tested) and the machine was also designed to dig away anti-tank earthworks when the rotor was lowered to ground level and revolved slowly so that projections on it would loosen and disperse the soil, which could then be pushed level.

Trials of the Baron Mark II showed that power for the flail drive was still insufficient; that a somewhat lower height for the rotor arms was desirable and that the cooling system for the auxiliary engine (taken from the main engines) was unsatisfactory and so a final model, Baron Mark III (Mark IIIA in its production form) was built and completed by the end of 1942. In this model it was decided to dispense with the turret and a fixed, square armoured super-structure for the flail operator was built in its place. Two Bedford flail engines each of 73bhp were fitted in armoured boxes, one each side of the hull, and these transmitted their power to the rotor by means of universally jointed shafts to worm reduction gears at each end of the rotor. A path 10ft wide could be cleared through a minefield at a speed of about ⅓mph. The Baron Mark III had defects which revealed themselves in trials, but a limited production order was placed with Curran Bros Ltd for 60 for delivery by July 1943 so that regiments destined to use flail tanks in battle should have machines on which to train.

Valentine III Scorpion   [*Imperial War Museum*

In the meantime, parallel development of flail tanks had been going on in the Middle East and when details of the Middle East Scorpion flail tanks were received in the United Kingdom at the end of 1942 it was decided to build a similar form of flail equipment on a Valentine tank. The Middle East Scorpions had a reasonably good mine detonating ability, but were much less complicated than the Baron and being narrower could be driven through the doors of existing tank landing craft, which Baron could not.

Like the later Middle East Scorpions, the auxiliary engines of the UK Scorpion Mark III (or Valentine Scorpion) were mounted on top of the hull. The Middle East vehicles retained their turrets, but in the Valentine the turret was removed and replaced by a large fixed structure built up from 8 to 14mm armour plate, which housed the two engines to drive the flail rotor as well as the tank commander, flail device operator and controls for the equipment. No hydraulic equipment to raise or lower the rotors was incorporated and the side arms followed the lattice design of the Middle East Scorpions, although the open-structure type of rotor developed in the Barons was used on the Valentine Scorpion. The two flail engines were Canadian-built Ford V-8s, each of 80bhp at governed speed and interconnected to drive the rotor arm via a carden shaft each side. In order to provide extra protection for the crew against anti-personnel mines (although full protection against unswept anti-tank mines was impracticable) a $\frac{1}{2}$-in mild steel plate spaced 2in below the underside of the tank was included in production Valentine Scorpions. The Valentine II and III (AEC 131bhp diesel main engine) were used as the basis of the Valentine Scorpion, which could clear a lane 9ft 6in wide at speeds of between $\frac{1}{2}$mph and $1\frac{1}{2}$mph, provided the anti-tank mines were buried not deeper than 3in from the surface. One hundred and fifty of these vehicles were built, sufficient to train in 1943 and 1944 the three regiments of 30th Armoured Brigade, which, however, were re-equipped with Sherman Crabs by the time they went into action in Normandy.

Adaptation of the flail device for attachment to the Sherman tank (by 1943 coming into widespread use in the British Army) was the logical development of the Matilda Baron and Valentine Scorpion and design work on this project was commenced in mid-1943 by AEC Ltd, who also built the first proto-

Sherman V Marquis   (*AEC Ltd*

type, on a Sherman V tank. This flail tank, called Marquis, was turretless and had a fixed central armoured structure housing the flail engines (two 85bhp Fords) similar to that of Valentine Scorpion, but the rotor side arms were single girders (more like those of Baron) and the hydraulic rams to raise or lower the rotors were again introduced, although this time solely as a means of reducing the space taken up by the vehicle when carried in landing craft. The rotors were of "solid" cylindrical type, unlike the open structures used in the earlier UK flail tanks. The Marquis was a better vehicle than Baron and Scorpion as it incorporated improvements found desirable from trials of both these types, but the prototype of the Sherman Crab, in which power for the flails was taken off the main tank engine, was ready shortly before the first Marquis. Although Marquis was tested it was apparent that the Crab was the better device and the one on which future development should be concentrated, and Marquis was accordingly dropped.

Sherman Pram Scorpion   [*RAC Tank Museum*

Flail Tanks—**Pram Scorpion, Crab and Lobster**

The earliest flail device in which the power for the flail rotors was taken not from auxiliary engines but from the tank's main power unit was the Pram Scorpion. The suggestion for this came from Samuel Butler Ltd of Leeds. It consisted of a flail rotor carried on two side arms attached to the sides of the tank—a Sherman with the turret and main armament retained—but supported in front of the vehicle by four castor rollers (two, close together side by side in front of each track). Investigation into a device on these lines had been carried out in 1942 and not completed, but the main change in the new model was that the auxiliary engines were eliminated and drive for the flail rotor transmitted from the tank main engines via the track front sprockets. The drive for the rotors was taken each side from a sprocket fitted to the same shaft as the tank driving sprocket, back to another sprocket to the rear of the end of the side arms and thence forward through two geared-up chain drives inside the side arms to the rotor which, to facilitate steering when flailing, was constructed in two halves, so that either half could slow down or speed up in response to turning movements by the tank. The Pram Scorpion prototype was ready by the end of May 1943 only four months before the Sherman Crab prototype appeared. Disadvantages appeared in trials but the Crab showed so much greater promise that little further development work was undertaken on the Pram Scorpion.

In the Sherman Crab the most important features were the flail drive taken from the tank main engines and the retention of the turret and main armament. These points had appeared before but the Crab was the most effective design of flail tank which had been built by 1943 and was the model selected for production in quantity for use in the North West Europe campaign in the following year. The prototype Crab was designed and produced by AEC Ltd in September 1943; it was based on the Sherman V, one of the standard versions of this American tank used by the British Army. The rotor was a cylinder, to which the flail chains were attached, carried on pivoted side arms. The power take off from the tank's main engine (a Chrysler 30-cyl unit, rated at 350bhp, built up from five

Sherman Crab I flailing   [*Imperial War Museum*

Sherman Lobster   [*Imperial War Museum*

207

6-cyl petrol engines geared to a single propellor shaft) was by means of a chain drive to a shaft, through an aperture in the right hand side of the hull to a universal-jointed carden shaft and a bevel gear on the end of the rotor. Although absent from the first prototype, hydraulic rams, one each side, were added to subsequent models to raise and lower the rotor arms in order to facilitate transport.

Trials with the prototype were generally very satisfactory and a lane 9ft 9in wide could be cleared of mines at a maximum flailing speed of 1¼mph, although the weight of the flail equipment reduced the Shermans top speed, when not flailing, to 20mph. Armour protection for the flail transmission where it came through the tank hull and the bevel gear at the top end of the rotor side arm were asked for, however, together with special navigational equipment for guidance when flailing. A production order for 300 Crabs was divided between four main contractors; this was later increased to an order for 689, to be completed during 1944. The special equipment referred to above for the Crab included a yardometer, a device driven by a belt to record the exact distance flailed; and directional equipment consisting of a direction indicating gyroscope, to enable the tank driver to follow a pre-arranged course, and a magnetic compass which could be projected from the turret roof and used for periodically checking the gyroscope.

One disadvantage of most flail tanks up to and including the Sherman Crab I was that, as the flail rotor was at a constant beating height, mines buried in hollows in the ground could be passed over without being detonated. The Sherman Crab II was designed to overcome this shortcoming. The hydraulic ram on the left hand side of the vehicle was eliminated and a counterweight fitted to the rear end of the rotor arm. This weight balanced the weight of the rotor arm and flail chain so that a regular beating height of 4ft 3in over the contours of the ground could be maintained automatically.

In the early trials of the Crab I although the design was satisfactory in most respects it was found that the flail chains suffered more damage from mines than those of the Baron, and so it was decided to incorporate the Baron type of open rotor and flail layout with the Crab type of flail drive in a new experimental model. The prototype built on this principle by AEC Ltd in early 1944 was known as Sherman Lobster. It turned out to be satisfactory on its trials, and a contouring device, as on Crab II, was worked out for it. However, the Lobster was both heavier and larger than the Crab and since, by experiment, a longer life for the Crab flail chains had been attained, proposals to put Lobster into production were abandoned.

The three armoured regiments of 30th Armoured Brigade began training with Sherman Crabs in November 1943 and took part in the North West Europe Campaign from D-Day onwards with a good measure of success. The value of primary armament in flail tanks was fully demonstrated right from the outset, because for the first few hours of D-Day on some of the landing beaches Crabs were the only gun tanks ashore. The equipment in use by the Brigade consisted almost throughout of Crab Is since the contouring flail Crab IIs did not become available in quantity before the War ended.

Matilda Scorpion Mark I   [*Imperial War Museum*

Middle East Types of Flail Tanks

The most effective method for clearing minefields evolved in World War II was a device consisting of rows of chains attached to a power driven revolving drum. This apparatus, which exploded mines on contact, was the invention, in August 1941, of a South African officer, Major A. S. J. du Toit. This officer, who was a motor engineer in civilian life, constructed a working model, a film of which was shown to General Auckinleck, then Commander-in-Chief Middle East. Auchinleck realised the potential value of the device and ordered du Toit to England so that development work could be undertaken. *En route*, however, the South African officer gave details of his invention to the Middle East Mechanical Experimental Establishment and (after a period during which experiments were banned because of the fear of inadequate security) development work, which had started with an experimental device attached to a lorry, was carried out.

The earliest application of the device to a tank was to a Matilda. The flails were cables with short lengths of chain attached to the ends and were driven by a Ford lorry engine mounted outside the tank in a compartment on the right hand side. The drive was taken via a cardan shaft to a bevel box at the end of the supporting girder arm on the right hand side and thence to the rotor to which the flails were attached. An unfortunate extra member of the tank crew sat in the rear part of the flail engine compartment (where he was nearly choked with dust and engine fumes) with the job of operating the auxilary engine. In this model the engine overheated so badly that the petrol vaporised after the tank had covered only 200 yards flailing, and most minefields were deeper than this. The Matilda tank engine air filters were found to be inadequate to cope with excessive dust thrown up when flailing so that the more efficient type of air filter used on Crusader tanks eventually had to be substituted.

Twenty-four Matilda Scorpion Mark Is were ordered and, with as many faults as could be eliminated in the time, were ready in October 1942, two days before the battle of Alamein. The Scorpions had a flailing speed of only ½mph and sometimes they broke down in the minefields they helped to clear, but on the whole they were reasonably successful.

An improved model, Matilda Scorpion Mark II, was developed from the Scorpion Mark I and a number was ready for use by early 1943, towards the end of the North African campaign. In the new type, the man operating the flail was in the fighting compartment of the tank itself and the design of the lattice side girders was improved. Unlike the Mark Is, these tanks did not all retain their 2pr main armament.

Grant Scorpion Mark III with turret removed—flailing   [*RAC Tank Museum*

Matilda Scorpion Mark II   [*Imperial War Museum*

[*RAC Tank Museum*

Grant Scorpion with twin Dodge flail engines

[*Imperial War Museum*

Sherman Scorpion flailing

The Matilda Scorpion II pattern of flail device was adapted for the Grant tank (the General Motors diesel-engined model) and the combination was known as Grant Scorpion Mark III. One advantage of this type was that, although the hull 75mm gun was removed, the upper turret could be retained, with a relatively unimpeded field of fire for its 37mm gun. Some tanks, however, had the top turret removed in order to reduce the dimensions for loading in landing craft. Of the few Grant Scorpions built some took part in the Sicily campaign in July–August 1943.

A further pattern of Scorpion, also on the Grant tank, had two Dodge engines, mounted on the rear deck plate, connected by universal-jointed shafts each side to drive the flail rotor. The lattice side girders and rotors were removable for transport purposes.

The final Middle East flail design was the Sherman Scorpion which had the flail equipment driven by two Dodge engines as developed for the Grant tank. The Sherman Scorpion had the big advantage of retaining its main armament, the 75mm gun. This type of flail was used in the Italian campaign.

[*Imperial War Museum*

Valentine flamethrower—cordite-operated (Ministry of Supply design)

Early Experimental Types of Flamethrower Tanks

The earliest work on mobile flamethrowers in World War II commenced in October 1940, following the production of various sorts of flamethrowers for static defences, when a Commer armoured vehicle was fitted with an annular type of flamethrower. This was followed shortly afterwards by another design of flamethrower actuated by a three stage pump and known as the Heavy Pump Unit, on a six wheeled armoured AEC chassis; and by a Bren Carrier-mounted flamethrower called the "Adey-Martin Drainpipe". All these models were completed by the Petroleum Warfare Department by early 1941. By the end of the same year the Ronson Flamethrower on a Universal Carrier had also been designed and built by the Canadian Petroleum Warfare Experimental Unit working under the Petroleum Warfare Dept.

The first British tank-mounted flamethrowers were two rival designs, both on Valentine tanks, one designed by G. J. Rackham and C. S. R. Stock of AEC Ltd for the Petroleum Warfare Dept and the other by the flamethrowing research section of the Ministry of Supply at Langhurst, near Horsham, under L. V. Thomas, their chief designer.

The AEC tank flamethrower system consisted of a high pressure vessel, containing the oil to be burned, mounted in a trailer, in which the pressure was obtained from compressed hydrogen bottles (at a pressure of 300/350lb/sq in) connected to the oil container through a reducing valve. The oil under pressure was carried via the trailer coupling through to the flame projector (based on the gun used in the Heavy Pump Unit referred to above) and ignition device in the tank itself. All the controls were operated by the tank crew and the trailer could be jettisoned in emergency, whether the oil was under pressure or not.

The Ministry of Supply design also carried the flame fuel in a trailer towed behind the tank, but projection of the ignited oil was by means of gas generated by cordite sticks. Unlike the AEC design, this model could not operate continuously but fired in bursts at intervals of ten seconds.

In order that a comparison could be made between these rival systems a joint demonstration was arranged for the War Office towards the end of March 1942. The AEC system developed for the Petroleum Warfare Dept was chosen

Valentine flamethrower—gas-operated (AEC design for PWD)

to form the basis of subsequent designs and as a result of this decision the Ministry of Supply flamethrowing section was absorbed by the PWD.

Also in the summer of 1942 work was started on a flamethrower for use in Churchill tanks. The basis of the design, which was suggested by a tank officer, Major J. M. Oke, consisted of an early Wasp flame projector (developed for use in Carriers) the fuel for which was carried in a standard jettison fuel tank mounted at the rear of the Churchill's hull. The design work was carried out by Lagonda and production was rushed through at great speed (without reference to the Director of Tank Design) so that a number of Churchill tanks with this equipment could be used in the Combined Operations raid on Dieppe which took place on 19th August 1942. Three Churchill II tanks of the Calgary Regiment equipped with Oke flamethrowers were sent to Dieppe but never had the chance to go into action as all three were sunk in their landing craft before reaching the beach. As an alternative method to the jettison tank for carrying the flame fuel, a single-wheeled castor trailer was tested at about this time for use with Churchill tank flamethrowers, but the idea was not followed up.

An entirely different form of tank-carried flamethrower can be briefly mentioned at this point. This was the 9.75in chemical mortar fitted in the fighting compartment of a turretless Valentine tank. The mortar fired a combustible projectile which had a far greater range than any flamethrower of the Wasp and associated types, but development of this equipment was not pursued beyond the experimental model.

Flamethrower Tanks—**Crocodile and Later Experimental Models**

The type of flamethrower designed for Carriers having proved satisfactory, the prototype vehicle of a successor to the Churchill Oke, designed to carry the Carriers' Wasp equipment, was in hand before the Dieppe operation. Subsequently, on 30th July, 1942, the War Office ordered twelve pilot models of what became known as the Churchill Crocodile. In September, however, policy changed as it was then felt that a tank would not have sufficient protection for close range flamethrower work and that the smaller and more mobile carrier would be a better vehicle for this purpose. However, work was allowed to continue on the Crocodile design, under R. P. Fraser of the Lagonda firm, although more slowly than before, and as a result it was not until January 1943 that the prototype was running. Supporters of the project succeeded in getting the September decision reversed and in March the prototype was successfully demonstrated to the War Office. This led, a month later, to an order for 250 Crocodiles, subject to user trials being satisfactory and production capacity being available. The prototype was then sent for the first troop trials under battlefield conditions with the 79th Armoured Division in Suffolk.

The first Crocodiles were built on the Churchill IV; initially Wasp Mark I type of equipment (with the long barrelled projector) was used but when the Wasp II equipment had been proved successful this was standardised for both Churchill tank and carrier use. The production Crocodiles were based on the later Mark of Churchill—in which the frontal armour was increased from 102mm to 152mm—the Churchill VII. The layout was similar to that of the AEC Valentine design which had been chosen for further development as a Churchill flamethrower. The flame fuel (400 gallons) was contained in a 9-ton armoured trailer: pressure was obtained from compressed gas cylinders and fire could be maintained for up to 100 seconds in short bursts. The fuel was led through a three-way coupling from the trailer to the projector, which replaced the hull machine gun in the front of the tank. Maximum range was between 100 and 200 yards.

The original production order was increased by stages to 1,000, of which about 800 were completed under the production parentage of the Lagonda

Churchill VII Crocodile in action at a demonstration in the United Kingdom

company by the end of World War II. Crocodiles were used in action during the later stages of the Italian campaign and quite extensively in North Western Europe, where eventually a whole Armoured Brigade was equipped with this weapon.

A Sherman version of the Crocodile was designed for an experimental contract placed with the Petroleum Warfare Department by the United States, and four vehicles were supplied. Other experimental flamethrowers on the Sherman tank were the Salamander and the Adder. There were several versions of the Sherman Salamander, all of which, however, had the Wasp flame projector mounted in the turret. In the Sherman Adder, the flame fuel and pressure apparatus were carried in an extension attached to the rear hull and the projector was mounted over the co-drivers position. The Churchill Cobra was another experimental flamethrower which was not produced in quantity.

The only other tank flamethrowers apart from Churchill Crocodile to be used in action during World War II by British Commonwealth troops were the Ram Badger and the Matilda Frog. The Ram Badger was the Canadian Ram tank equipped with a Wasp II flamethrower and flame fuel carried internally. One of these vehicles is said to have wiped out an entire parachute batallion in the Canadian attack on a strong-point at Minnethal in 1945.

The Matilda Frog was developed for use with the Australian Armoured Brigade assembled for the Pacific campaign: one reason for the use of the Matilda in this role was that it was still employed operationally by the Australian Armoured Corps. The flame fuel was carried in the tank itself and the projector replaced the main armament in the turret. Four troops of these tanks were included in the Brigade which took part in the island battles of Aitape, Wewak, Bougainville and Borneo in 1945.

Matilda Frog—with the Australian Armoured Corps

Churchill VII Crocodile

Matilda CDL   [B.T. White

Searchlight Tanks

As long ago as 1916 it had been proposed that searchlights should be mounted on tanks for use in night action but little practical effort was made to follow this up, although some interest was revived in the Army in the early 1930s. In 1933, however, Commander Oscar de Thoren, RN—proposer of the 1916 suggestion—formed a private syndicate to further the development of tank searchlights. Mr A. V. M. Mitzakis was manager and technical adviser to this body and Major-General J. F. C. Fuller after his retirement from the Army was retained as military advisor. Mr Mitzakis designed a searchlight projecter that could be fitted to armoured vehicles and was practically invulnerable to small arms fire. The War Office eventually showed interest in the project and the equipment, mounted on a carrier of the Carden Loyd type, was demonstrated on Salisbury Plain early in 1937. As a result, the War Office bought the design and a tank turret incorporating the invention was ordered. This was completed in September 1939 and, after tests, six further turrets with an improved type of projector, also designed by Mr Mitzakis, were ordered. The trials of the new model in April 1940 were so impressive that a production order was given for 300 searchlight turrets for Matilda tanks. This equipment was known for secrecy as Canal Defence Light (CDL) and training in the United Kingdom with Matilda CDL tanks began in 1941; in the following year two regiments were also training in the Middle East. Later, Churchill tanks were also fitted with CDL turrets and then Grants. The Grant was finally standardised for CDL work because, with the 37mm gun turret replaced by the searchlight turret, the hull 75mm gun could still be retained for offensive action.

The CDL device consisted of a high intensity arc lamp that, by means of two reflectors, projected a beam through a vertical slit 2ft high and 2ins wide, but which, at 1,000yds, would illuminate a width of 350yds. The light could be oscillated by means of a steel shutter, creating a flickering effect that dazzled enemy gunners. In the Matilda CDLs, power for the searchlight was taken off the tanks' own engines but in the more roomy Grants a special generator was built in for this purpose. The carbon arcs of the lamps lasted only 30 minutes and had to be changed by the crews wearing asbestos gloves.

The two regiments equipped with Matilda CDL tanks in the Middle East had not completed their training in time for the Battle of Alamein in October 1942 and for various reasons were not used in the Mediterranean theatre subsequently. At home a CDL Brigade of three regiments (two of which were eventually replaced in January 1944 by the two regiments from the Middle East) was included in 79th Armoured Division and landed in Normandy in August 1944, but was not employed. It was not until the Rhine crossing battle, by which time the Brigade had been re-equipped with other AFVs, that there was a call for CDL tanks to protect the assault craft and the bridges. Twenty-four CDL tanks were got together and did useful service in which only one tank was

[*Imperial War Museum*
Grant CDL

[*Imperial War Museum*
Grant CDL tanks in a night training exercise in the United Kingdom

217

disabled. The same function was carried out for the Elbe crossing a few weeks later.

In these two river crossings improvised Ram searchlight tanks—not CDL—also took part. The searchlight—a 90cm projector—was mounted in the turret ring of one tank and its generator similarly mounted in another, and the tanks operated in pairs.

Tetrarch **DD** with screens raised. Note the screw for water propulsion

Duplex Drive Tank—**Tetrarch**

The DD device was an effective and relatively simple means of converting an ordinary battle tank into an amphibious vehicle capable of sea-going under moderate conditions and yet remaining an effective fighting vehicle with all the main armament available once it had reached dry land.

The device—known as DD from Duplex Drive, a name which concealed its function—was the invention of Nicholas Straussler and was a means of increasing the freeboard of the tank and so raising the vehicle's bouyancy to a level when it would float. Straussler was the inventor of a number of ingenious items of military equipment, including an earlier amphibious tank, created by the addition of two pontoons to a 3-ton light tank of his own design. A similar device was tried out on a British Army Light Tank Mark II in 1931. Straussler also designed a collapsible assault boat with a canvas hull and the DD device amounted to a collapsible boat fitted over a tank hull. A Tank, Light Mark VII—Tetrarch was first equipped with the device and was tried out on a reservoir at Hendon, north west London, in June 1941. The canvas screen was attached to a platform welded on all round the hull at the level of the track guards. The screen was erected by means of inflatable rubber tubes and held in the erected position by metal struts. The hull below this level was, of course, fully water-proofed and when the tank was floating the hull was below water level. Water propulsion was by means of a single forward-facing propeller mounted on a bracket at the rear of the tank and driven through a shaft taken off the main engine. The propellor mounting incorporated a rudder and the whole assembly, like an outboard motor, could be turned for steering. The Tetrarch was tested during 1941 at the same time as a contemporary version of Straussler's earlier tank amphibious device—a Crusader tank fitted with a large pontoon either side and special tracks for water propulsion. In spite of certain disadvantages—such as vulnerability of the canvas screen and the fact that the armament could not be used whilst the tank was waterborne—the DD device was compact and effective and was adaptable to most types of tank and was accordingly selected for further development and eventual production.

[*RAC Tank Museum*

Crusader with pontoons for floatation and special tracks—tested at the same time as Tetrarch DD

Valentine IX DD with screens lowered   [*Imperial War Museum*

Duplex Drive Tanks—**Valentine**

The first prototype DD device on a 7½-ton Tetrarch Light Tank was used successfully to demonstrate the feasibility of the concept as a whole, but when production in quantity was decided on a more powerful fighting vehicle was needed and the Valentine, then in mass production, was chosen.

To adapt the DD device to the Valentine, exactly the same type of equipment was used but a rather higher freeboard was needed to give extra bouyancy for the Valentine's weight of 16 to 17 tons. Propulsion was again by means of a single screw at the rear. This faced rearwards and could be hinged upwards out of the way when not in use. The Metropolitan-Cammell Carriage and Wagon Co Ltd (a company associated with Vickers-Armstrongs Ltd, designers of the Valentine) was asked to develop the Valentine DD in conjunction with the inventor and then put it into quantity production. Three prototype Valentine DDs were built and a contract was placed with Metro-Cammell in July 1942 for conversion of 450 Valentine tanks, to be taken from the company's current production line. This order was subsequently increased to one for 625 Valentine DD tanks. Army trials of the prototypes continued in 1942, including the first sea trials in August, in which technical staff of Metro-Cammell and Nicholas Straussler Ltd (the inventor's firm) took part.

The first production Valentine DD tanks were delivered in early March 1943 and the whole order for 625 had been completed in the following year. The Valentine itself was progressively modified during this time so that Valentines Marks V, IX and XI, with essentially the same amphibious equipment, appeared as DD tanks. All three marks had General Motors' diesel engines, although the Valentine V had armament of a 2pr gun and Besa machine gun in the turret; the Mark IX had a 6pr gun, and the Mark XI had a 75mm gun and Besa MG.

The Valentine DD tanks were used extensively from about April 1943 onwards to train crews for the D-Day campaign although only Sherman DD tanks were actually used in combat in North West Europe. Valentine DDs were also used for training in the Italian theatre of operations from August 1944 onwards and a small number was also used operationally (when sent as replacements for Sherman DDs, which were in limited supply) in North Italy in the spring of 1945.

Valentine V DD tanks in a Tank Landing Craft. The nearest Valentine has the screens lowered

Valentine DD swimming

Sherman DD with screens lowered, although rear part is not quite down

Duplex Drive Tanks—**Sherman**

The Sherman tank began arriving for the British Army from the United States in increasing numbers from September 1942 onwards and during the course of production of the Valentine DD tanks, in 1943/4, plans were made for a Sherman version. Prototypes were prepared and underwent trials both in fresh water inland (in Norfolk) and in the sea. The tanks themselves were, of course, completed as normal gun tanks in the United States but the conversion work (as for the Valentines) was again undertaken by the Metropolitan Cammell C & W Co Ltd. An order for 573 Sherman DD tanks was given to this company and deliveries began in time for training for the D-Day landings to be well under way by spring 1944. Early in the same year, at the behest of General Eisenhower, the Allied Supreme Commander, the United States also joined in to produce more Sherman DD tanks and in fact, enough were built to equip three US tank battalions (in addition to the five British and two Canadian tank regiments) by June 1944.

The Sherman DD conversion was very similar in principle to that of the Valentine but because the weight was almost double, more bouyancy had to be provided, and of the tank's height of 13ft with screens raised, about 9ft was under water, the freeboard ranging from 3 to 4ft. Twin screws were used for water propulsion and steering. The power for the screws was supplied, as in earlier DD tanks, by the tank's main engine. In the Sherman, however, this was transmitted via the tracks and the rear idler wheels, which were incorporated into a new assembly with stub axles. From the stub axles the drive was taken via

Sherman DD with screens raised

[*Imperial War Museum*

bevel gears through universally jointed shafts to the three bladed screws. The propellors were designed to hinge upwards when not in use, but even so often sustained damage going cross-country and a means of protecting them had to be devised later. Since with this system of drive the tracks were always running when the tank was in the water it was prepared to climb ashore immediately it touched ground. The speed afloat of the Sherman DD was 5-6mph and steering (normally by the tank commander standing on a platform using a tiller with mechanical linkage to the screws, although a hydraulic system was also available) on a straight course took a lot of practice. A periscope was provided for the driver. The main turret armament of the Sherman was retained but the hull armament was not usable in tanks converted to the DD role.

Experience with the Sherman III DD and Sherman V DD (the two marks of Sherman used for this conversion) showed the need to stiffen the top rails of the screen, and struts to the turret were added; in addition eight self-locking struts to hold the screen erect were introduced. Vehicles with these improvements were known as Sherman III DDI and Sherman V DD I. Further improvements were incorporated in Sherman III DD II and the wholly American-built DD tanks in British nomenclature were styled Sherman III DDIII.

To assist Sherman DD tanks in certain types of opposed or difficult landings various experimental devices were prepared. These included Ginandit, a folding mat which could be extended in front of the tank for crossing mud flats before reaching firm ground; rockets fitted in two banks of five either side to help the tank climb a difficult river bank or similar obstacle; and Belch, a device to spray the canvas screens with sea water to protect them in anticipation of the sea being ignited by the defenders in the D-Day landings. Trials in the months before D-Day showed that a DD tank could emerge unscathed through a flame barrage.

Sherman DD tanks were first used in action on D-Day and achieved a tactical surprise since during the run-in little enemy fire was attracted because of their boat-like appearance. Rough seas in some sectors prevented DD tanks being launched and they were landed direct on to the beaches, but those that did swim ashore stood up very well to sea conditions worse than any experienced during training. They were in fact, because of their underwater weight a little too steady in a cross sea and so more susceptible to damage. Sherman DD tanks were also used in the Rhine crossing in March 1945 and in the final operations in north Italy. Preparations were made for employment of Sherman DD tanks in the Far East theatre, although the war ended before this was necessary. However, before this an attachment known as Topee armour, which would protect the folded screens of DD tanks from damage by undergrowth in jungle operations, was hurriedly designed and produced.

———

Churchill ARV Mark I with jib erected

[Imperial War Museum

Armoured Recovery Vehicles—**Mark I Types**

The equipment available at the outbreak of World War II for the recovery of disabled tanks from the battlefield consisted only of six-wheeled breakdown lorries, supplemented later by a quantity of tracked Caterpillar D8 unarmoured tractors. The latter, although more efficient than the wheeled vehicles under bad conditions, had to be transported for any distance on wheeled trailers.

The success of the German Afrika Korps in the North African campaigns in 1941/2 in recovering tanks from the battle line itself, repairing them close behind the battle area and returning them into action, often within hours, stressed the need for a comparable British organisation and also for the development of armoured recovery vehicles.

From February 1942 investigation was made into the possibility of conversion of various types of tanks into armoured recovery vehicles and by the middle of the year several experimental types had been produced by the REME Experimental Recovery Section at Arborfield. These vehicles were all adaptations on similar lines, the turrets being removed and the type of recovery equipment carried was common to all. After trials, however, both the Covenanter ARV and the Crusader ARV prototypes were rejected as unsuitable—more from the basic vehicle characteristics than anything—whereas the Grant ARV and the Churchill ARV were both considered good.

The Churchill Armoured Recovery Vehicle, Mark I, as it became known in full, was intended principally for use with Regiments equipped with Churchill tanks, but the changes made in adaption of the standard fighting vehicle and the equipment carried were typical of ARV Mark Is on other chassis. A jib with a maximum lift of 3 tons for removing tank engines, gearboxes or other major assemblies was carried, stowed on the hull for travelling, but mounted on the

Sherman V ARV Mark I   [*Imperial War Museum*

B.T.F.V.—H

front of the vehicle for use. For the recovery of bogged down AFVs a 100ft length of 1⅛in diameter steel wire rope was carried, together with a snatch block (pulley) and ground anchors for indirect pulls and difficult operations. Two types of drawbars for towing British-built or North American AFVs were also carried in the ARV.

Other equipment included a high pressure oxy-acetylene cutting and welding plant and a 4½in vice mounted on the front of the vehicle, and extra fire extinguishers.

The turret opening was covered by a roof plate with two opening hatches, and twin Bren guns on a collapsible mounting could be operated from this position both for AA and ground use. In addition the normal front hull Besa of the Churchill was carried.

The Grant ARV Mark I, referred to earlier, carried similar equipment to the Churchill, including the twin Bren AA mounting. The hull 75mm gun position was blanked off. Cavalier and Centaur ARVs Mark I were also produced, followed by the Cromwell ARV Mark I, for employment with armoured regiments equipped with these types of tanks.

A Sherman counterpart of the Churchill ARV Mark I was produced in prototype form shortly after the Churchill model and the production version, based on the Sherman V (Medium M4A4) chassis became the most widely used ARV with British armoured divisions, many of which from 1942 onwards were, of course, equipped with Sherman gun tanks. The Sherman ARV Mark I carried the same equipment as that described for the Churchill ARV, including the twin Bren AA mounting. The fixed armament was the bow 0.30 Browning machine gun of the basic Sherman tank.

Cromwell ARV Mark I with jib erected   [*Imperial War Museum*

Churchill ARV Mark II. Note spade earth-anchor and 9½ ton jib at rear and 3½-ton jib erected at front of tank

Armoured Recovery Vehicles—**Mark II Types**

A few Churchill Armoured Recovery Vehicles Mark I were produced in time to accompany the 1st Army to North Africa in 1942 but production in 1942/3 to meet the need for this model and the Sherman ARV Mark I was slow because of the lack of spare industrial facilities. In the meantime, a number of United States Tanks, Recovery, T2, with winches and high lift jibs was supplied to the British Armies in Italy, where they were known as Lee ARVs. These were efficient and popular vehicles and underlined the need for a corresponding British vehicle equipped with a winch and heavy lift jib. The design of such a vehicle, the ARV Mark II, had been undertaken by the REME Experimental Recovery Section and production was carried out, as for earlier ARVs, by two Ministry of Supply establishments—one at Hayes, the other the London Passenger Transport Board Railway Workshops, Fulham—so that issue to the armoured units, to replace earlier vehicles, began in 1944.

The ARV Mark II was produced in two main versions, on the Churchill III or IV chassis and on the Sherman V chassis. The equipment on both types was similar; the most obvious change from the ARV Mark I being a fixed turret (mounting a dummy gun) in which was housed the operator of the winch. This winch, produced by Croft's, had a pull of 60 tons. A fixed jib with a 9½-ton lift was fitted at the rear and a detachable 3½-ton jib (similar to that of the ARV Mark Is) was carried, and in use was mounted at the front of the vehicle. A hinged earth anchor to enable the rear jib or the winch to be used to their maximum capacity was fitted at the back of the ARV.

Sherman V ARV Mark II

In Canada, ARVs comparable to both the ARV I and the ARV II were produced in limited numbers on Ram chassis. Also, for the record, it should be mentioned that quantities of the American Tank, Recovery M32 were taken into British service as Sherman II, ARV Mark III.

Sherman III BARV
[*Imperial War Museum*

[*Imperial War Museum*

Churchill BARV towing a Universal Carrier ashore during an excercise

Beach Armoured Recovery Vehicles

One part of the detailed planning for the D-Day invasion of Europe included provision for the recovery of "drowned" or disabled armour and vehicles from the beaches, both above and below the tide level. For this work the REME Experimental Beach Recovery Section, based at Budleigh Salterton on the Devon coast designed and experimented with, in 1943, Churchill and Sherman Beach Armoured Recovery Vehicles.

These early Beach ARVs were ordinary Sherman and Churchill tanks with the gun turrets replaced by a fixed rectangular structure and the engine air inlets and exhaust had tall metal cowls added. The hulls were completely waterproofed so that the vehicles could wade in up to about seven or eight feet of water. The BARV crews were trained to use shallow diving apparatus so that towing ropes could be attached under water to vehicles to be recovered.

The Churchill BARV was abandoned at the prototype stage since the hull with its side entry doors needed more waterproofing attention than the Sherman and three cowls were needed for the engine compared with the Sherman's one. BARV development was concentrated on the Sherman (the Ford petrol-engined model earlier, the Diesel-engined Sherman III standardised later) therefore, and a new multisided upper structure was designed which enabled the tank to operate in up to 10 feet of water, according to weather conditions. The hull form can be seen clearly in the photograph, although the outward-flared top edge to deflect spray from the commanders position was added after early trials. In addition to towing equipment, two wooden railway sleepers were attached to the front of the BARV for use in pushing vehicles or nudging off stranded landing craft. A trackway round the hull top was provided for the crew's use and the vehicle had hanging ropes (as on lifeboats) at the sides. Production of Sherman BARVs was undertaken, as with other types of armoured recovery vehicles, under REME supervision at two small Ministry of Supply workshops.

These vehicles were very successful in helping to keep the D-Day beaches clear and one BARV even caused local consternation as a "secret weapon" to the enemy at a very early stage of the proceedings, since the Landing Craft carrying it happened, through a miscalculation, to be the first to touch down on the beach.

The REME were responsible also for the design and production of an armoured amphibian tractor. This was based on the Caterpillar D8 and also did useful work, similar to that of the BARV, on the Normandy beaches, although it did not have the same submersible capacity.

Matilda Dozer— with the Australian Armoured Corps   [*Australian War Memorial*

Tank Bulldozers

For clearance of earthworks and other obstacles in the battle area and for various other earthmoving tasks under fire, several of the main types of tank in British service during World War II were converted to take Bulldozer attachments. The earliest of these were the turretless Valentine Dozer and the Matilda Dozer, although the latter type probably performed its most useful service with the Australian Armoured Corps near the end of the war in the Pacific theatre in 1945. The Matilda retained its turret and main armament, as did the Churchill AVRE when fitted with the bulldozer blade.

The largest production of tank bulldozers was, however, on Crusader and Centaur chassis and these were converted from gun tanks by the MG car factory at Abingdon of Nuffield Mechanisations. The turrets were removed and a square cupola was built on for the vehicle commander. The same pattern of girder structure was added to the sides of both types of vehicles to take the arms holding the bulldozer blade and in both cases the blade was raised or lowered by means of a block and tackle operated, via a tripod jib on the front, by a winch in the fighting compartment.

The work of Centaur Dozers, in particular, in clearing a passage for armour through rubble-strewn German towns after the Rhine crossing came in for special praise. One unusual job for a Crusader Dozer in the United Kingdom was in removing crates of live bombs from the area following a fire at a Royal Ordnance Factory in 1945. This tank was fitted with a special grab, an armour plate was added in front of the dozer blade and the front of the tank was heavily sandbagged.

Centaur Dozer

[*Imperial War Museum*

Two further types of dozers, built late in the War, were on the Alecto chassis with gun omitted (a light vehicle suited to airborne operation), and on the Crusader Gun Tractor chassis. In both these models, neither of which went into quantity production, the bulldozer blades were operated by hydraulic rams.

Part 4

SELF-PROPELLED GUNS
& CARRIERS

Universal Carriers coming ashore at Salerno, Italy, in 1943

Development

THE EARLY IDEAS in Britain for a cross-country fighting vehicle eventually crystallised to produce the tank—in essence a cannon- or machine gun-armed tracklaying armoured tractor. Before this, however, although the desirability of the tracklaying form had emerged fairly soon, thoughts on the tactical use of such a vehicle had encompassed both armoured infantry carriers as well as self-propelled mountings for artillery. Both these functions had been considered in the early Admiralty Landship Committee designs of 1915.

Once the tank, in the form set by "Mother" and Mark I was chosen, production facilities did not allow much diversion to other types of tracked fighting vehicles beyond the Gun Carrier Mark I, the infantry and cargo carrier Tank Mark IX (both of which used many components of the normal tank series), and the Newton tractor which, had the War not ended when it did, would have been mass produced, using the facilities of the automotive industry rather than heavy engineering.

After the end of World War I when more time was available, many interesting experimental vehicles were built for the War Office both by the government Tank Design Department and later by industrial armaments concerns. Tracked chassis were experimented with as artillery transporters; self-propelled mountings; artillery tractors; infantry weapons carriers and so on. Advanced features, like built-in amphibious capability and track warping steering were tried out, but the vehicles in each class which were finalised for production were fairly conventional in their technical specifications.

This main types, with which this Part is concerned, to emerge by 1928 from the experimental stage, were the Birch self-propelled 18pr guns, the Carden-Loyd Mark VI carrier and the Dragon artillery tractor. The Birch Guns (evolved from transporter vehicles—from which the weapons could be demounted) were well-tried in field exercises but were eventually abandoned through a change in policy rather than any particular technical shortcomings.

The Carden-Loyd, from its origin as a one man "tankette" was developed into a family of vehicles using the same chassis and performing as infantry machine gun, mortar and anti-tank vehicles and artillery light field gun tractors. The Carden-Loyd Mark VI after having given excellent service (and incidentally introducing many foreign armies to mechanisation) was superseded in 1935 by the bigger, more powerful Vickers carrier, but most of the various tactical functions established by the Carden-Loyd had their counterpart in the World War II Universal Carrier series which evolved from the Vickers Carrier.

The Dragons of 1928, built on chassis comparable in dimensions to the Vickers Medium Tanks, were used for towing both field and medium artillery but were soon joined by a series of Light Dragons (sharing mechanical features with Light Tanks) which were faster, smaller and better adapted for field artillery traction.

Of these three types of tracked vehicles—self propelled guns, infantry carriers and Dragons—only the carriers enjoyed an unbroken line of development in the British Army from the late 1920s through to the end of World War II.

No self-propelled field guns were in use by the British Army at the outbreak of war and none was in the course of development; not until nearly two years later was work again started on a field self-propelled mounting. Following this, increasing importance was allotted to the design and production of both 25pr field gun and heavy anti-tank self-propelled carriages. Much greater attention was, by the end of the War, given to the design of proper chassis rather than slightly modifying existing tank chassis.

The Dragons—both Medium and Light—were obsolescent in 1939 and were being supplanted by wheeled vehicles with multi-wheel drive. The advantages of this change in policy at the time of increasingly urgent rearmament were in quicker mass production of the less complex wheeled artillery tractors which also needed less training for new recruits in driving and maintenance. Also, in Western Europe, at any rate, tracked tractors for artillery did not offer enormous advantages over four-wheel-drive lorries in most situations, but there was later a reversion to tracked artillery tractors when Universal, Loyd, Windsor and T16 carriers in turn were employed for towing light anti-tank guns. Late in the War tank chassis were converted into tractors for 17pr anti-tank guns, although mainly for special missions.

The Vickers Carrier was of such excellent basic design that it continued in production—as Bren Carrier, Universal Carrier and other variants—unaltered in essentials throughout World War II, although the needs of the many new functions it was called upon to undertake brought its laden weight at times to $1\frac{1}{2}$ tons more than its originally designed $3\frac{1}{4}$ tons.

Two types from the past to be revived in the British Army in World War II were tracked amphibious carriers and armoured personnel carriers. Amphibious qualities were called for in various tanks and carriers immediately following the Great War but experimental work was given up after a few years and the British

Universal Carriers in Burma, 1944

[*Imperial War Museum*]

236

A Bishop firing at night   [*Imperial War Museum*

Ronson Carrier flamethrowers in action during an exercise   [*Imperial War Museum*

Neptune and Argosy of 1944/5 owed more in concept to American designs than any earlier work carried out in the United Kingdom. Infantry casualties in Normandy in 1944 stressed the need for armoured protection for infantry moving up in the battle area and turretless tank and SP gun chassis were converted into "Kangaroo" armoured personnel carriers in British and Canadian workshops.

It is interesting to see that in the post-war British Army the process of standardisation has again brought together with the same basic chassis types of vehicles which in the past have had features in common. The basic vehicle of the current (1969) FV432 series is an armoured personnel carrier comprising the functions of the wartime Kangaroos and Universal Carriers and which is adaptable to mortar, ambulance, recovery, radar and guided weapons roles, and much of the basic chassis and running gear is shared with that of the Abbot SP 105mm gun. Both the APC and the Abbot have built-in amphibious qualities.

Universal Carriers climbing up to Centuripe, Sicily, 1943   [*Imperial War Museum*

Nomenclature

SERVICE DESIGNATIONS are included in the appropriate places in the text in this book, but in connection with the many experimental vehicles that did not receive service designations which are referred to, it should be explained that the War Office General Staff specifications in the "B" series covered Dragons, Tractors and Carriers and the "C" series (of which there was only one example), self-propelled mountings. In the example B6E1, the B6 signified the specification (for a Dragon chassis to transport the 18pr field gun) and E1 was the first vehicle built to this specification. B6E2 was the second vehicle produced to meet the same requirement but with some different features. Hence, in these GS series, the suffixes E1, E2, and so on, always denoted *individual* experimental vehicles, which before 1930 did not receive a WD number.

The full ordnance designations for self-propelled guns in the earlier part of World War II were very cumbersome—for example, "Mounting, Valentine, 25pr Gun, Mark I on Carrier, Valentine, 25pr Gun Mark I" for what was more commonly known as SP 25pr—Bishop.

A new War Office specification series for self-propelled guns was commenced with SP1 for the SP 17pr Valentine mounting (Archer) of 1942. SP2 which followed was Avenger, SP3—Alecto and SP4 a projected 32pr Sp mounting.

The output of Carriers during World War II was enormous and nearly all had Ford V-8 engines of either British, Canadian or US manufacture, so a ready means of identifying the engine type in the designations was introduced, with various suffixes to denote alternatives in mechanical specification or form of hull construction. The Mark number indicated differences in the basic design, layout and/or stowage of the vehicle itself. The most important of these descriptive letters or numbers were:

> No 1—Carrier with British-built Ford V-8 engine
> No 2, No 2A—Carrier with US-built Ford V-8 engine
> No 3—Carrier with Canadian-built Ford V-8 engine
> Z (following No)—Carrier with US-built axles
> W (following No)—Carrier with welded hull
> * (following Mark No)—Canadian-built Carrier

Gun Carrier, Mk I

Weight:	34 tons (with gun)	Armour:	8mm
Length:	35ft 5in (29ft 9in without tail)	Armament:	1 × 60pr gun or
Width:	8ft 1½in		1 × 6in howitzer
Height:	9ft 4in	Engine:	Daimler, 105hp
Speed:	3.7mph	Crew:	4 plus gun detachment
Range:	35 miles		

The state of the Western Front in 1916 after a year of trench warfare made it very difficult to bring up artillery and ammunition over shelled, entrenched ground and this was particularly noticeable at Verdun early in the year, when the Germans were unable to keep up the initial momentum of their offensive for this reason. Major Gregg of the Metropolitan Carriage, Wagon and Finance Company suggested that a gun-carrying tank, able to transport medium artillery and ammunition, should be built. A design was ready by April 1916 and in June an order for fifty was approved by Lloyd George. The first Gun Carrier was completed in January 1917 by the Metropolitan CW&F Co at Oldbury. Most of the balance of the order were built by Kitson & Co at Leeds and 48 were ready by July and sent to France. The last two of the batch of fifty were completed as salvage vehicles.

Mechanically, the Gun Carrier Mark I was based on Tank, Mark I, although to accommodate the gun a central compartment was left clear and the driver and brakesman were carried in small armoured cabs in the front, one at either side. The engine, transmission and even the steering tail wheels were used in the Tank, although the latter were later abandoned. Driving control also needed the services of four men, the other two crew members who operated the secondary gears being accommodated in the body of the machine. The maximum speed—about 3½mph—was about the same as Tank Mark I but the greater length of track in contact with the ground made it more sluggish to manœuvre than the tank. The gun, either a 60pr or a 6in howitzer with wheels removed, was winched on a skid platform into the vehicle through the front, so that when the weapon was secured it pointed forwards. It could be fired from the vehicle in this position although there were some practical difficulties in employing the 60pr in this way. Mounted 6in howitzers were used on a few occasions to shell German positions at night from different locations. The apparent presence of a number of unlocated guns was a source of puzzlement to the enemy at this time of static warfare, when every feature of the opposing positions was recorded in detail on large scale maps. In general, however, the Gun Carriers were used more for the carriage of ammunition and supplies than transporting artillery and in the summer of 1918 the two Gun Carrier Companies, each with 24 Gun Carriers, were permanently converted into supply companies.

The Gun Carriers, Salvage, referred to above, were similar in appearance to the standard machines but the twin armoured cabs at the front were eliminated (incidentally, these were absent in the original design of the Gun Carrier) and a revolving jib was mounted at the front. The two built were sent to France where they performed useful work. A Priestman steam-powered excavator, with grab was also mounted on a modified Gun Carrier chassis.

Gun Carrier, Mark I, carrying a 60pr gun   [*Imperial War Museum*

240

Gun Carrier, Mark II
—wooden mockup

A Gun Carrier, Mark II was designed in 1917 although, apart from a wooden mock-up, was not built. It was similar in form to the Mark V tank, with overall tracks. The 6in howitzer or 60pr gun (complete with wheels) was carried at the rear, hauled into position by means of block and tackle apparatus mounted on the roof of the vehicle and attached to the trail of the carriage. A Mark II Salvage vehicle based on the Mark V tank was also projected at this time although, likewise, was never built.

It is appropriate to mention here the interesting series of "Emplacement Destroyers" which were designed in 1916 as a private venture by Col R. E. B. Crompton following his work for the Landship Committee. Four different types—ED1, ED1A, ED2 and ED3 were designed, all except the last having two sets of Killen Strait tracks in tandem and all were to be powered by two 38hp Lanchester engines. They were intended to carry 4.5in howitzers (two in the case of ED1A). Each layout differed, but in all of them, the howitzer was carried in the vehicle so that the muzzle projected through armour plate at the front, through which it could be fired. Only scale models of these vehicles were built: probably because, apart from any mechanical disadvantages in the Crompton machines that may have emerged, once production of the "Mother" series of tanks was embarked on it was obviously easier to build any gun carrying vehicles using as many of the same components as possible, and the Gun Carriers, Mark I were the result.

Birch Guns

DATA FOR Mountings, SP, QF, 18pr, Mks IA-ID

Weight:	12 tons	Armour:	—
Length:	19ft 4in	Armament:	1 × 18pr gun
Width:	8ft 0in	Engine:	Armstrong-Siddeley 82hp
Height:	8ft 5in	Crew:	6
Speed	13.5mph	Range:	150 miles

The first tanks ever to be ordered from Vickers-Armstrongs Ltd were three Light "Tropical" Tanks—a War Office contract for these, to be tested against tanks built by the Royal Ordnance Factory, was awarded in 1921.

Numbers one and two of the Vickers tanks did not come up to expectations and the War Office instructed that the third vehicle was to be completed instead as an 18pr gun Transporter. This transporter did not resemble the tanks (which were roughly of the appearance of the wartime Marks I-V, with the addition of a dome turret) in any way although the same tracks and suspension units were used. The engine was re-positioned in the front of the vehicle—like the fresh design by Vickers for a Light Tank (the famous "Vickers Mediums" as they were later known)—and the hull was a low open-topped structure with an open compartment at the rear. This had a downward-opening rear door, through which the 18pr and mounting could be loaded.

A second vehicle with a different engine was built, but trials with both 18pr Transporters (eventually given the experimental designations B6E1 and B6E2) evidently led the War Office to abandon the idea of demountability, and in the next self-propelled artillery carriage, ordered from Vickers at the end of 1923, the mounting was an integral part of the vehicle. The 18pr gun was given all round traverse and could be elevated to 70deg for anti-aircraft fire. In other respects the new vehicle, which was the first type of what came to be known as the "Birch Gun" (after the Master-General of Ordnance, Sir Noel Birch, who was a protagonist of the idea of making the artillery more mobile) resembled the Vickers 18pr Transporter. It was longer, however, and the suspension (road wheels in pairs sprung on vertical coil springs) had extra units added and was improved, together with the tracks, in many ways. The engine—an 82hp Armstrong Siddeley air-cooled unit—was at the front and the final drive sprockets at the rear. This vehicle was issued to the 28th Field Battery of IX Field Brigade, Royal Artillery in 1925 for trials. The weapon showed promise and an order for four further "Birch guns" incorporating modifications was given to Vickers towards the end of the year.

The battery of four new Birch guns of the second type in 1926 were also issued to the IX Field Brigade (20th Field Battery) and were tested extensively over the next few years. The principal external differences between the new vehicles and the first type were the armoured skirting over the suspension, the addition of a gun shield, and the mounting of the 18pr so that the recuperator was now under instead of on top of the barrel. The fire control instruments were improved (and differed in arrangement between all four vehicles) and could be linked to a predictor for anti-aircraft fire.

Vickers 18pr Transporter—rear view

[*Imperial War Museum*

Mounting, SP, QF 18pr, Mark I

[*RAC Tank Museum*

Mounting, SP, QF 18pr—typical of Marks IA-ID

[*F. Mitchell*

Two vehicles of a third and final type of Birch gun were ordered from Vickers in December 1927 and were delivered just over a year later. These do not appear to have been issued to a Royal Artillery unit for field trials (as were the earlier types) and seem to have been regarded as close support tanks rather than self-propelled artillery weapons. They had full all round protection for the gun crew in the form of a large circular armoured structure, incorporating the shield of the 18pr gun, which was not capable of anti-aircraft fire. In trials, these vehicles were associated with Vickers Medium Tanks equipped with 15pr mortars for close support work, and the latter form was chosen for further development for use in the tank battalions: all later British tanks had versions fitted with a mortar or howitzer firing high explosive projectiles to supplement the normal tanks equipped with high velocity guns. Little was heard of the Birch guns after the early 1930s—there were mechanical difficulties arising from lack of power and faults in the design of the steering system—and for various reasons effort in the Royal Artillery was instead concentrated on the development of towed field artillery. The Birch guns were quite capable of improvement into reliable vehicles but this form of field weapon in the British Army was dropped until 1941 when the 25pr s-p Bishop was produced to meet an emergency.

For convenience, the three types of Birch gun that appeared in 1925, 1926 and 1929 have been referred to here as "Birch Guns", 1st, 2nd or 3rd types, respectively, although the official designations for these vehicles was "Mounting, SP, QF 18pr"—Mark I (the first vehicle), Marks IA, IB, IC and ID (the second batch of four), and Mark IE (the last two vehicles).

A contemporary of the Birch guns, although designed for lighter field pieces, was the Light Artillery Transporter built by Sir W. G. Armstrong, Whitworth & Co Ltd in 1924. This vehicle, which carried a 13pr gun (although a 3.7in howitzer could be substituted) had the engine—a 48hp AEC 4-cylinder type—at the rear and the gun mounted low at the front. There was no armour protection for the crew, but the Transporter was designed to be inconspicuous to make it more suitable for close support work. Only the prototype of this experimental machine was built.

Mounting, S.P., Q.F. 18pr, Mark IE   [*Imperial War Museum*

Light Artillery Transporter (1924)   *[Imperial War Museum*

S-P 25pr, **Bishop**

Weight:	17.2 tons		Armour:	60mm/8mm
Length:	18ft 2in		Armament:	1 × 25pr gun
Width:	8ft 7½in		Engine:	AEC diesel, 131hp
Height:	9ft 1in		Crew:	4
Speed:	15mph		Range:	90 miles

SP 25pr Bishop—note sandbags for extra protection   *[Imperial War Museum*

An urgent call from the Middle East in June 1941 for a self-propelled field mounting for the 25pr gun led to the Birmingham Railway Carriage & Wagon Co Ltd being asked to design and produce a prototype mounting on the Valentine tank chassis. This was done with speed and the prototype vehicle was ready for firing trials at Shoeburyness in August, although some delay ensued before a production order was placed—in early November—for one hundred vehicles. The majority of these was delivered by July 1942 when a contract for a further fifty was given, although this appears later to have been cancelled.

This vehicle was known in ordnance nomenclature as "Mounting, Valentine, 25pr Gun Mark I on Carrier, Valentine, 25pr Gun, Mark I", although the name of Bishop was generally used, in conformity with the gunner practice of World War II of giving ecclesiastical names to self-propelled mountings. The gun when mounted had a total traverse of 8deg; elevation was 15deg and depression 5deg. Additional 25pr ammunition was carried in a towed limber.

Nearly all Bishops built were sent to North Africa where some served with the Eighth Army and others with the First Army; they were not very satisfactory and after the Sicily campaign were eventually dropped.

Carrier, Churchill, 3in Gun, Mark I   [*Imperial War Museum*

Carrier, **Churchill, 3in Gun, Mk I**

Weight:	39 tons	Armour	88mm/16mm
Length:	26ft 1in (over gun)	Armament:	1 × 3in (20cwt) gun
	(25ft 2in hull only)	Engine:	Bedford, 350hp
Width:	10ft 8in	Crew:	4
Height:	9ft 1in	Range:	90 miles
Speed:	15.5mph		

This self-propelled mounting was proposed towards the end of 1941 in order to make the best use of an existing supply of guns for Home Defence in the event of invasion of the United Kingdom. The prototype was completed as a matter of urgency by February 1942; trials were satisfactory and 24 vehicles were ordered. This order was increased to 100 when Vauxhall Motors Ltd, design parents and production parents for Churchill tank manufacture, pointed out that a production run could not be taken on such a small number, but the order was finally reduced to 50. The production vehicles were delivered from the end of July 1942 onwards.

The weapon used in the mounting was the 3in AA gun—"Ordnance, 3in, 20cwt Marks III, IIIA and III*"—for which special 12½lb shot was provided for use in the ground role. (For the record, a further 50 of these guns were mounted on 17pr field carriages as anti-tank weapons; half of these was sent to the Middle East and the balance allocated to Home Forces.) The mounting in the front plate of the heightened fighting compartment of the Churchill allowed only a total traverse of 10deg; elevation was 15deg and depression 10deg.

The mechanical details of the Churchill 3in Gun Carrier were the same as the earlier marks of the Churchill tanks and the basic vehicles were produced by manufacturers of the Churchill production group. A leading part in the final assembly of the Gun Carriers was, however, taken by Beyer, Peacock & Co Ltd of Gorton, Manchester.

Later in the War some Churchill Gun Carriers, less guns, were put to other purposes—as experimental carriers for Snake demolition charges, for example.

S-P 25pr, **Sexton**

Weight:	25.4 tons	Armour:	32mm
Length:	19ft 3in	Armament:	1 × 25pr C Mk II or III
Width:	8ft 11in		2 Brownings (unmounted)
Height:	8ft 0in	Engine:	Continental 400 or 484hp
Speed:	25mph	Crew:	6
Range:	180 miles		

This self-propelled mounting for the British 25pr field gun was a major Canadian contribution to British armour: in 1944–5 Sextons formed the most important artillery component in British and Canadian armoured formations. Intended to replace the Bishop and the American-produced Priest, the Sexton was designed by the Canadian Army Engineering Design Branch and the pilot model was completed towards the end of 1942. Production in Canada (at the Montreal Locomotive Works Tank Arsenal) commenced early in the following year and continued until late 1945, when a total of 2,150 had been manufactured.

The chassis of Sexton was based on that of the Canadian medium tank Ram II and the lower hull, including the suspension, engine and transmission, was virtually identical to that of the tank. The upper hull was a fairly simple welded open-topped armoured structure, with the 25pr mounting slightly to left of centre of the front plate and the driver's vision port was at the right. The Ram itself had running gear derived from the US M3 medium tanks, from which the M4 (Sherman) was developed in the United States. The Sherman was later produced also in Canada (known as Grizzly I) and the Sexton during the course of its production reflected various changes (such as replacement of the three-piece bolted hull nose for a single piece structure and re-location of the track guide rollers) made in the design of the Canadian and US tanks.

The 25pr gun had a traverse of 25deg left of centre and 15deg right; elevation of 40deg and depression 9deg. It was primarily intended for indirect fire as a field piece but in addition to the 87 HE and smoke shells carried there were 18 armour piercing projectiles for use against tanks.

Auxiliary armament included two Bren guns—unmounted—and certain vehicles in Europe had the addition of a 0.5in Browning machine gun on a mounting on the left hand front corner of the hull top.

Sextons equipped the field regiments of British and Canadian armoured brigades in the campaign in North West Europe and also in Italy in 1944–5. There was also a version without the gun and equipped with a second No 19 wireless set and other fittings, as a gun position officer's vehicle—Sexton GPO.

Design studies for several other types of self-propelled mountings of 25pr, 17pr, 5.5in, and 3.7in guns were also carried out in Canada and prototypes of a 3.7in (AA) mounting on a Ram chassis were built, although production in quantity was not called for.

SP 25pr Sexton

S-P 17pr, **Archer**

Weight:	16 tons	Armour:	60mm/8mm
Length:	21ft 11in	Armament:	1 × 17pr gun
Width:	9ft 0½in		1 Browning (unmounted)
Height:	7ft 4½in	Engine:	General Motors diesel, 192hp
Speed:	20mph	Crew:	4
Range:	140 miles		

By the middle of 1942 a self-propelled mounting for the new 17pr anti-tank gun was needed and it was at first proposed that the Bishop 25pr S-P mounting—then in production—should be used for this purpose, with the 17pr in place of the field weapon. This proved to be impracticable, however. A design investigation of the Crusader cruiser tank chassis showed that little protection of the 17pr gun and mounting could be provided and it was decided to design an entirely new s-p mounting using the Valentine chassis as a basis. (It may be mentioned here that about 1941 the Valentine had been used for an earlier S-P anti-tank mounting—the 6pr with a shield mounted in the turretless tank. This remained experimental only because it was relatively easy—and much preferable—to redesign the Valentine tank turret to take a 6pr gun.)

A contract for two prototype carriers for the 17pr gun was awarded to Vickers-Armstrongs and the first of these vehicles was completed by March 1943; the gun and mounting was added about a month later and the equipment was tested at Shoeburyness and Larkhill.

SP 17pr Archer—right hand side view   [*Imperial War Museum*

A rearward-facing mounting for the 17pr was adopted, with only limited traverse, and this resulted in a fairly compact design and the advantages of low silhouette to some extent compensated for the lack of all-round traverse. It was also argued that the gun facing rearwards conferred some benefits when it was necessary to get out of a hot spot in a hurry. The upper hull was all-welded and the vertical protection varied between 20mm and 14mm; on some of the later production vehicles a light steel roof was added. The lower hull, engine, transmission and running gear were very much the same as the later models of Valentine tank fitted with the General Motors' 6-cylinder two-stroke diesel engine. The 17pr gun had an elevation of 15deg, depression of 7½deg and a total traverse either side of the centre line of 45deg; 39 rounds were carried. Subsidiary armament was one Bren gun; no permanent mounting was provided for this, although in some vehicles in addition a Browning machine gun was mounted at the front on an A-A mounting.

After various modifications in the design had been agreed, including some rearrangement of the traverse system, inclusion of a new gun sight and redesign of the frontal armour and the engine cooling gills, production went ahead and deliveries began in the first half of 1944. Apart from the two prototypes, a contract for 800 vehicles was given to Vickers-Armstrongs Ltd at Elswick and 665 of these were completed before the end of the War led to cancellation of the balance of the order.

The usual designation for this weapon was "SP 17pr Valentine", although the Royal Artillery name of "Archer" was also used fairly widely, although not consistently.

The Archer was employed by anti-tank regiments in both the North West Europe campaign and, towards the end of the campaign, in Italy. User opinion varied. One British regiment in Italy (mainly equipped with M-10s, and after somewhat limited experience) was strongly critical of the armour—inadequate against mortar fire, the limited traverse and the fact that the driver had to be removed before the gun could go into action. However, the vehicle itself was very reliable and the 17pr gun a powerful weapon and the Archer was put to useful employment. At the end of the War and for some years after, SP 17pr Valentines were used in the new organisation of Divisional Anti-Tank Regiments, Royal Armoured Corps, when this role was taken over from the Royal Artillery.

SP 17pr A.30—Avenger

[*Imperial War Museum*

S-P 17pr A30, **Avenger**

Weight:	31 tons	Armour:	—
Length:	28ft 7in (over gun)	Armament:	1 × 17pr gun
Width:	10ft 0in	Engine:	Rolls Royce Mekar 600hp
Height:	8ft 3in	Crew:	4–5
Speed:	32mph	Range:	90 miles

This anti-tank self-propelled mounting was developed late in the War and, in fact, the first production vehicles were not ready until December 1945, after the War was over. This design was an improvement on the SP 17pr Valentine, which lacked all round traverse, and was more or less a completely British equivalent of the American SP 17pr M-10 which had been supplied in numbers to the Royal Artillery, where it was popular.

Existing components were used to a great extent, notably the hull, engine, transmission and running gear, which were slightly modified from those of the Challenger 17pr gun tank (built to the GS specification A30). Avenger was an artillery weapon and not a tank, however, and the turret, which had all round traverse, lacked a co-axial machine gun and had only a light splinter-proof roof, spaced a few inches above the top line.

Development of the Avenger was entrusted to the Birmingham Railway Carriage & Wagon Co Ltd which had performed the initial design work on the Challenger. A contract for 500 of these s-p guns was given to the company, although only a small proportion of this order was, in fact, completed.

SP 95mm Howitzer Alecto

[Imperial War Museum

S-P 95mm, **Alecto**

Weight:	8 tons	Armour:	10mm
Length:	18ft 1in (over gun)	Armament:	1 × 95mm howitzer Mk III
Width:	8ft 10in	Engine:	Meadows, 158hp
Height:	6ft 2¼in	Crew:	4
Speed:	30mph	Range:	120 miles

A General Staff requirement made in April 1942 called for a light self-propelled infantry gun which would be able to give close support to infantry in the attack and be a readily available form of artillery fire power for the use of infantry commanders. The weapon chosen for this purpose was the 95mm howitzer, already being developed as a close support weapon for tanks (it was later carried in certain Churchills, Centaurs and Cromwells) and a carrier was designed for it by Vickers-Armstrongs using the Harry Hopkins (Light Tank Mark VIII) as a basis.

The most interesting feature of the Harry Hopkins (and its predecessor the Light Tank Mark VII, Tetrarch) was the method of steering whereby all road wheels could be turned in an arc, curving the track so that the vehicle could be driven round gentle corners, with skid steering coming into use only for abrupt turns. This feature was retained in Alecto, the new s-p 95mm mounting, where, both for general manœuvrability and in aligning the gun, it was a desirable asset.

The armour of Alecto was on a 10mm basis and was all welded. The fighting compartment was open and the gun mounted low, right at the front, with the commander (at the right of the vehicle) loader and gunner immediately behind. The driver sat behind the gun crew in the centre of the vehicle in a small raised compartment.

A contract for 300 Alectos was placed with Vickers-Armstrongs but because of later indecision over the original role, production never really got under way and only a small proportion of the 300 was actually completed before the War ended, and Alecto was never used in action. It was eventually decided that Alecto should be used as a reconnaissance vehicle for the Royal Armoured Corps—for which its low silhouette and better cross-country performance than an armoured car and good speed made it quite well suited—and some of the pilot vehicles for this role were fitted with 6pr guns in place of the 95mm howitzers. Experiments also took place with the Alecto (less gun) as a field artillery tractor for the 25pr gun and limber.

[*RAC Tank Museum*

Carrier, 2pr (40mm)—Vickers-Armstrongs commercial prototype

Carrier, Armoured, 2pr (1937)   [*Imperial War Museum*

S-P Mountings on Carrier Chassis

An interesting variety of mountings for the 2pr anti-tank gun was tried out on different chassis of the Bren and Loyd Carrier types. These had varying degrees of success, but no further attempts were made to mount the 2pr after 1943 by which time it was obsolescent as an anti-tank gun.

The earliest of these designs, which appeared around the beginning of 1935, was a Vickers-Armstrongs commercial project and carried a 40mm Vickers gun on an open mounting (without gun shield) behind the driver's armoured compartment. The gun was pivoted in the centre of the vehicle and theoretically had an all round traverse. However, the mounting incorporated a trail with the gunner's seat and this effectively limited the arcs of fire to forwards only, unless the gunner were to leave the vehicle to serve the gun. This vehicle is of interest as being the earliest of the type of chassis which culminated in the Universal Carrier series.

The commercial design was followed by one built for the War Office in 1937 and consisted of a 2pr Mark IX or X mounted in a Carrier, MG, Armoured of the same basic layout. The gun was, however, mounted behind a fixed shield and had a limited traverse of 20deg either side of centre. The frontal armour for the driver and, beside him, the commander was extended either side of the vehicle for about two-thirds of its length, but no rear protection was provided for the gunner and loader in the rear compartment. This carrier was experimented with in 1937–8 but the design was not adopted for further production—amongst other disadvantages the shape of the shield was found, when the vehicle was moving, to cause dust or sand to be drawn into the rear compartment so as to make difficult the operation of the gun.

What amounted to a revival of the same idea was built by the Canadians in 1942 on a Canadian-built Carrier, Universal and known as "Tank Hunter".

253

The 2pr gun was mounted in the same position but this time with a shield (of the 6pr anti-tank gun pattern) moving with the mounting. Traverse was limited, for practical purposes, by the restriction on movement of the gun crew who served the gun from the rear compartments of the carrier either side of the engine.

A wider traverse was attained in a 2pr mounting built on a specially adapted Loyd Carrier, known unofficially as the "Stacey-Loyd" and officially as Carrier, 2pr Mounting, Mark I. The engine of the Loyd carrier was moved forwards to a position just behind the driver's compartment, leaving a flat platform on the rear half of the vehicle. The 2pr gun, complete with front shield and hinged side shields was mounted on this platform from which it had a traverse of 225deg in an arc to the rear and sides. The design was finally abandoned in December 1942 after production of only a limited quantity had been undertaken. The Loyd Carrier was used also for a 25pr field gun s-p mounting in which the gun, without shield, was mounted low at the front, pointing forwards. This vehicle was experimental only.

In Australia in 1942 work was carried out independently on self-propelled mountings for the 2pr anti-tank gun. Two models were built, one using a standard Australian pattern Carrier Universal on which the gun was mounted on a pivot immediately behind the driver's compartment. The mounting could be raised by means of a hydraulic jack so that the gun had a 360deg traverse, although this was limited from the practical point of view by the fact that for fire outside a forward arc the gunner would have to leave the protection of his compartment. In the lowered position the gun crew were fairly well protected both by the carrier's armour and the gun shield, but only a very limited traverse was possible. The other Australian 2pr carrier consisted of a lengthened chassis specially built up from Australian Universal Carrier components: the front idler wheels were placed further forward than on the standard carriers and the engine was brought forward to the front left hand side of the vehicle. The 2pr gun was

Carrier, 2pr Mounting, Mark I ("Stacey-Loyd") [*Imperial War Museum*]

Carrier, 2pr (Aust.)

Carrier, Bren with Smith Gun

mounted at the rear and had a full 360deg traverse, although this was limited in depression in the forward arc by the front hull of the carrier. The whole equipment was comparable to the United Kingdom-built Loyd s-p 2pr. Some of the disadvantages were that the chassis was found to be overloaded and as a consequence underpowered, slow and mechanically unreliable and the gun crew were felt to lack adequate protection, so that, like the Carrier 2pr (Australian) with Hydraulic Hoist, it did not go into quantity production for the Australian Army.

It is of interest to mention two improvised gun mountings on Carriers—one British and one German. The 3in Ordnance Smooth Bore—commonly known as the Smith Gun—which could fire a range of projectiles from 3in mortar bombs to 6pr anti-tank shells, was mounted in the gunner's compartment of a modified Carrier, Bren, with a limited forward traverse. The high frontal armour at first used was later modified to reduce the height. This vehicle was intended for home defence but, as far as is known, it was never built in quantity.

The German conversion made use of Bren and Scout Carriers, large numbers of which were captured in France in 1940. The 3.7cm Pak 35 or 36 complete with shield was mounted fairly high behind the driver's compartment where it had an all round traverse, although, like the similar British and Australian conversions, this was limited at most times to forward fire only.

Newton Tractor (with Ford engine)

Newton Tractor

The Newton Tractor was a cross-country supply vehicle or infantry carrier designed to be mass produced at low cost: about 22,000 were planned to be built in the United Kingdom and the United States but the Armistice in 1918 caused work on them to be ceased after between 200 and 300 had been completed.

The design was kept as simple as possible and was based on standard motor vehicle engines and components—Fords in England and Studebaker and Buick in the USA were manufacturers involved in the scheme. The tracks were conveyer chain links, and boiler plate was used largely in the construction. In layout the Newton Tractor consisted of a large open cargo compartment at the front and the engine mounted at the rear with the driver sitting behind it on a farm tractor type of seat. Immediately below him was the transmission to the track-driving sprockets. The road wheels, as in the wartime tanks, were unsprung. The first experimental type of Newton Tractor differed in many details from the final model but notably in that the top line of the tracks was depressed, apparently in order to facilitate side loading of cargo.

An outgrowth of the Newton Tractor was a fully armoured vehicle known as the Studebaker Tank—this never got beyond the experimental stage.

Early Experimental Carriers and Dragons

Before development of Carriers and Dragons settled down in the early 1930s into progressive improvement of the Vickers-Carden-Loyd and Vickers-Armstrongs series of tracked vehicles, a variety of different types was experimented with.

The first post-war cross-country supply vehicle was the little Ammunition Carrier (or Carrier, 1 ton, SAA) with a Ford engine, designed by Lt-Col P. H. Johnson's Tank Design Department. Two were built by the Royal Ordnance Factory between 1921 and 1922. The hull was watertight, with a curved deck, and propulsion in water was effected by a single screw at the rear. The suspension of the Ammunition Carrier was of the cable type as used by Lt-Col Johnson in the Light Infantry Tank, in which all the bogie wheels on each side were sprung by means of a single cable tensioned by one spring only. Steering was assisted by curving the tracks through movement of the front idler wheels. The amphibious capabilities of the Carrier were successfully demonstrated on Fleet Pond near Aldershot in June 1922 but following the closing down of the Tank Design Department at the end of the year, both Ammunition Carriers were scrapped.

Armstrong-Siddeley Motors Ltd was given a contract in 1922 to design and supply a Light Dragon. This vehicle, known as B1E1 was followed by a second, B1E2, in 1924. Both Dragons employed a steering system involving track curving by pivoting the front "horns" carrying the idler wheels—this was a development of the method used on the Ammunition Carrier designed by the Tank Design Department. In fact, when that establishment closed down some members of the design staff joined Armstrong Siddeley Motors.

257

The function which these Dragons were to perform does not seem to have been defined very closely and the carrying of supplies and towing 18pr field artillery were considered. Also the 1924 Dragon was at one stage equipped as a Machine Gun Carrier, with two Vickers machine guns on pillar mountings, suitable for use against either terrestrial or air targets.

The 1922 Dragon was built to a specification calling for it to be able to float. The engine was an Armstrong-Siddeley air-cooled eight-cylinder Vee-type, but in the 1924 Dragon a water-cooled four-cylinder engine was fitted with a front radiator and in this model floatation was not required.

A third Dragon, B1E3, was built by Armstrong-Siddeley's in 1925. This was similar in overall layout to the 1924 model but was larger and there was a reversion to an air-cooled engine—this time a 60hp four-cylinder type. The suspension, including provision for track warping, was much like that of the 1924 Dragon and consisted of bogies independently sprung but, because of the increased length of the vehicle, there were ten of them each side instead of eight.

Unfortunately, no satisfactory way could be found of preventing the Armstrong-Siddeley Dragons, with their track curving devices, shedding their tracks and none of these vehicles ever reached a production stage. The 1925 Dragon was eventually handed over to Roadless Traction Ltd, Lt-Col Johnson's firm (formed when he left the Army), to be experimentally fitted with tracks of his design.

In the meantime, in 1924 the Royal Ordnance Factory had completed an experimental Dragon to specification B1E4. The purpose of this vehicle is not clear but its main feature was good trench crossing ability for its size. Two large rollers extended at the front of the vehicle, together with a pair of laterally grooved rollers at the rear being driven by a take off from the main drive at the rear track sprockets. These rear rollers would assist the vehicle in climbing out of ditches. Called the "Dragon PT", the initials standing for "protected track", this vehicle had, as its name implied, the track fully enclosed. The bogie wheels, excepting the first and last, were sprung in pairs on vertical coil springs—a system similar to that of the Vickers medium tanks.

In the efforts to decide on the best form of Machine Gun Carrier, widely differing types of vehicles, ranging from unarmoured half tracks to tanks, were

Ammunition Carrier (1922)   [*RAC Tank Museum*

Armstrong Siddeley Dragon (1924)   [*RAC Tank Museum*

Carrier, MG, No 1 (1926)   [*Imperial War Museum*

experimented with in the late 1920s. The largest of these was the 6¾-ton "Carrier MG No 1" of 1926 which was originally intended, when ordered in 1925 from the Royal Ordnance Factory, as a cheap, three-man tank. The two Vickers machine guns, ball-mounted in turrets at the front and rear of the vehicle, were not readily demountable and experiments proved this rather clumsy vehicle to be no more acceptable as a MG Carrier than it was as a light tank.

In the summer of 1928 a Section of 2nd Battalion Kings Royal Rifle Corps

Dragon PT (BIE4)   [*RAC Tank Museum*

Carrier, MG, Armoured, 30cwt, Burford-Kegresse   [*RAC*]*Tank Museum*

was equipped experimentally with armoured Burford half tracks (officially designated later "Carriers, MG, Armoured, 30cwt, Burford-Kegresse). Lorries of various makes fitted with Kegresse rubber tracks at the rear were popular in the Army as cross-country vehicles at this time, and the Burford MG Carrier was a standard chassis armoured by Vickers. The prototype had one Vickers 0.303in water-cooled machine gun on a ring mounting (of the type used in aircraft), although in the later vehicles twin machine guns were fitted. Two other sections of 2nd Bn KRRC were equipped respectively with unarmoured 15cwt Crossley-Kegresse half tracks and full-tracked Carden-Loyd Mark Vs with auxiliary wheels. The latter were considered the most satisfactory vehicles for infantry MG Carriers from several points of view—not least their inconspicuousness—and experiments with both the Burfords and the Crossleys were discontinued.

Carden-Loyd Tankettes

The Carden-Loyd Mark VI Carrier, which was the predecessor of the well-known Universal series of carriers of World War II, was itself descended from the "one man tanks" of 1925–6.

The concept of mechanised infantrymen armed with automatic weapons advancing under fire in small cross-country armoured vehicles had occured to Colonel G. le Q. Martel and, being a practical engineer, he himself built and completed a small one-man tank in pursuit of this idea. The same idea had occured—independently—to Mr John Carden of the Loyd garage, who also produced a prototype one-man tank. Once publicity was given to Martel's vehicle, Carden in conjunction with Loyd produced further and improved models.

Martel's home-built prototype was followed by an improved model built to his design by Morris Motors and subsequently by two-man tanks on similar lines. Eight of the latter were ordered for the Army (together with eight Carden-Loyds) and were used with the Mechanised Force in 1927, not as intended—as mechanised infantry—but as scout light tanks with the reconnaissance group. As machines they were more successful than the contemporary Carden-Loyds but the Morris-Martels faded from the scene since neither the inventor nor Morris Motors had the time to spare to further their development. Carden, on the other hand, had improved his original design through a series of models and was able to continue development steadily. The Carden type following the prototype was a small tractor with an open top box hull with the engine at the rear. The suspension consisted of 14 small road wheels each side attached to a frame sprung on coil springs. There was no cover above shoulder level for the driver.

The following model, known as Carden-Loyd Mark I, was similar in layout but a 3-sided rotatable shield (open at the rear), in which a stripped Lewis light machine gun was mounted, enclosed the driver's head and shoulders. Another version of this vehicle, known as Carden-Loyd Mark I* had the addition of a tricycle wheel device, consisting of two pneumatic-tyred wheels, one either side near the front of the hull and a small steerable solid-tyred wheel at the rear between the track horns. These wheels could be lowered and used in place of the tracks for faster running on roads, also saving track wear. Power transmission on wheels was by means of chain drive to the two large side wheels and a top speed of 35mph could be attained; on tracks it was 24mph.

The Carden-Loyd Mark II was very similar in layout to the Mark I but the suspension was improved in that the fourteen small wheels each side were replaced by four larger rubber-tyred track road wheels. The Mark III was the same but was a wheel-cum-track machine with a tricycle similar to that of Mark I*.

At about this time the first two-man Carden-Loyd appeared. The general layout and suspension were similar to those of the Carden-Loyd Mark I but the vehicle was wider, lower and had no turret, the gunner sitting at the right-hand side beside the driver.

Carden-Loyd Mark IV was an improved two-man model with a new six-sided hull designed to give better protection. Track suspension was on the lines of that of the Mark II. In its final form the Mark IV (like its predecessors only a prototype vehicle) had leaf springs, attached to the track frames, for each pair of bogie wheels, but it is not clear if it had these springs originally. Later, this model also had the addition of five return rollers each side on the upper track supporting frame.

A reasonably advanced state of development had by now been reached with the Carden-Loyd series, which had already been tried out experimentally by the Army, and a contract was given to the Carden-Loyd firm at the end of 1926 for eight machines to be ready for use in the Mechanised Force manœuvres in 1927. The eight Tankettes, Carden-Loyd Mark V (as they became known) were two-man vehicles with hulls like the Mark IV but with tricycle wheel-cum-track undercarriages similar to that of Mark III.

The eight Carden-Loyd Tankettes were employed in the 1927 manœuvres in the same way as the Morris-Martels—as scout light tanks—but in the following year they took part in experiments conducted by the 2nd Battalion KRRC to find out the best type of armoured machine gun carrier for the infantry machine gun company. A section of four Carden-Loyds were fitted out as machine gun carriers, with Vickers 0.303in water-cooled machine guns mounted so that they could, if necessary, be fired from the vehicle; one Carden-Loyd was in reserve and a sixth machine was the section commander's vehicle. This had a shield in

Tankette, Carden-Loyd Mark V

front of the gunner's position and a mounting suitable only for a light machine gun. In 1928, the pneumatic wheels had been removed from some of the Carden-Loyd Mark Vs, although all still retained the operating screw jacks for the wheel-cum-track equipment.

The Carden-Loyds were judged to be satisfactory both as machines and in the function as machine gun carriers and towards the end of 1927 the first of several orders were given by the War Office for a similar model, but improved in detail, the Carden-Loyd Mark VI. As a matter of interest, some or all of the Carden-Loyd Mark Vs which had been first used in the 1927 manœuvres were later rebuilt to the same standard as the Mark VI, and took their place in the Army, re-designated Mark V*, alongside the newer vehicles as 0.303in Machine Gun Carriers.

Carden-Loyd Mk VI

DATA FOR STANDARD VEHICLE (MG CARRIER)

Weight:	1.5 tons	Armour:	9mm/5mm
Length:	8ft 1in	Armament:	1 0.303in Vickers mg
Width:	5ft 9in	Engine:	Ford, 40hp
Height:	4ft 0in	Crew:	2
Speed:	25mph	Range:	90 miles

The patent rights of Carden and Loyd were acquired by Vickers-Armstrongs in 1928, the contracts for Carden-Loyd vehicles already placed were taken over and all subsequent orders fulfilled by Vickers. John Carden joined Vickers as the principal designer for light tanks and tractors.

The improved model of the Carden-Loyd, which became known as Mark VI, was very similar externally to the eight tankettes used in the 1927 manœuvres. The main point of difference was that the tricycle wheel device was eliminated entirely—the road speed on tracks was found to be adequate and improvement in design had produced a short pitch track which wore much better than the earlier types. Secondly, the road wheels were sprung in pairs on leaf springs attached to the underside of the track frames. The most obvious of the various other minor improvements over the Mark V was the addition of a curved plate to protect the differential casing at the front of the vehicle. The four-cylinder Ford Model T type engine was retained—as in the Mark V—between the driver and the gunner, which must have made the Carden-Loyd a warm vehicle for its crew. Also, the small six sided armoured engine and crew compartment, and the hull generally, remained as before.

Between the end of 1927 and 1930 about 270 Carden-Loyd Mark VIs were supplied to the British Army. They appear to have been delivered ex-works in a standard form without mountings and only when received by the Army were fitted out for the function they were to perform. Most, in fact, were destined for the infantry as 0.303in Vickers Machine Gun Carriers but the list of official designations included Carrier 0.303in MG, CL, Mk VI; Carrier 0.5in MG, CL, Mk VI; Carrier Mortar, CL, Mk VI; Carrier Smoke, CL, Mk VI; Tractor 3.7in How, CL, Mk VI; Tractor 0.8in MG, CL, Mk VI.

Of the various vehicles, the 3.7in howitzer and the 0.8in anti-tank machine gun were on towed tracked mountings and the crews were carried in tracked trailers towed by the Carden-Loyd. In addition, there were two types of specially designed GS trailer and an artillery forward observation officers' trailer.

Several variants of the basic Carden-Loyd Mark VI existed. The vehicles (armed with 0.303in Vickers machine guns) used by some battalions of the Royal Tank Corps for training purposes, pending receipt of real light tanks, had an open rectangular structure added at the rear (apparently to enable them to be more readily identified as simulated tanks) and prototypes of the Indian Pattern (B11E3 and B11E4) had overhead protection. A completely enclosed version of the Carden-Loyd Mark VI had hinged pyramid-shaped head covers for the driver and gunner and numbers of this type were supplied commercially by Vickers-Armstrongs to several countries. Another model, not used by the British Army, but sold abroad, was a self-propelled 47mm gun mounting.

Amongst the countries supplied by Vickers-Armstrongs with "Carden-Loyd Light Armoured Vehicles"—various types of Carden-Loyd Mark VIs—were Japan, Italy, Bolivia, USSR, Belgium, Czechoslovakia, Chile, Holland, Poland, Portugal and Siam. Carden-Loyds built under licence, or similar vehicles strongly influenced by the Carden-Loyd design, appeared in France, Belgium, Italy, Poland, USSR and Czechoslovakia.

Experimental development for the War Office of the Carden-Loyd Mark VI proceeded on several lines—mainly in fitting alternative engines, in testing the feasibility of a three-man version and in improving the armoured protection. Of the latter, with armour raised in height and better cover for the machine gun mounting, four only of the improved Carden-Loyd—Carrier, 0.303in MG, CL, Mark VIA, were built by Vickers-Armstrongs for the British Army, although twelve similar vehicles were supplied to Canada in 1932. This model had a four-

Carrier, 0.30in MG, CL, Mark VI

[*Vickers Armstrongs*

Carrier, 0.30in MG, CL, Mark VIB   [*Imperial War Museum*

sided upper hull with inward sloping armour in place of the six sided structure
of the Mark VI. Other modifications included two guide rollers each side in
place of the track guide rails. A generally similar version, Carrier, 0.303in
MG, CL, Mark VIB was produced by the Royal Ordnance Factory, which
earlier had built 57 of the Carden-Loyd Mark VIs. This model, of which ten
were supplied to the Army, was much the same in appearance and specification
as the Mark VIA, but the top line of the hull side plates sloped to the rear.

Meadows engines were used in some of the later Carden-Loyd Carriers and
an Armstrong-Siddeley air-cooled engine was tried out in the experimental
model B11E1, which had a hull similar to that of the CL Mark VIA. An experimental three-man version of the Carden-Loyd, B11E10, had the engine
moved over to the left hand side, the driver was in the centre and the third man
was accommodated behind the gunner at the left. The general design of this
vehicle was like that of the Carden-Loyd "Patrol" tank without its turret and, in
fact, its construction appears to have taken the place of a cancelled War Office
experimental order for a number of "Patrol" tanks.

The Carden-Loyd Mark VI was an excellent vehicle, but the desirability
of adding one or more extra men to the crew of the Carrier for various functions
led eventually to the design of a larger model—this turned out as the "Vickers
Carrier" and its enormous progeny of Bren and Universal Carriers, and the like,
of World War II.

Carrier, MG—the 1935 prototype vehicle   [*Vickers Armstrongs*

Carriers—Machine Gun, Bren, Cavalry & Scout

DATA FOR CARRIER, BREN NO 1, MK 1

Weight:	4 tons	Armour:	12mm
Length:	12ft 0in	Armament:	1 Browning mg
Width:	6ft 11in	Engine:	Ford 65hp
Height:	4ft 6in	Crew:	3
Speed:	30mph	Range:	160 miles

By the end of 1934 Vickers-Armstrongs had developed from its long and successful series of Light Tanks and Light Dragons a new chassis for a Carrier in succession to the Carden-Loyd Mark VI type.

The new suspension arrangement used consisted of, each side, one two wheel "Horstmann" type unit with coil springs and behind it a generally similar single wheel unit. The idler wheel was at the front and the drive sprocket at the rear. The interesting feature of this suspension was that the twin wheel units were carried on a cross tube (running through the vehicle) which could be moved sideways, so displacing the tracks laterally for gentle turns. For sharper turns, further movement of the steering wheel operated the track brakes on either side.

The first vehicle using this chassis was built as a commercial project and mounted a Vickers 40mm gun. This machine, which appeared about early 1935, is described more fully elsewhere. It was followed by a machine gun carrier, also built commercially, using the same chassis.

War Office interest became aroused in the potential of the new vehicles and, following discussions with Vickers-Armstrongs on 1st February, 1935, contracts were awarded about two months later for two experimental machines—one to be

Carrier, Bren, No 2, Mark I   [*Imperial War Museum*

Carrier, Cavalry, Mark   [*RAC Tank Museum*

built as a machine gun carrier and the other as a Light Dragon. The latter became known as Dragon, Light Mark III, and is described separately.

The new machine gun carrier built for the War Office had suspension identical with that of the Dragon although both differed in detail from the commercial prototypes—principally in that the front idler wheel was now the same type as the road wheels and the rear bogie unit bracket was cleaned up in design. The superstructure consisted of an armoured compartment for the driver (sitting at the right) and the gunner, behind which were longitudinal seats over the tracks on which the four other members of the crew sat either side of the engine casing, facing inwards. The seats were open in the commercial prototype carrier, but in the War Office experimental vehicle hinged metal covers could be lifted to form backrests. The Vickers 0.303in machine gun was on an open mounting, without a shield, as in the Carden-Loyd Mark VI. Open stowage bins were carried on either side of the front compartment.

After trials, a small contract for a further 13 similar vehicles was given in April 1936. The first production machine gun carriers differed from the prototype mainly in that the armoured compartment was extended the full width of the vehicle, the external bins were eliminated and stowage racks were provided inside the armour. Also, since it had in the meantime been decided not to carry the full crew for ground operation of the Vickers machine gun, a seat was provided for only one man at the rear. For the protection of the gunner a small shield, which moved with the barrel of the gun, was added.

In the next batch of 41 more carriers ordered from Vickers towards the end of 1936 an armoured extension of the gunner's position housed the machine gun, which then projected through an aperture in the front of the armour. These vehicles were designated Carriers, MG No 2, Mark I, the new nomenclature indicating that they were fitted with a more powerful engine. Side armour and a sloping rear plate was added for protection of the third man of the crew.

During 1936 it was decided to produce three further types of carrier— Cavalry, Bren and Scout—to fulfil other functions.

The 0.303in Bren light machine gun was then being introduced into the infantry battalions of the British Army and the Carrier, Bren was intended to take this weapon forward under fire, to be used for support either mounted or dismounted. One vehicle of the first batch of MG Carriers was completed as the prototype Bren Carrier. This vehicle had the same armour arrangement as the second batch of MG Carriers (No 2 Mark I), the main external difference being a hood over the aperture for the Bren gun. Keeping step with the supply of the new light machine guns to the infantry, approximately the latter half of contracts for MG Carriers awarded to some manufacturers in 1937 were completed with Bren Carriers. When the demand for MG Carriers was met later contracts were for Bren Carriers alone.

The prototype of the Carrier, Cavalry Mark I was completed as part of the first production batch of MG Carriers which also included the Bren Carrier prototype. This type of vehicle was intended for a proposed new role for mechanised cavalry units—to carry forward with their weapons cavalrymen who could then dismount rapidly and go into action. For this purpose there were longitudinal seats capable of carrying two or three men each side over the tracks at the rear. To facilitate rapid dismounting, the seats faced outwards and curved shields (wire mesh on the prototype, solid metal on later vehicles) were fitted to protect the men's legs from the tracks and mud etc. To avoid involuntary departure from the vehicle a hinged hand rail could be lowered in front of the seats and a metal framework could be erected to carry canvas overhead protection. The usual light weapons could be mounted at the front in the gunner's compartment which was cut down slightly in height.

268

Carrier, Scout, Mark I   [*Imperial War Museum*

A first contract for 50 Cavalry Carriers was awarded to Nuffield Mechanisations towards the end of 1937, and although some of these vehicles were taken to France with the BEF in 1939–40 they appear only to have been used as personnel carriers and not in action as originally envisaged. This particular idea of using cavalry as a sort of mechanised mounted infantry was soon abandoned—the Cavalry Carriers must have been very uncomfortable and rather dangerous vehicles for the men sitting at the rear to whom they gave no armour protection whatsoever.

The Carrier, Scout Mark I was also intended as a vehicle for mechanised cavalry—a light reconnaissance vehicle for use in divisional cavalry regiments, which were also equipped with light tanks. It was also to be the equipment of infantry motor battalions in armoured divisions. For this job the Scout Carrier carried armament equivalent to a light tank, consisting of a Boys anti-tank rifle in the front compartment, a Bren gun on a pillar anti-aircraft mounting, where it could be operated by the man in the rear compartment, and a 3in smoke discharger on the right hand side of the hull. A wireless set was carried in the back of the rear compartment in some vehicles. As a matter of interest, an early experimental version of the Scout Carrier (which was, in fact, the War Office prototype MG Carrier rebuilt) carried the Bren gun in the front compartment and the anti-tank rifle was mounted on a rail which ran all round the top of the left hand side of the front part of the hull. The Scout Carrier was mechanically identical to the MG, Bren and Cavalry Carriers but the hull arrangement differed slightly—the armour of the rear compartment at the right hand side of the vehicle was square and had a vertical rear plate, unlike the Bren and MMG Carriers, although the frontal armour of the gunner's compartment resembled the latter.

Contracts for a grand total of 667 Scout Carriers was given to Nuffield Mechanisations and Aveling Barford in 1938 and many of the vehicles gave useful service in France in 1939–40 and in the early Desert campaigns.

Carrier, Universal—towing 6pr anti-tank gun   [*Imperial War Museum*

Carriers—Universal, AOP, Mortar and MMG Mk II

DATA FOR CARRIER, UNIVERSAL, NO 2, MK II*

Weight:	3.95 tons	Armour:	12mm
Length:	12ft 4in	Armament:	1 Bren Lmg and/or Boys atr
Width:	6ft 11in	Engine:	Ford 85hp
Height:	5ft 3in	Crew:	4–5
Speed:	32mph	Range:	160 miles

The position that had been reached where four different types of hull were being produced for the same basic vehicle clearly left some scope for a measure of standardisation. The function for which the Cavalry Carrier was designed was not required by 1939 and sufficient Carriers for the Vickers Medium Machine Gun were delivered or on order, but later requirements for Bren and Scout Carriers were met by the design of a new hull suitable for equipment for either of these tasks. The result was the Carrier, Universal for which the first contracts were awarded in April 1939 and which continued in production with only quite minor changes throughout World War II.

The "Bren Carrier" is probably one of the best known—and certainly one of the most successful—vehicles ever used by the British Army although, oddly enough, nearly all the carriers colloquially referred to as "Bren Carriers" were, strictly speaking, Universal Carriers, since the original Carrier, Bren was produced in relatively small numbers (some 1,280) and not later than about 1940. The exact figure for Universal Carriers built is not available but it appears to have been at least 35,000 in the United Kingdom alone.

A square armoured hull at the rear was adopted for the Universal Carrier, similar to that of the right hand side of the Scout Carrier but with a crew compartment on either side of the engine. This added to the total weight of armour, but the vehicle was well able to bear it and the additional protected crew space increased the usefulness of the carrier for a variety of tasks and, later, greatly simplified waterproofing for wading operations. A number of Scout and Bren

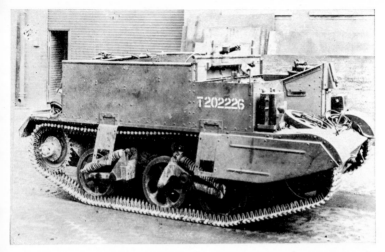

Carrier, Universal—a late Mark II vehicle

Carrier, Armoured OP, Mark II

Carriers was converted to the new standard and became known as Carriers, Universal, Mark I, the first of the normal production vehicles being Universal Mark II. The uses of Universal Carriers included, by 1944, an adaptation as a towing vehicle for the 6pr anti-tank guns of some infantry battalions, although Loyd Carriers or, later, Windsor Carriers were more often used for this purpose. A later version, Mk III, had modified air inlets and engine cover and in many examples a hull of welded instead of rivetted construction.

The Carrier, AOP, or Armoured Observation Post, was produced to meet the need for a cross-country vehicle for artillery observers. In earlier experiments for this function, a vehicle known as D5E1 or Artillery Observers Car was built in 1929. This was an armoured vehicle which had the same lower chassis as the slightly later and better known Dragon, Light Mark I. About 1936 a Dragon chassis, unarmoured this time (the prototype Dragon Light Mark III in fact), was fitted experimentally with cable reel winding gear for the OP function.

The first batch of AOP vehicles using the new Vickers Carrier chassis was ordered in March 1939, and when delivered from 1940 onwards they took over from modified Light Tanks Mark VIB and armoured cars which had been used as improvised artillery observation vehicles. These AOP Carriers differed externally from the contemporary Universal series in that the front left hand compartment had no aperture for a weapon—the Bren gun carried was on a pillar mounting from which it could be operated from the rear compartment—and in the cable drum carried at the rear. A wireless set was housed in the rear right hand side of the vehicle. Modifications included in the Mark III vehicles, which carried a crew of four instead of the three normally carried in the earlier Marks, included a sliding observation shutter—large enough to permit the use of binoculars—in the front and an additional cable drum mounted on the front glacis plate. As with the Universal Carriers, Mark IIIw was a welded hull version.

The demand for AOP Carriers was quite small compared with that for infantry carriers and the approximate numbers built were 95 Mark Is, 746 Mark IIs and 4,577 Mark IIIs.

A specialised carrier for the transport of the three-inch mortar and crew does not appear to have been ordered before 1941, although at least a proportion of certain contracts for Universal Carriers given towards the end of 1940 was completed as (or possibly converted to) Carriers, 3in Mortar. The main difference between the Universal and 3in Mortar Carriers lay in the stowage arrangements at the rear—in the latter a mortar barrel was carried strapped across the rear plate and the legs and baseplate of the weapon were in a container over the back axle. Two special bins over the rear track guards were used to carry mortar bombs. The Mortar Carriers carried a crew of five.

The number of Carriers, 3in Mortar to be built during World War II is difficult to ascertain because the early vehicles were not ordered as such, but it was around 14,000: the principal contractors were Wolseley Motors and the Sentinel Waggon Works.

Production of carriers specifically for the Vickers machine gun was recommenced in 1943 or early 1944 and many were used in the North West Europe campaign. Known as Carriers, MMG, Mark II they were basically almost identical to contemporary Universal Carriers but a pedestal mounting for the Vickers gun was provided in the centre of the vehicle over the engine casing: from this position the gun could be used in action with a wider field of fire than would be possible from the front compartment, although at the expense of protection for the crew. Variants in stowage allowed for use of the Carrier, MMG without the gun as a Platoon Commander's vehicle, a Platoon Sergeant's vehicle or as a Section Commander's vehicle in an infantry machine gun company.

Carrier, 3in Mortar

[*Imperial War Museum*

[*Imperial War Museum*

Carrier, MMG, Mark II—note the Vickers machine gun on a pedestal mounting and all the spare equipment on this vehicle in 1945

273

Carrier, Universal (Aust.) (LP No 2)   *[RAC Tank Museum*

Australian, New Zealand and Canadian Carriers

In Australia there was little pre-war experience of building armoured vehicles and drawings were obtained from Britain for a basic design of carrier. The first Australian Carriers, designated LP No 1 (LP—"Local Pattern"), had rivetted hulls of similar form to the British-built Bren and MG Carriers, with a rear crew compartment at the right hand side and rear-sloping armour. These vehicles had streamlined head lamps set more closely together than those of the British Carriers. One hundred and forty Australian Bren Carriers were built up to June 1940, when they were succeeded in production by the Australian Universal Carrier, LP No 2. External changes introduced in production of this model included welded-construction hulls, in which the front glacis plate was carried higher up, to a level just below the gun aperture in the front compartment, and shielded headlights. There was an armoured rear crew compartment either side of the engine, as in British Universal Carriers. Mechanically, the LP No 2 differed from LP No 1 mainly in that the track displacement form of steering of the original British designs—absent in the first model, which had lever steering controls—was included.

As a Carrier for the 3in mortar, the Australians used a modified version of the Universal type in which the track base was extended by repositioning the bogies so that there was a wider gap between the front bogie and the idler wheel. The engine was transferred to the left front of the vehicle (in place of the gunner's compartment) so leaving an unobstructed rear compartment. The 3in mortar on its normal mounting could be fired from this position: mortar bombs were stowed in bins round the inside of the hull. This same front-engined chassis was also used for an Australian 2pr anti-tank gun self-propelled mounting, described separately.

Carrier, Mortar (Aust.)   [*RAC Tank Museum*

Carrier, MG, LP No 2A (New Zealand)   [*Imperial War Museum*

Another rather unusual Australian machine was the Tracked Truck (Aust). This was a simple little unarmoured vehicle, built on lorry lines, and featuring left hand drive, tracks, and driving sprockets in place of rear wheels. The track road wheels consisted of three Universal Carrier single unit bogies each side, the front one reversed. There was an open cargo body at the rear.

Australian-made Carriers were used by the 2nd AIF in the Middle East, together with British-built vehicles' and for Home defence and in New Guinea and the Pacific area. In all, nearly 5,600 were manufactured in Australia.

Carrier production in New Zealand commenced in 1940 with the Carrier, MG, LP No 1 which, apart from the different pattern of headlamps used, was identical in appearance to the British Bren Carrier. However, the Ford V-8 95hp engine was fitted, instead of the 85hp version used in the British vehicles, and because of the shortage of armour plate they had to be constructed with mild steel.

A total of 420 Carriers was ordered in 1940 for the New Zealand forces at home and in the Pacific area and this number was increased to 520 in 1942. The first 40 Carriers to be built were of the LP No 1 type; subsequent vehicles (LP No 2 and LP No 2A) were very similar to the later Australian Carriers, with sloping glacis plates, welded hulls and, compared with the British vehicles, heavier suspension and wider tracks. The New Zealand carriers were all built at the Hutt Railway Workshops and by General Motors NZ Ltd at Petone.

Large quantities of Universal series carriers—nearly 29,000 in total—were produced in Canada between 1941 and 1945, the Canadian Ford Company and Canadian Bridge Company being the principal contractors. Little need be said about them in this part of the book since they closely followed the pattern of their British counterparts, although some minor changes in design were made in order to substitute Canadian standard components, such as lighting equipment.

Tracked Truck (Aust.)

Carrier, Universal (TI6EI)

Carrier, Universal (T.16) and Carrier, Windsor

CARRIER, UNIVERSAL (T.16) MK 1

Weight:	4.25 tons	Armour:	12mm
Length:	12ft 8½in	Armament:	1 Bren
Width:	6ft 11in	Engine:	Ford, 100hp
Height:	5ft 0½in	Crew:	2–4
Speed:	33mph	Range:	120 miles

CARRIER, WINDSOR, MK 1*

Weight:	5.35 tons	Armour:	12mm
Length:	14ft 4½in	Armament	1 Bren
Width:	6ft 11in	Engine:	Ford, 95hp
Height:	4ft 9½in	Crew:	2–5
Speed:	33mph	Range:	276 miles

Two enlarged developments of the Universal Carrier, the T16 and Windsor carriers, were built in the United States and Canada respectively. In both of these models the opportunity was taken to increase the track base and with it the length of the hull by substituting a two wheel rear bogie for the single wheel unit used in all the standard Universal Carriers: this change brought the suspension more closely in line with that of the Loyd Carrier series.

Both the T16 and the Windsor had a hull layout (including right hand drive) and general appearance very similar to that of the Universal Carriers—this is very apparent in the front view of the Windsor Carrier shown here—and most of the other characteristics were retained. In the steering of the T16 Carrier however, the lateral movement of the front bogies was eliminated and the driving control was by lever instead of a steering wheel. The engine used in both cases was a Ford V-8 of 95-100bhp.

The increased hull space for crew and stowage made the North American vehicles particularly well adapted as 4.2in mortar carriers and 6pr anti-tank gun tractors and Windsor Carriers were sent from early 1945 onwards to replace Loyd Carriers in the latter role in 21st Army Group. The Windsor Carrier was claimed to be more reliable than the Loyd Carrier and to have a better performance. A total of 5,000 was assembled at the Ford Motor Company of Canada's plant (at Windsor, Ontario) with hulls made by the Canadian Bridge Company.

There were three versions of the T16 Carrier, of which nearly 14,000 were built in the USA. Two of these models were used in numbers in the British Army, Carrier Universal (T16) Mark I and Carrier Universal (T16E2) Mark II. The T16 and also T16E1, an intermediate model, had reversed rear bogies and the wheels in the latter were "solid" instead of spoked. The T16E2 had the suspension repositioned and the rear bogies were identical in arrangement to the front pair. Frontal protection in this version was improved by the adoption of a sloping front glacis plate.

A T16 carrier was used in an interesting experiment in 1944 to try to produce a vehicle capable of crossing anti-tank minefields, whilst setting off anti-personnel mines. For this, a vehicle, known as Carrier Tugboat, was built in which the complete suspension of the T16 carrier was duplicated, doubling the track width with consequent decrease in ground pressure.

T16 carriers were in use with the British forces in the Far East at the end of the War; subsequently some were sold to the Swiss Army.

[*Imperial War Museum*
Carrier, Windsor, Mark I*—this vehicle is in use as a 6pr anti-tank gun tractor

Carrier, Tracked, Towing (Loyd)—towing a 6pr anti-tank gun

Loyd Carriers

TYPICAL DATA

Weight:	4 tons	Armour:	normally none
Length:	13ft 7in	Armament:	normally none
Width:	6ft 9½in	Engine:	Ford, 85hp
Height:	4ft 8¼in (without hood)	Crew:	various
Speed:	30mph		

The Loyd Carrier was designed by Captain Vivian Loyd—of the former Carden-Loyd association—as a simple cross-country tracked vehicle using, as far as possible, only well tried components. The basis of the vehicle was the 15cwt 4 × 2 Fordson (UK Ford) truck to which were added tracks and suspension units of a pattern that had been used for several years on light tanks, dragons and machine gun carriers.

The Ford engine and radiator, gear box, transmission tube and differential—all standard—were mounted so that the radiator was at the rear and the drive was taken to front driving sprockets. This meant turning the axle upside down so that the direction of drive was reversed. The track passed over idling sprockets at the rear which, like the front sprockets, carried brake drums so that steering was attained by steering levers which applied front and rear brakes on one side or the other, the differential allowing a difference in track speed. The track warping device used in the Bren and Universal series of carriers was not employed. The hull was of simple open top design and was unarmoured, although light armour plates could easily be added if required and special provision was made for this later on. Access to the vehicle (apart from over the top) was via either side of the engine at the rear. The suspension units were the same as the Hortmann type slow motion forked double units used on the Bren, Scout and

279

MG carriers, then in production. On the Loyd Carrier two of these double units (the rearward one reversed) were used each side, creating a longer track base than that of the Bren type carriers.

The prototype vehicle, known then as "Loyd GS Carrier" was tested by the Army and found satisfactory in late 1939 and a first production order for Captain Loyd's firm for two hundred followed soon afterwards.

The earliest production vehicles (and many of those of the subsequent production orders) were primarily intended as personnel carriers with a capacity for seven to eight men and equipment and were designated "Carriers, Tracked, Personnel Carrying" but before long this useful machine came to be used in other roles. These were either factory-built in specialised forms or, particularly in the earlier cases, modified Personnel Carriers, since the conversion in most cases required little more than rearrangement of the internal stowage of the vehicle.

Some of the earliest variants on the basic type were Slave Battery Carriers (or officially, "Carriers, Tracked, Starting and Charging"), needed to assist in starting tanks engines and also to act as mobile charging vehicles for all the batteries of the tank unit. For this purpose a power take-off located by the gearbox was used to drive, though universal couplings and pulleys, a 30 volt dynamo and a 12-volt dynamo housed inside the carrier to the left of centre. The slave battery used was a 30-volt, 300amp/hr unit; thirty volts being used to start vehicles with 20V equipment and, suitably tapped, twenty volts for vehicles with 12V equipment and ten volts for 6V equipment. The series of batteries comprising the Slave Battery Unit was accommodated against the hull plates on both sides. The remainder of the interior of the vehicle behind the driver's compartment (which was separated by a canvas bulkhead) was taken up with the control panels, stowage for spare batteries (carried as appropriate to the tank unit) and starting cables and platforms to carry batteries being charged.

Mechanical cable laying for the Royal Corps of Signals was a function generally taken over by Loyd carriers—"Carriers, Tracked, Cable Layer Mechanical—from the lorries previously used for this task. The cable laying unit was mounted on a pivot in the centre of the rear compartment, just forward of the engine, and could eject the telephone cable to the rear at either side. The stowage of the Carrier, CLM included light poles and ladders for the use of linesmen, carried in racks either side of the hull.

The Loyd Carrier was also produced as a towing vehicle (although a towing hook at the rear was included in nearly all Loyd Carriers except the earlier-built vehicles) with stowage appropriate to this role. This type was known as "Carrier, Tracked, Towing", and by 1944 was in wide use in infantry battalions for hauling 6pr anti-tank guns or trailers and for the 4.2in mortar role.

A similar but slightly more specialised vehicle was designated "Tractor, Anti-Tank, Mark I" and was adapted to tow the 2pr Anti-tank gun and carry a crew of five (including the driver) as well as a supply of ammunition, and a spare wheel for the gun. The side shields of the 2pr gun could be hung at the sides of the driver's compartment as a measure of protection for the crew when in the vehicle. The carrier was later adapted in a similar form to act as a 6pr anti-tank gun tractor. These Loyd towing vehicles were a reversion to the function as well as in almost the appearance of the Light Dragons Mark IIC-D which had become obsolete some years earlier.

Experimentally, the Loyd Carrier was used as a mobile welding plant with a transversely mounted generating engine; as a carpetlayer and as an A-A vehicle. Two forms of the latter existed with quadruple mounted Bren guns with drum magazines; in both cases the gunner was protected by an armoured steel box shield and the driver by an armoured steel cab. There was also a self-propelled

[*Imperial War Museum*

Carrier, Tracked, Cable Layer, Mechanical (Loyd)—three-quarter rear view

Loyd Carrier with quadruple Bren anti aircraft mounting   [*Imperial War Museum*

2pr mounting on the Loyd carrier and a 25pr mounting, both described separately.

During the course of production of the Loyd Carrier the external appearance altered only slightly, although two brackets (sometimes only one) from the hull to the bogie assemblies each side were added after the first vehicles to give extra rigidity. The vehicles designated Mark I all had Bendix brakes but later Girling brakes were also used and Loyd carriers equipped in this way were designated Mark II. The original Loyd carriers all had British built Ford V-8 engines of 85bhp but later, American built Ford V-8s of 90bhp and similar, but Canadian-built, engines of 85bhp were introduced into the series.

The first contracts for Loyd carriers and those following until late 1941 were taken by Vivian Loyd & Co Ltd but after this, other larger firms took the major part in production, including Aveling & Barford, Dennis Bros Ltd, the Sentinel Waggon Works and the big mass producers, the Ford Motor Company and Wolseley Motors (of the Nuffield group). The last two firms alone produced more than 13,000. An accurate figure of the total number of Loyd carriers built during World War II is not available, but it appears to have been around 26,000. They were used in the major British theatres of war and their rugged, comparatively simple and accessible components and driving simplicity earned them popularity.

[*B. T. White*

Dragonfly—amphibious Ronson Carrier—with DD screens folded down

Carrier Flamethrowers

The first experimental Carrier-borne flamethrower was devised by Mr S. W. Adey and Lt-Col Martin as one means of defending anti-tank ditches in the 47th (London) Division's area of Southern England when invasion was expected in October 1940. This device mounted on a Bren Carrier, known graphically as the "Adey-Martin Drain Pipe", was demonstrated by the Petroleum Warfare Department to a gathering of senior officers, including General McNaughton, the Canadian Army Commander. Although it had a favourable reception, some delay in giving a decision to encourage further experiments was caused by an argument as to whether development should not be continued under the appropriate War Office weapons branch. A go-ahead was given in July 1941, however, and a new design which became known as the "Ronson" or "Ronson Lighter" was developed by R. P. Fraser of the Lagonda company with the strong support and co-operation of the Royal Canadian Engineers; it was ready by November. The Ronson consisted of a flame projector mounted on the front top left hand side of the gunner's compartment of a Universal Carrier, the flame fuel being fed via an external pipe on the left side of the vehicle from two interconnected cylindrical pressure containers mounted on the rear of the carrier. Although the Ronson broadly satisfied the laid down War Office requirements and met with the approval of the Commander-in-Chief Home Forces (General Sir B. Paget), when demonstrated to him in January 1942, changes of opinion as to the weapon's suitability for use in the infantry carrier platoon and doubts as to the adequacy of its range of 40 yards led to a full scale production order for the War Office being withheld, although 73 sets were produced by Lagonda. Nevertheless, General McNaughton had sufficient faith in the weapon to place an order, on his own authority, for production of 1,300 Ronsons in Canada. The design details were accordingly passed over to the Canadians by the Lagonda company and a total of 500 was eventually completed, the balance of the order being changed to later types of flamethrower.

Mr Fraser then commenced design of a new flamethrower with longer range than Ronson so that the objections of the War Office on this score at any rate could be overcome. The first experimental model of the new type was undergoing trials by the end of July 1942. This vehicle became known as Wasp I. It had a clumsy projector externally rather like that of Ronson, although longer, but the flame fuel was carried in a single large cylinder inside the armour of the Universal Carrier in the left hand rear compartment. One thousand sets of this equipment were ordered and quantity production was in progress by the spring of 1943. An improved model, Wasp II, had been developed by this time, however, and this new model, which had a much handier design of projector mounted in the gunner's compartment of the Universal Carrier, succeeded the Wasp I in production. In all 3,500 Wasp sets were manufactured by a group of manufacturers under the "parenthood" of the Lagonda company.

The Wasp II became the standard carrier flamethrower in the field, but a number of other experimental vehicles was produced both in the United Kingdom and in Canada. Hornet, also designed by R. P. Fraser of Lagonda, had a longer range than Wasp I, which it followed, but it was rejected in favour of Wasp II. In order to meet a possible demand for carrier flamethrowers for use in assault landings, six Ronsons were fitted with DD floatation screens (similar to those used on tanks) for experimental purposes. Known as Dragonflies these vehicles were quite successful but the idea was not proceeded with as it was decided that tanks alone should be used in the seaborne assault. In Canada, the Army Engineering Design Branch developed the Barracuda from the Ronson in conjunction with the Stewart Warner Alemite Corporation and these two bodies also were responsible for the Rattlesnake, a Universal Carrier-mounted flame-thrower using gell-type fuel. Only pilot models of Barracuda and Rattlesnake were built.

Wasp I

Wasp IIc—note plastic armour added round front compartments

284

The Wasp I was used only for training purposes (in the Middle East as well as in the United Kingdom) but Wasp II was used increasingly in action towards the end of the War. The Canadians designed an improved model in which the flame fuel cylinder was carried outside the armour, mounted transversely across the rear of the vehicle. This allowed more room inside the vehicle and this pattern, known as Wasp IIc, became standardised by the end of 1944. Because of doubts as to the manpower situation, special carrier flamethrower units were not formed for the 21st Army Group but crated sets of equipment (for conversion of standard Universal carriers to the flamethrower role) were sent to Normandy for use if required. It was not, in fact, until August 1944 that Wasps were first employed in action. They were successful and increasing use was made of them (on an establishment of 6 Wasps per infantry battalion), particularly by the Canadians, until the end of the War. The Canadian Army was responsible for fitting supplementary plastic armour to the front of their Wasp Carriers. In Italy Wasps were also used with success, reaching a peak in the Senio River offensive in April 1945 in which 127 Wasps took part.

Praying Mantis

This revolutionary design of fighting vehicle is perhaps closer to a light tank than a carrier, but since it was built on a Universal Carrier chassis it is described here.

The original concept in 1936 of a one-man tank was, in effect, a revival of the "tankettes" of the late 1920s but with the important difference that the driver-cum-gunner could raise himself and his machine gun by mechanical means up to six feet higher at will. This enabled him to shoot over walls or other cover and then lower himself out of sight again.

This machine was the invention of Mr E. J. T. Tapp; the War Office took some interest in the design and authorised the construction of a prototype by County Commercial Cars Ltd, Mr Tapp's firm at Fleet, Hants. The prototype was demonstrated at Minley, near Sandhurst, before the Commandant of the Royal Military Academy and later to members of the General Staff not long after the outbreak of War in 1939. The old objections to the one-man "tankettes" —mainly as to the difficulties of one man to command, control and fight a vehicle—again came to the fore, although the generals were sufficiently impressed to give authority to Mr Tapp to carry on with a further design on the same lines, but to carry two men.

The drawings for the two-man machine were delivered to the War Office in December 1939 but the Ministry of Supply delayed work on construction of the vehicle in January and nothing further was done until October 1941 when after a fresh demonstration of the original (one man) machine to General Martel (Commander, Royal Armoured Corps) and General Richardson and officials of the Department of Tank Design, a new go-ahead, after a delay of some six months, was ordered. Two experimental vehicles were to be built by County Commercial Cars Ltd and these were completed towards the end of 1943.

The machine collected a name—"Praying Mantis" at this time but not a production order because although the design was brought to an improved state of efficiency, following further trials, it was finally decided that there was no official military requirement for such a vehicle and the project was cancelled in July 1944.

"Praying Mantis" consisted of a slightly lengthened Universal Carrier chassis (the bogie units were more widely spaced) with the Ford V-8 engine in approximately the normal position. In place of the usual front and rear crew compartments, however, was an armoured chamber in which the crew—gunner and driver—lay prone. The chamber was pivoted at the rear and could be elevated by means of a power take off from the main engine to a height of 11½ feet above the ground. Mounted on top of the crew chamber, with an all round traverse, was an armoured box containing two 0.303in Bren light machine guns. These were periscope-sighted and were fitted upside down in order to give the gunner easy access to the magazines for reloading from within the crew chamber.

The "Praying Mantis" was an ingenious idea but the device was insufficiently reliable to be used in the field and the light weapons it mounted were inadequate to justify a machine which, it was felt at the time, would have only a limited role.

[B. T. White

Praying Mantis—three quarter rear view with crew chamber elevated

Carrier, Universal with steel roof   [*Imperial War Museum*

Universal Carrier Series—Special Adaptations

The Universal carrier series were about the most readily available tracked vehicles in the Army during World War II and for this reason, if no other, were not infrequently adapted for special purposes, some of which are now described.

In 1940 steel roofs were added to the Universal carriers of certain Cavalry regiments engaged in Home Defence after Dunkirk. With Boys anti-tank rifle and/or a Bren gun these vehicles with added protection were better able to act in the role of light tanks. A much more complete conversion of the Universal Carrier into a light tank was carried out by the Japanese in the Far East when they added both a roof and a small turret to some vehicles captured in Malaya.

The Universal Carrier was modified as an anti-aircraft vehicle in which the driver's and gunner's compartments were fully enclosed and a small turret, with two Vickers "K" machine guns on a high angle mounting, was mounted on the roof of the gunner's compartment. This design was experimental only and was apparently not produced beyond the mock-up stage, modified Light Tanks, Mark VI being preferred as AA vehicles.

An unusual Canadian modification of a Universal Carrier about 1944 was the addition of a wooden framework at the rear to take a battery of PIAT projectors. These were mounted in two rows of seven each so that they could fire a barrage.

The Universal Carrier was used as the basis of several forms of specialised armour—in some cases smaller editions of equipment carried or operated by tanks. A carpet device for crossing soft ground consisting of a long strip of reinforced hessian carried on a reel mounted on side arms in front of the vehicle was made in versions for laying by Carriers as well as tanks. The carpet unwound itself in front of the Carrier, which ran over it leaving behind a track, which could be used by following infantry or vehicles. This equipment was developed in 1941 and 500 sets were built in 1942–3: there were three patterns of Carpet Device—Mark I (Infantry), 11ft 6in wide; Mark II (Infantry), 11ft wide, and Mark III (LCM), 8ft, for use in assault landings from the small Landing Craft, Mechanised.

Kid was a smaller version, for use with the Universal Carrier, of the Goat demolition device designed for operation by Churchill AVREs. A tray of 600lb explosive was pushed by the carrier against the wall or fortification to be destroyed. The driver of the vehicle "baled out" at a safe distance.

Conger was a gutted AOP Carrier used for minefield clearance. Filled with liquid nitro-glycerine, the Carrier was towed to the edge of the minefield by an AVRE and a canvas hose (up to 300ft long) was fired across the minefield by means of a rocket. The nitro-glycerine was then pumped from the carrier through the hose and detonated, bringing about a sympathetic detonation of mines laid in the area. Gutted, engineless Universal type Carriers were also used towed by AVREs to carry assault engineer stores.

The Germans also used the chassis of Universal-type carriers as demolition vehicles. Captured British carriers were stripped of their upperworks and modified as a variant of the Goliath remote controlled vehicle carrying 50kg of explosive.

Various amphibious devices were tried out on Carriers, including the DD system on a Dragonfly flamethrower carrier (described separately here). Nicholas Straussler, the inventor of the DD, also tested a pontoon floatation device on an AOP Carrier, consisting of two boat shaped pontoons, one either side of the hull. Other means of floatation, ranging from oil drums to kapok bags surrounding the hull were tried out, but the only amphibious system used extensively for carriers

Carrier, Universal—AA (mockup of mounting)   [*RAC Tank Museum*

was an adaptation for deep wading. Extra plates were welded on all round the hull, increasing its freeboard by about 2ft, so that the carrier could wade in between four and five feet of water. One difficulty lay in overcoming the carriers tendency to float and so get out of control. Many carriers of the Universal type were modified in this way for the D-Day landings.

Two less warlike tasks for carriers were as Ambulances and in clearing beach mines. For the former only slight modifications to carry stretchers were necessary and sometimes a canvas hood was added. In clearing mines from British beaches towards the end of World War II and afterwards, a Carrier "Monitor" was used in conjunction with a Hippo 10-ton armoured trailer. A pump mounted in the trailer drew water in and delivered it under pressure through a flexible pipe to a nozzle in the Carrier which had extra high frontal protection added to it. The high pressure jet of water uncovered mines buried in the sand.

Carrier, Universal with Carpet Device   [*Imperial War Museum*

Dragon, Mk I

Weight:	9 tons	Armour:	none
Length:	16ft 7in	Armament:	none
Width:	9ft 3in	Engine:	Leyland, 60hp
Height:	7ft 0in	Crew:	11
Speed:	12mph	Range:	90 miles

The experimental vehicles designed by the Tank Design and Experimental Department headed by Lt-Col P. H. Johnson soon after World War I included a Light Tropical Tank and a companion Supply Tank: both were intended to be capable of operation in hot countries.

The Supply Tank (or Tropical Tank No 4 as it was sometimes called— three of the Light Tanks were built) was a vehicle with a Tylor water-cooled engine and the driver at the front, both enclosed in one compartment, and an open body at the rear for the carriage of personnel or supplies. After mechanical trials, following delivery from the Ordnance Factory at Woolwich, the Supply Tank was handed over in August 1922 to the 9th Field Brigade, Royal Artillery for experiments. Following experience with the Tropical No 4, a new vehicle was designed and two experimental models were built, this time with their employment definitely as Field Artillery tractors in view. The two experimental vehicles, which became the prototypes of Dragon Mark I, were similar in general layout to the Tropical No 4 but the cable suspension of the latter, which was advanced in concept but unreliable, was replaced by a system consisting of pairs of road wheels on vertical coil springs.

The two experimental Dragons were followed by a production series (differing from them only in detail) of eighteen Dragons, Mark I which were issued to Field Brigades of the Royal Artillery for towing 18pr guns. They were found to be underpowered and really too slow for a field artillery tractor and the engine cooling system was evidently unsatisfactory because the radiator grilles were removed from the Dragons in service. One of the two experimental Dragons was sent to India (where it was known as "AT2") in 1923 for trials and the cooling difficulties with the water-cooled engine were underlined there. This led to the adoption of air-cooled engines in later Dragons and also in the new Vickers tanks.

One Dragon Mark I was subsequently modified to take the body of a Rolls-Royce Armoured Car, as an experimental light tank. The vehicle was fitted with an armoured cab for the driver, although it is not known if the armoured car body was ever added. A Dragon Mark I was also adapted as a Bridge Carrier and this is described in more detail elsewhere.

[*RAC Tank Museum*
Supply Tank (Tropical No 4)

[*RAC Tank Museum*
Dragon, Mark I towing 18pr field gun

Dragon, Mark II

Dragons, Medium, Mks II, II*, III, IIIA, IIIB, IIIC and IV

DRAGON, MEDIUM MK III

Weight:	10 ton	Armour:	—
Length:	16ft 5in	Armament:	—
Width:	7ft 9in	Engine:	Armstrong-Siddeley, 82hp
Height:	6ft 2in	Crew:	11
Speed:	10mph		

DRAGON, MEDIUM MK IV

Weight:	9.25 tons	Armour:	—
Length:	15ft 5in	Armament:	—
Width:	8ft 2in	Engine:	AEC diesel
Height:	6ft 7in	Crew:	11
Speed:	—		

The decision to replace the underpowered commercial type of water-cooled engine used in the Dragon Mark I with a new type of air-cooled engine led to a new design in which at the same time other better features were incorporated. Twenty-eight vehicles of the new pattern, Dragon Mark II, were built by Armstrong-Siddeley Motors Ltd and these were introduced into service in 1924. The engine used was the Armstrong-Siddeley V-8-cylinder air-cooled engine of about 90hp, which was fitted also in the contemporary Vickers medium tanks. The extra power of this engine gave the Dragon Mk II a speed of 16mph compared with the Mk Is 12mph, and an extra man could be carried. Unlike the

Dragon Mark I, the Mk II had enclosed sides, which offered the crew a greater degree of comfort and protection.

At this time it was decided to adopt a similar type of vehicle for towing medium artillery—the 60pr gun and the 6in howitzer—and the Dragon, Mk III (later known as Dragon, Medium, Mk III) was the result. Introduced into service in 1925, the Mark III had revised gear ratios appropriate to the greater weight towed and some revision of the design of the side skirting and mud chutes, but was otherwise about the same as Mark II. The top speed was reduced to about 10mph.

Twenty Dragons Mk III were built by Armstrong Whitworth & Co, and this firm also completed a further ten in 1927 of an improved pattern—Dragon, Medium, Mk IIIA. These were similar in performance, but the design of the side skirting was again revised and the frontal layout of the vehicle was cleaned up.

From about 1927 onwards a variety of vehicles was tested out for field artillery transport, including half tracks, both as tractors and as portées, and at this time it was decided to convert the Dragon Mk IIs into Medium artillery tractors by changing the gear ratios and altering the stowage. In their modified form these were then known as Mark II*.

A further demand for Medium Artillery Tractors in 1928 was met by Armstrong Whitworth & Co building another ten vehicles (again with modification to the side skirtings and mud chutes) known as Dragons, Medium, Mark IIIB. Finally, between 1932 and 1935 a total of 11 vehicles of this series was built by the Royal Ordnance Factory. This was in line with the general policy of sharing War Office orders for tracked vehicles between private industry and the government factories. Known as Dragons, Medium, Mark IIIc these were similar to earlier vehicles but had a somewhat higher superstructure and the track return rollers were sprung on leaf springs in pairs.

The last type of medium artillery Dragon was the Mark IV. The origin of this vehicle lay in the commercial Vickers-Armstrongs tractor, two of which, in a slightly modified form, were purchased by the Army in 1931 and given the experimental designations B12E1 and B12E2. These tractors had the suspension— two units of four wheels each side, sprung on leaf springs—and the Armstrong-Siddeley 80hp 4-cylinder air-cooled engine of the famous Vickers-Armstrongs 6-ton tank, which had been sold to many countries abroad. An order for two

Dragon, Medium, Mark IV—first pilot model

[Imperial War Museum

more vehicles, to be completed as artillery tractors and designated Dragons, Medium, Mark IV was given in 1935, followed by a further ten in 1936. The tractors had no upper works beyond a shield in front of the driver, but the Dragons were completed with body sides in which stowage bins were incorporated. More important, however, was the fact that an AEC diesel engine replaced the air-cooled petrol engine.

Of all the Dragons described above, only the Mark IV type is known to have been used in action—a number was sent to France with the BEF at the beginning of World War II. Even at this stage, however, wheeled tractors had largely replaced Dragons for towing medium artillery.

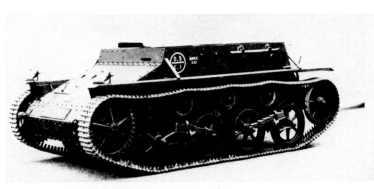

Artillery Observer's Car (D5E1)   [*RAC Tank Museum*

Dragons, Light

DRAGON, LIGHT MK IID

Weight:	4.15 tons	Armour:	—
Length:	12ft 10½in	Armament:	—
Width:	6ft 9in	Engine:	Meadows
Height:	6ft 3in	Crew:	6
Speed:	30mph		

DRAGON, LIGHT MK III

Weight:	3.25 tons	Armour:	—
Length:	12ft 1¼in	Armament:	—
Width:	6ft 9in	Engine:	Ford, 81hp
Height:	6ft 6in	Crew:	6
Speed	30mph		

The first of the British Army Light Dragon series for towing field artillery were ordered in 1930 following trials with Vickers-Carden-Loyd tractors based mechanically on the contemporary Light Tanks, Mk I. The Carden-Loyd 2-ton tractor (B9E1) had Horstmann leaf spring type suspension identical to that of the tanks, as had also another experimental vehicle, B3E3, or Carden-Loyd 3-ton tractor which, unlike the smaller vehicle, was armoured and in a fashion similar to the Artillery Observer's Car (D5E1).

The successor to the Carden-Loyd 2-ton tractor, a generally similar vehicle B9E2, was accepted as the design for the small production order of 1930 as Dragons, Light, Mark I. These tractors had the horizontal coil spring type of Horstmann suspension which had been introduced also into the later light tanks of the Mk I-IA type. The driver was at the front left hand side of the Dragon with one man beside him and three others behind. One Dragon Light Mk I was modified with raised sides, the driver was moved over to the right and seating was provided for six men behind him at the left side and centre of the vehicle. In this new form it was known as Mk IA and a further four were built making a total of 20 of all these early types. The Mks II and IIA which followed—41 were manufactured by Vickers and the Royal Ordnance Factory in 1932—were generally similar.

Dragon, Light, Mark I   [*Imperial War Museum*

Dragon, Light, Mark IID towing 3.7in howitzer   [*Imperial War Museum*

Dragon, Light, Mark III   [*Imperial War Museum*

Apart from the introduction of the improved Horstmann suspension with twin sloping coil springs (again following the pattern of contemporary light tanks—Mks IIA, IIB and III) the next batches of Light Dragons, Mks IIB, IIC and IID were little changed in appearance. Two hundred and thirty-seven of these later marks of Dragon were ordered between 1933 and 1935, the larger proportion from the Royal Ordnance Factory. Of these, two were sent to India and eight supplied to the South African government.

All these light dragons were fitted with Meadows 6-cylinder water-cooled engines and Wilson gearboxes which gave them a reasonable performance when towing the 18pr field gun or 3.7 howitzer or, latterly, the 2pr anti-tank gun.

A new chassis designed by Vickers was offered to the War Office in 1935 as both a Machine Gun Carrier and a Light Dragon. Both types were accepted after trials and the latter became Dragon, Light, Mark III. The principal feature of this vehicle was the Ford V-8 engine and the more refined form of steering in which, by lateral displacement of the front bogie units, the track could be warped for gentle turns, clutch and brake coming into operation for movements of smaller radius. Orders for 119 of these Dragons (excluding the prototype) were given to Vickers and the Royal Ordnance Factory in 1936, although it is not clear if all were, in fact, completed. Two were supplied to the Egyptian Government and one each to Canada and Australia. The Mark IIIs turned out to be the last Dragons to be built as such, because the War Office was turning increasingly in favour of wheeled tractors for field artillery, at first 6 × 4 vehicles and later four-wheel-drive Guy and Morris "Quads".

Some Light Dragons, Marks IIB-C-D and III were in action with the BEF in France; the earlier Marks performed useful service during the 1930s and for training in the early War years.

During the time the Light Dragons were being built for the British Army, Vickers also produced various vehicles on rather similar chassis which were

295

available for sale commercially. The most successful of these was the vehicle variously known as the Carden-Loyd 75mm A-A gun tractor or Vickers-Carden-Loyd Artillery Tractor. This tractor which first appeared in 1929 had a body similar in appearance to the Light Dragons and a shortened version of the leaf spring suspension of the B9E1 in which the rear idler acted also as a road wheel. Some of these with varying modifications were sold to foreign countries including China. With a lorry-type cab and various bodies the same chassis was known as the Vickers Tractor-Truck. Some were sold to civilian concerns in different forms as farming, logging, pipe carrying or airfield vehicles and a few were purchased and tested by the British Army, although none was subsequently ordered for general service.

Vickers-Carden-Loyd Tractor Truck

[*RAC Tank Museum*

Gun Towers

DATA FOR CRUSADER GT MK 1

Weight:	15 tons
Length:	20ft 8in
Width:	8ft 10in
Height:	7ft 6in (over canopy)
Speed:	25mph
Armour:	33mm
Armament:	—
Engine:	Nuffield Liberty, 340hp
Crew:	8
Range:	110 miles

Gun Towers using converted tank chassis represented a further stage during World War II in the British Army of reversion to tracked vehicles for artillery traction following the abandonment of the Dragon about 1940.

The earliest 17pr anti-tank guns on field carriages were towed by standard Field Artillery Tractors of the four wheeled, four-wheel-drive type. Battle experience in Italy in 1943–4, however, showed the need both for armour and better cross-country performance in the towing vehicle and turretless Sherman tanks or US-built half-tracks were sometimes used in the role of 17pr anti-tank tractors.

For employment in the invasion of Europe an armoured tractor for the 17pr was specially designed, using the chassis of the obsolete Crusader tank as a basis. Six hundred of these vehicles, known as Crusader Gun Tractor Mark I or Crusader Tower, were ordered and the first of them was completed in March 1944 so that numbers were able to take part in the D-Day landings in June. The contract for reconstruction of Crusaders for the new role was undertaken by Ruston & Hornsby Ltd of Lincoln, part subcontracted to their subsidiary of Ruston-Bucyrus Ltd. The last Crusader GT was delivered in April 1945. The Gun Tower retained the Christie type suspension of the Crusader and was mechanically the same as the tank in most respects but in place of the turret and driver's cab was built a rectangular open-topped armoured superstructure which housed the driver, beside him the commander, and behind them the gun crew. In the rear was stowage for 17pr ammunition.

Crusader Gun Tractors were used in the North West Europe campaign from D-Day (where for deep wading they had the sides of the crew compartment heightened with extra plates welded on) onwards. The outstanding employment of Crusader Gun Tractors was in the dash to link up with the 6th Airborne Division at the Rhine Crossing in 1945. For the later operations in northern Europe, Crusaders were augmented as 17pr tractors by Ram Kangaroos which were slightly modified for the task.

A much lighter vehicle, tested as an armoured tractor for the 25pr field gun and limber, was a modified Alecto, which was designed originally as a self-propelled mounting for the 95mm howitzer. This vehicle, however, never progressed beyond the experimental stage.

Crusader Gun Tractor, Mark   [*Imperial War Museum*

297

Priest Armoured Personnel Carrier ("Kangaroo"), Normandy, 1944

Armoured Personnel Carriers

The Tank, Mark IX, designed as an infantry carrier, had appeared before the end of World War I but no comparable British vehicle was produced in the inter-war years, although the concept of armoured infantry to accompany tanks had often been envisaged during this period. It was not in fact until well into World War II, in the later stages of the Normandy campaign, that tracked armoured infantry carriers were again employed, although United States wheeled and half-tracked armoured personnel carriers had earlier been supplied to the British Army. The vehicles first used were American S-P 105mm howitzer carriages—Priests—with the guns removed and the openings plated over. These "unfrocked Priests", as they were called, could each carry 12 infantrymen. This was the idea of Lt-Gen G. G. Simonds, commander of 2nd Canadian Corps, and the conversions of the Priests were hurriedly undertaken by REME workshops in time to carry infantry of 2nd Canadian Division and 51st Highland Division in 2nd Canadian Corps' attack in the breakout south of Caen starting on 7th August, 1944.

A similar kind of conversion of Priests was undertaken by REME workshops in Italy, when 102 Priests, together with 75 Sherman IIIs with turrets removed, were turned into armoured personnel carriers between October 1944 and April 1945. The modifications in Italy did not have to be performed in such haste as was necessary for the Normandy attack, and the new frontal armour protection on the Priests was better designed. Some, at least, of the Priests later had exhaust cowls fitted to suit them for deep wading in actions in the marshy areas of North Italy in April 1945.

In the meantime, a somewhat more satisfactory armoured personnel carrier known as Kangaroo using a turretless Canadian Ram chassis had been devised and two armoured regiments—one British and one Canadian—had been equipped with them. By December 1944 these two units, with a combined strength of about 300 Kangaroos, had been incorporated in 79th Armoured Division, which controlled all 21st Army Group's specialised armour. Ram Kangaroos could carry an infantry section of eight men each and gave useful service up to the end of the War in Europe. An armoured ammunition carrier version, externally similar to the Kangaroo, was known as Ram Wallaby.

A similar kind of conversion to the Ram was the Centaur Kangaroo which was not, however, used in action.

All these vehicles filled a need, and the tank armour of the Ram, in particular, gave good horizontal protection, but all lacked overhead cover and infantry disembarking out of the top of the vehicle (as none had quick-exit hull doors) were vulnerable. These shortcomings were overcome in post-war designs which brought together on similar chassis a range of infantry vehicles covering the functions of the war time Kangaroos and the Universal series of carriers.

Ram Kangaroo   [*Imperial War Museum*

Tracked Amphibians

DATA FOR AMPHIBIAN, TRACKED, 4-TON GS (NEPTUNE)

Weight:	17 tons (unladen)	Armour:	—
Length:	30ft 2½in	Armament:	—
Width:	11ft 8in	Engine:	Meadows, 270hp or 280hp
Height:	10ft 6½in	Crew:	2
Speed:	19mph (land) 5½mph (water)	Range:	—

British needs for tracked amphibians were not great before 1944, although a few American built Alligators—LVT 1—were supplied and allotted to the Royal Army Service Corps as 2-ton load carriers. For the Walcheren operations and the great Rhine Crossing and the 1945 campaign in the lagoons of northern Italy, much larger quantities of the heavier LVT(A)2 and LVT4 were supplied by the USA for the British Army, by which they were sometimes known as Buffalo II ("Fantail" in Italy) and Buffalo IV respectively.

In 1944, however, with the prospect of intensified amphibious operations by the Army ahead after the European War was won, steps were taken by the War Office to design and have built in quantity a British tracked amphibian.

The contract for design and production of a pilot model to GS specification AF1 was accepted by Morris Commercial Cars Ltd, drawings were commenced in May 1944 and the prototype vehicle, known as Neptune, was ready by December—a remarkably short time. A contract for 1,400 Neptunes was given to Morris (some of which were to be constructed by the Milner Safe firm) and a contract for 600 to the Metropolitan-Cammell Carriage & Waggon Co Ltd.

The design of the Neptune owed a lot to the American LVTs—particularly the Buffalo IV, with the rear loading ramp. The Neptune was bigger, however, with a cargo compartment of 120 square feet area and capacity of up to 4 tons—it could accommodate a 17pr anti-tank gun or a range of vehicles up to 4 tons laden weight which could be driven in through the rear ramp. The end of the War led to the cancellation of contracts for Neptune after only a small proportion of the 2,000 ordered had been completed. Recovery and Machinery (workshop vehicle) versions of Neptune known respectively as Sealion and Turtle, were built in prototype form.

The Argosy Amphibian Freighter was another project undertaken by the Nuffield Group and prototypes were under development by Morris Commercial at the end of World War II. More like a boat on tracks than anything, the Argosy used suspension and tracks of design derived from the Valentine and Valiant tanks. The hull form was refined during the development work but as by then there was no longer a call for such a vehicle production did not follow.

As mentioned earlier, the tracked amphibians mainly used by the British Armies were the American-built LVTs, but there were several important British modifications and conversions of these US vehicles. These included the LVT(F)—known as "Sea Serpent", an armoured Buffalo IV, equipped with two small turrets, each mounting a Wasp flamethrower; and the LVT(R) another modified Buffalo equipped with rocket projectors capable of putting up a barrage of 72 rockets in three minutes. These types, together with an LVT4 fitted with a 3.7in howitzer in the cargo compartment, were all destined for operations against Japan, the plans for which were cancelled by the sudden end of the war in the Far East.

[*Imperial War Museum*

Amphibian, Tracked, 4 ton GS (Neptune)—rear view showing loading ramp down

A Neptune at sea   [*Imperial War Museum*

[*British Motor Corporation*

Argosy Amphibian Freighter—one of the prototype vehicles

For use by British forces in the European theatres of War—in Italy and
North West Europe, American LVTs were modified (mainly in REME workshops) to enable them to carry larger loads such as the 25pr gun, or a Jeep and
2pr anti-tank gun; as recovery vehicles with a jib at the rear, and as carpet-
layers for crossing soft ground at the approaches to water obstacles. The latter
type performed useful work in Northern Italy and in the German river crossings
in 1945.

An American-built LVT was also used as the basis of an interesting wireless-
controlled amphibious demolition vehicle (carrying 1 ton of high explosive)
constructed in 1943–4 by DMWD, an experimental department of the Admiralty. The LVT could be remote-controlled either from the ground, the sea, or
from an aircraft.

Tractor, Light, GS, Mark I

Miscellaneous Tracked Vehicles

DATA FOR TRACTOR, LIGHT, GS, MK I

Weight:	1.3 tons	Armour:	—
Length:	6ft 7in	Armament:	—
Width	4ft 0in	Engine:	Ford, 52hp
Height:	3ft 11½in	Crew:	1
Speed:	20mph	Range:	—

A simple tracked load-carrying vehicle was produced in 1924 by Vickers Ltd by adding tracks to a Peerless lorry. This "Caterlorry", as it was called, was strongly reminiscent of the Daimler Marienwagen full-tracked lorry built in Germany about 1918, which may have been the inspiration of the War Office General Staff specification B5E1 which called for the Caterlorry's production. Most of the normal lorry driving controls were retained and the "Caterlorry' could probably have been handled by most Army MT drivers without much extra training, but the type was not proceeded with. An earlier essay in tracked load carriers was the "Roller Track Waggon" which had four tracks, the front pair steering. Although the engine and cargo body were of conventional layout, much of the vehicle was suggestive of railway waggon practice—the suspension consisting of external semi-elliptic leaf springs, for example. Vickers-Armstrongs Ltd and Mr John Carden took out patents in 1928 and 1929 for a four-track lorry and a vehicle of this type was built about 1931 and offered for sale commercially—for military or civil use—as the Vickers-Armstrongs Heavy Cross-Country Lorry. The rear suspension unit was a modified version of the type used on the Vickers 6-ton tanks and incorporated the driving sprockets. The front suspension unit was mounted on a turntable, had hydraulic steering brakes, and a turning circle for the vehicle of 30ft was possible. Steering operation by the driver was by means of a conventional wheel and the other controls corresponded to those of an ordinary lorry, so the vehicle presented no particular driving problems. The payload of the cross-country lorry was 6½ tons and a further 3½ tons trailer load could be hauled.

A cheap and simple little tracked tractor was produced by Vickers-Armstrongs about 1932—this was known as the Vickers-Carden-Loyd Utility Tractor and a military version was called the Vickers-Carden-Loyd Army Transport Tractor. One of these tractors was bought by the War Office early in 1933 and a further twelve were ordered later in the year. Fifty-one more were ordered in 1934 and another 83 in 1935. The Army designation for these vehicles was Tractor, Light GS, Mark I and, for the last 89 built with heavier suspension and certain other new features, Mark IA. The tractors had an overall length of only 7ft and were hardly ideal military vehicles, but they were of straightforward construction and fitted with a Ford 4-cylinder engine. At a cost of about £375 each they were a cheap method of furthering the mechanisation of the Army. Vickers-Armstrongs sales brochures illustrated a wide variety of potential civilian and military uses for these tractors, but in the British Army they appear to have been used mainly as cross-country supply vehicles towing two-wheeled trailers, and as carriers for the Vickers machine guns of infantry battalions, until they were replaced by the more suitable Vickers Machine Gun Carrier. A fully armoured version of the Vickers-Carden-Loyd tractor was supplied to the Belgian Army.

Two Vickers-Armstrongs 6-ton Tractors, of a design based on that of the successful 6-ton tank, were purchased by the War Office in 1931 and given the experimental designations B12E1 and B12E2. They appear to have been tested mainly for their suitability as artillery tractors, rather than carriers, and a

Tractor, Light, High Speed (Armoured)—supplied to Belgium   [*RAC Tank Museum*

modified version was eventually ordered as Dragon, Medium Mark IV. However, 26 vehicles of the original model, equipped with 40mm (2pr) pom-poms were sold to Siam by Vickers-Armstrongs as a commercial venture in 1933.

Metropolitan-Vickers Ltd inspired a series of remote-controlled small tracked vehicles for demolition purposes, although later research with these machines was directed towards clearance of anti-personnel minefields. The first "Beetle" was completed by Metro-Vick in 1940. It was driven by electric motors, powered by storage batteries, up to a speed of 18mph and was controlled by means of a cable, 300yds of which was carried on a reel. Detonation of the explosive charge of 170lb was by impact or by remote control. Following demonstration of the prototype, the War Office ordered six more Beetles for experiment, including an amphibious type which was waterborne at a speed of about 5 knots. The 500yd cable of the later prototypes was increased to 900yds for control of the amphibian Beetle which could, by remote control, jettison the floats which supported it on water, sink to the bottom of the sea or river and continue out of sight the last part of the journey to its objective. A limited production order for fifty Beetles, renamed for security "MLM" (Mobile Land Mine), was given in 1941. Later development of the remote control vehicle was as a quick means of making minefields safe for infantry crossing by springing anti-personnel mines and yet, by low ground pressure, passing safely over anti-tank mines. A tractor known as "Agag" was built by the School of Military Engineering, using motor cycle components and a Petter engine. An improved version of Agag was constructed in 1944 with a lengthened Beetle hull and Universal Carrier tracks and track rollers employed as road wheels. Later experiments with low ground pressure vehicles were with a modified T16 carrier, described in another part of this book.

No operational use was made of the Beetles. However, the Germans who had developed a somewhat similar type of vehicle to "Beetle", used this in action against Allied beachhead positions at Anzio in 1944, when no less than 14 were knocked out by gunfire on one day and so the War Office decision to discontinue development of Beetle appears to have been justified.

To cut down the casualties to the crews of bulldozers working near the front line, armour protection was introduced. The armoured bulldozers used by the British Army were the American-built D6 and D7 but the armour appears to have been added in the United Kingdom.

[*Vickers Ltd*

Vickers-Armstrongs Carrier with 40mm automatic gun ("pom pom")